Route 66 Still Kicks

Advance Praise for

Route 66 Still Kicks:

"We've all traveled some part of Route 66, if only in our dreams. Road-tripping 66 is largely a young person's rite of passage—when everything is possible and nothing is certain. Rick Antonson comes to this mythic road in later years and his Mustang-enabled journey with a buddy represents a life "without restrictions or obligations." His tale is a middle-age Woodstock in motion, an encounter with an America that isn't as lost as we think. Off he goes in a cratering economy, summoning the voices of Woody Guthrie and John Steinbeck, singing from the hymnal of the road—the Eagles's anthemic "Take It Easy"—and thrumming through obscure towns like McLean and Romeroville and Bellemont, across landscapes made iconic in the movies of Errol Flynn and Ronald Reagan. It is, of course, the characters he encounters that make this funny, warmly rendered little treasure of a road-trip chronicle so winning. And in the end Antonson proves that Route 66 indeed still kicks—as does America."

—Keith Bellows, editor in chief of
National Geographic Traveler

"*Route 66 Still Kicks* is an informative, entertaining, and emotionally charged quest of the occasionally secluded, fabled highway . . . the most impressive account of a road trip I have ever read."

—Paul Taylor, publisher of
Route 66 Magazine

"There are two ways to take a Route 66 trip. You plan ahead or you don't. The lead characters here, Rick and Peter, chose the latter.

"Planning ahead—using all the information you have available—helps assure comfort and safety. And, well, you get the point. Had they asked my advice before leaving, I could have saved them angst with a relatively problem-free expedition. Yet, they wouldn't have had a book to write. Who would have watched the TV series, *route 66*, if Buz and Tod wouldn't have opened that creaky door or wandered down that perilous path? I watched Rick and Peter open such doors and take such paths. And like an audience, I'd cringe in anticipation because I knew what dangers lay ahead.

"There are many Route 66 books but none are a full-length road trip like this. So what? Well, if you plan to motor west and get your kicks doing it, I suggest you read it. Rick and Peter fell into many well-known pits, but in so doing, they also made some very interesting discoveries—discoveries they probably wouldn't have made if they'd planned their days well. Here you can find out what to avoid and also a lot of things the guidebooks won't find for you."

—David Knudson, executive director,
National Historic Route 66 Federation

"It was by far the best book I have read about the Road in many, many years. An excellent read. Two guys went in search of Route 66 and found America. This is a fun, entertaining and, at times, tantalizing read as the erstwhile new millennium Buz and Tod (from the 1960s TV series *route 66*) find their way from mud-hole to mud-hole and meet the people who continue to make Route 66 a wonder of the world. Their 'ten-second' rule guides them past many of the things we all vow to see and yet does not color the journey as they find their Mother Road with humor and understanding. Highly recommended."

—Bob Moore, co-author of *The Complete Guidebook to Route 66* and *The Complete Atlas to Route 66*

"Every once in a while, each of us is privy to something that will have a major impact on what we enjoy or the industry we are in. For me it was being given a copy of the manuscript of the new book Rick Antonson has written on his trip down the old road with his pal Peter.

I have traveled Route 66 more times than a long-haul trucker and this book is going to become one of the classics of the road.

"Reading Rick's account of his time spent on the road is forever etched in my mind and showed me things that I did not know. Rick has a style of writing that makes you feel like you are right there with them as they get stuck in the mud or meet people along the way. I can count on one hand the number of books I could not put down and this is one of them.

"Rick Antonson and his friend Peter took on one of the most respected yet least understood roads in history: Route 66. They were in no hurry to get from one end to the other and the side trips or detours they took are staples of America's history, its love of the open road, lore of the automobile, and the truly inspiring gift this "route" gave the country. They now possess the major secret of the road: it changes each of us just as it too has changed. Antonson's book will make you feel it, live it and love it—for make no mistake, this is solid proof that Route 66 'still kicks.'"

—Jim Conkle, director,
Route 66 Pulse newspaper and TV

Route 66 Still Kicks

Driving America's Main Street

Centennial Edition

Rick Antonson

Foreword by Peter Greenberg

SKYHORSE PUBLISHING

Skyhorse Publishing books may be purchased in bulk at special discounts for sales promotion, corporate gifts, fund-raising, or educational purposes. Special editions can also be created to specifications. For details, contact the Special Sales Department, Skyhorse Publishing, 307 Fifth Avenue, 4th Floor, New York, NY 10016 or info@skyhorsepublishing.com.

Visit our website at www.skyhorsepublishing.com.

10 9 8 7 6 5 4 3 2 1

Cover Design by David Ter-Avanesyan
Cover photograph: Getty Images

Library of Congress Cataloging-in-Publication Data is available on file.

ISBN: 978-1-5107-8519-9
eBook ISBN: 978-1-62087-555-1

Printed in the United States of America

For Riley and Declan—grandsons,
early travelers, inquisitive fellows—with the hope that
Route 66 is still there when you seek to understand
America for yourselves

America's Route 66 has been called
"The most famous highway in the world."

Contents

In the world of rust and decay, the days pass slowly; the years speed by. Rust seldom has a national identity. Yet American rust helps Route 66 signs cling to the perception of permanence. These, too, will fall.

You work and work for years and years, you're always on the go
You never take a minute off, too busy makin' dough
Someday, you say, you'll have your fun, when you're a millionaire
Imagine all the fun you'll have in your old rockin' chair

Next year for sure, you'll see the world, you'll really get around
But how far can you travel when you're six feet underground?

The years go by, as quickly as a wink
Enjoy yourself, enjoy yourself, it's later than you think.

"Enjoy Yourself (It's Later Than You Think)"
Lyrics by Herb Magidson; music by Carl Sigman; recorded by Guy Lombardo in 1949 (Lombardo made a guest appearance on NBC's *route 66* in 1963).

Foreword

If you believe, as I do, that travel is an experience that by definition is meant to be shared, then *Route 66 Still Kicks* is the inspiration you need to start that process. And great travel experiences almost always involve great storytelling—colorful, larger-than-life characters, sentiment, adventure, discovery, and yes, romance. There are travel books and there are travelogues—and then, if you're lucky, you come across storytelling like this, which actually takes you on a history-filled, magical mystery tour that becomes a remarkably accessible journey.

I drove Route 66 when I was twenty-one. It was one of my dreams to motor down that road and stop at every chance I had to savor the food, the people, and the myths—and hopefully create a few myths of my own. It was, at least for me, a rite of passage to head across the country the old-fashioned way—heading west from Illinois to California. It wasn't about how fast I drove. It was about how much I learned along the way.

Rick Antonson got my attention with his first book, *To Timbuktu for a Haircut*, and he more than keeps it with *Route 66 Still Kicks*. Gentlemen—and ladies—start your engines, but remember, this isn't a race. No need to speed down the road. This is America's favorite highway talking, and Antonson is a superb enabler—so sit back and relax as Route 66 gives up its legendary stories.

—Peter Greenberg, travel editor,
CBS News

A bricklayer's nightmare or a roadmaker's dream? Route 66's early surface varied from dirt to pavement, from loose-set gravel to craftsmanship like this still-maintained stretch of brickwork. Today, the once-upon-a-time Road of Dreams wanders warily through the heart of America.

Author's Note:

Route 66 Centennial (1926–2026)

Route 66 is the motorist's Mecca. Ramblers from around the world drive stretches of it every year. This year, we salute a century of travelers on the world's most famous highway. Happily, this book's reprint joins celebrations of that landmark anniversary. As the author, I still love hearing incidents and anecdotes from readers' trips on America's longest monument, Route 66.

April 30, 2026 marks 100 years since a 1926 telegram from Springfield, Missouri, to the Bureau of Public Roads in Washington, DC, accepting "sixty six" (sic) as designator for the "Chicago Los Angeles Road." It was signed by Missouri's highway commissioner, B. H. Piepmeier and Oklahoma's Cyrus Avery. "The road of dreams" consolidated bicycle paths, auto club roads, and fragments of existing streetways into a slanting, cross-country backbone of America.

In 1946, Bobby Troupe wrote the musical road map and travelers' anthem *(Get Your Kicks on) Route 66.* Nat King Cole's recording forever changed public references from "road" or "highway" to "route." For that, we say *thank you.*

Adventurers dream of finding *all* the old parts—including abandoned sections and ghost towns—as I once did. One hundred years on, researchers seek fresh perspectives on the route's harsh history, its ebb and flow of popularity and viability alongside America's economic and social upheavals, adding folklore and fresh fact findings.

When initially writing this book, I wished to portray the road's rise to fame, its segmenting by superhighways, and its fall from grace with the gazetteers—and Route 66's entrenchment in legend. You will discover, as did I, that Route 66 is America's podium, a 2,400-mile declaration of independence.

This memoir chronicles an exhilarating, heartrending drive down a forgotten road through an unknown America. In recent years, some diners we visited refreshed while others disappeared; committed restoration buffs we met passed away while new ones replace them with enthusiasm—much like every aspect of the Route 66 revival.

Now, while older maps pinpoint remote places barely accessible, GPS technology provides more confident routing. Thankfully, there are increased visual markers to remind drivers they are on the right road, Route 66—not lost, as so often happened with my travel companion, the inscrutable Peter.

Creating Route 66 a century ago was fraught with pavement politics and nearly thwarted by the rationale for a tidy coast-to-coast highway grid it did not fit within. "America's Main Street" would not have existed at all without one of my favorite characters in the USA travel industry.

Cyrus Avery, recognized as the "Father of Route 66," is among America's cathedral thinkers, those visionaries who realized, they—like European cathedral builders from centuries before—were setting in place the foundation upon which future generations would build, literally laying the groundwork to which communities would hinge their fate.

As you read on —in anticipation of your own trip or as an armchair fan of the "Route 66" mystique—I wish safe passage on your journey.

Rick Antonson
On the road in the USA, 2026

Introduction

The Most Famous Highway in the World

"Actually, all I know about it is that song . . . "
—World traveler

Years ago, I was sitting in a California tavern. One of the men I was chatting with, a truck driver—bald, squat, and a bit sassy—told me, "You'll never understand America until you've driven Route 66—that's *old* Route 66—all the way. It's the most famous highway in the world." He lifted his eyes over his Samuel Adams beer before revealing: "It runs through six states."

"Eight," said the lady he was with, as she sifted peanuts from shells.

"Seven," he countered, as though it were negotiable.

She began to hum, "Get your kicks on Route 66 . . . "

The truck driver mouthed the song's words as the fingers of his left hand tracked place names, while those of his right hand kept count of how many states were implied. His friend dropped the peanut shells on the tiled floor, freeing her own fingers in order to compete, first wiping them on her checkered slacks.

"Chicago," he said.

"Not a state," I offered.

"Illinois. Missouri, Kansas," he rattled.

"Texas," she said, pointing a finger to the wooden ceiling for some unknown reason.

"Missed Oklahoma," he said.

"New Mexico. Arizona," she added.

"California," they said in unison.

"Eight." She nodded to herself.

Their game over, the truck driver observed, "It's America's Main Street."

I didn't ask why Route 66 was important; being a teenager in the 1960s, I recalled the song made famous by Nat King Cole and remembered the television series named after the road. I knew little else, and what stuck in my mind was a question: Why did he think it was "the most famous highway in the world"?

The years passed. An excess of nostalgia for Americana ensured that Route 66 became known, if not understood, in the ensuing decades. Freeways had circumvented many small towns on the route during half a century of "progress," leaving a hodgepodge of memories where a roadway of hope had once run diagonally across the United States of America. Route 66 retreated to the back of my mind.

But not long ago, just months before what was intended to be a joint journey to Asia, my buddy Peter and I admitted that trip was hobbled by time constraints. We decided to abort it. Dispirited, we retreated to a bar, where we watched the waiter approach with a succession of pale ales.

Suddenly Peter brightened. "Maybe we do something closer to home. Shorter. Within the U.S. Maybe Canada. Mexico?" A long pause. "Maybe a cruise?"

I choked. "That'd be like spending seven days at a wedding reception." I was beginning to wonder about the wisdom of traveling with someone who'd even propose this.

But Peter was not so easily stopped. "What about Route 66?" He considered it a bit, having surprised himself, and then tried again, to make sure I got it. "Let's drive Route 66!" he said. "It goes through six or seven states."

"Eight," I said.

And drive it we did: on a crisp October day, five months after Peter and I made our ale-inspired decision to seek out the rough and lonely spots that remained of what was once a hectic Route 66, I was at the wheel of a top-down convertible, rumbling across a back road of gravel and cracked earth, out of sight of any other people or vehicles. The sun was bright and the wind was fast. I pressed the gas pedal for more speed. A bullet-riddled marker on a fence post confirmed that this remote and bumpy stretch of hidden history was old Route 66. I looked over as Peter scratched his unshaven chin and adjusted his sunglasses against the glare. He removed his baseball cap, held it out over the side of the car, and let it flap in the onrushing air as a little kid would on a family vacation.

We were halfway through our twelve-day road trip, commonly noted as 2,400 miles, although claims range from 2,200 to 2,448 miles—which tells us a lot about the variation of alignments over the years. By that time, I'd already shed enough misconceptions about the United States to fill our car's trunk, but I'd also confirmed that the myth is as important to America's self-esteem as is fact.

That nuance had been captured for me in a conversation the night before with a middle-aged waitress in a roadside diner. When I told her that Peter and I were intent on seeing "every part of the old road," she said, "I hope you're driving a Corvette convertible!"

"We're driving a Mustang. But it's a convertible."

"Ah. At least it's red, right?

"Why red?"

"Because red was the color of the Corvette those two guys drove in the TV show!"

I didn't have the heart to remind her that the program had been broadcast in black and white.

My equation of a nation is straightforward, I think: land + people + climate + commerce = country. America, the world's superpower, has a more elaborate formula, complicated by its distorted sense of importance. Many foreigners suspect that the United States rewrites its history away from facts—recasting them in a favorable light, and revising them to suit its sense of greatness. As a result, America is often accused of celebrating make-believe legends instead of the duller truths. But whatever the reputation of Americans in foreign lands, this national "species" is best viewed close up, in its indigenous setting, if one wishes to take its measure.

Many travelers begin their journeys, whether in their own country or another, with biases based on hearsay. Many of these people, both outsiders and residents, see America as arrogant, and getting away with it, in a world that often respects America's commercial thunder and little else. But if there is a place to see America at its truest, it is Route 66—the road first renowned for its attractions, then for its deterioration, and now for its attempts to reassert itself in the eyes of those who seek an authentic America. Americans love an underdog. Even more, they love stories about people who rolled high, lost it all, and fought to regain respect. In that way, Route 66 *is* America.

The road has an uncommon presence on the world stage. Route 66 is not a runner-up to any contender; it is *the* highway of highways. North America's Alaska Highway, Baja Highway, and Trans-Canada Highway are icon-lite by comparison. Route 66's peers are on other continents: perhaps the Asian Highway from Singapore to Bangkok, the Road of the Emperors from

Prague to Budapest, or the Golden Road from Baghdad to Samarkand.

Many tourists today want an instant "experience." Route 66 does not grant that. Tourism frequently offers up over-managed travel; Route 66 eschews that. It is possible to drive from Chicago to Los Angeles in three days on the interstate: you just need to get up each morning and chase the pavement. However, as a fellow traveler told me, "Seeing Route 66 in three days would be like having a smorgasbord on a coffee break."

Peter can be a stickler for daily minutiae (which drives me nuts). He set the tone of our drive by announcing, "If we're going on old Route 66, let's take the time and do it right. That means finding where it's ignored and abandoned, unpaved and unhappy—not just the smooth parts." That gave him a motive for the trip, a mini-quest that satisfied his need for a rationale that took him away from more reasonable obligations.

Our ambition became to search for the left-behind and forgotten pieces of Route 66, not merely to "touch it" between speeding along samples of cared-for sections. We aimed for the remnants and dead ends of 66 for no reason other than that they are dead ends—and were once of magical importance. Although today these fragments are often overgrown by weeds, they are compass points to the past. They remind us of pioneers and provenance.

While speaking to others—even world travelers—about our plans, I would hear, "I'd love to do that! I've always dreamed of driving Route 66." Then there'd be a hesitation, followed by: "Actually, all I know about it is that song . . . " Driving Route 66 was not infrequently a romantic notion accompanied by amnesia.

This cannot avoid being a tale of two boomers at the wheel—one with a love for America in all its exaggerations, the other with a sense that America had become the sum of its flaws.

This is us: two friends, simple as that. We are chalk and cheese, Peter and I; he veers right politically, and I lean to the political port. A friend, hearing of our Route 66 adventure, sized the two of us up as "road scholars, not Rhodes scholars."

Peter stretches taller than most men, weighs more than most men, and has a head described by his mother as "large and capable," which his body grew to match. He feigns pride, when in fact he is modest. He casts a long shadow on family and colleagues. He bought a grungy shirt and ill-fitting jeans specifically for this trip, but only brought them out when all his collared shirts and pressed pants had had their day. His hairstyle is unchanging—coiffed for years by the same barber, although his gray is becoming grayer (something he will not bother to hide). His lifestyle is overengaged, overcommitted—he'll be everywhere he's expected to be; he'd go to the opening of an envelope. He's generous to a fault, and gregarious—he could have a conversation with a stop sign. He believes that "the good things in life are easy not to do." And he is loud, and laughs vigorously—often in the face of potential danger, like a freight train whistles before a vehicle crossing.

And I should say that he's done a poor job in life of making time for himself a priority; he's more bound to an office than to the wilderness, more tied to a Daytimer than to the open road. This would be among his few attempts ever to spend a couple of weeks untethered.

Me? I didn't need to go far to find a grungy shirt or ill-fitting jeans; my closet is full of them. I bracket Peter's age by five years—five more in chronology, five less in emotional reliability. I dream of a life without restrictions or obligations. A man of many enthusiasms, I'm not always focused. I've hopscotched U.S. state lines throughout my life, visiting family, friends, and back roads, but seldom with a plan. I travel to reconcile my dreams.

I was witnessing workmates and friends afflicted with sufficient money and not enough life. That startled me. "You should save money; you're getting old," Peter said one day while we were driving on Route 66.

"I'm getting old, but I'm not old yet," I replied only a little defensively.

"Seriously, money can be important."

"I've never wanted to be the richest guy in the cemetery," I said.

Woody Guthrie wrote of the man who "lives for work's sake and works to dig up more work." I'd been guilty of that, and I wanted to change it.

Travel is my mistress. I sleep in forty or fifty different beds a year, pull up that many strange blankets, turn out that many bedside lamps, and wake up to that many different curtains, some torn.

Peter and I are in the autumn of our lives. I am still this side of curmudgeonly and, as Peter would say (and has said) of me, "You really can be a bit of an ass." That makes us each a little set in our ways.

Road trips, like marriages, are about compromises. We went in search of America without being sure exactly what that would mean. Might it mean seeing the country in pockets often overlooked? Perhaps hearing truths spoken by people who don't often get listened to? Maybe opening our closed minds to the wisdom of the open road? Freedom was our byword, and the extent of our planning was agreeing on our completion date. But we swore we'd avoid prepackaged foods, prearranged experiences, and predictable America.

En route, a conversation with an old-timer captured the openness of the road and of our plans. In a remote Oklahoma town on Route 66, a tall woman with weathered skin looked at our parked car with its top down and asked, "Where're you going?"

Peter replied, "Wherever the wind takes us."

The lady leaned forward, laughed with a hint of cunning and said, "Travelers *are* the wind."

1

The Road of Dreams

"I am an American citizen and feel I am entitled to the same rights as any other citizen."
—Nat King Cole

Peter and I arrived in Chicago on separate flights. We were to meet up that night at the once-famous Midland Hotel, which had since taken leave of that name and was now the W Hotel. The W stood mere blocks from Route 66's original starting point, where the next morning we would begin our road trip through history.

I had a monthly book club to attend as a guest author. A few months earlier, a book on my travels to Timbuktu had been published, and Rachael, a friend in Chicago, thought it would be a grand idea to have me appear at her club's gathering at her home. With that invitation in hand, I'd taken an earlier flight to Chicago. I'd been met at O'Hare Airport by her friend Zeke. En route from the airport to Rachael's house, Zeke listened carefully to my plans.

His response was sharp. "Get out of Illinois. There's nothing to see here. Might be a few hundred miles of 66 in this state, but it's not what you're after. Put it behind you. Route 66 is about open lands and backcountry, and for that you need Missouri. Oklahoma." I mentioned that Illinois's side roads might mean less to its residents than to someone in awe of Route 66. Zeke, though, was adamant. "Route 66 heads south and west, and it's been shifted and overpassed by more and more interstates every decade."

It was an early fall evening as Zeke delivered me to a Chicago neighborhood of elegant homes, where trees were shedding their autumn colors over cobblestone walkways. The scene felt bookish, and my mind turned away from the road trip and toward the evening's reading event.

A dozen of the club's members chose to attend that night, lured as much by Rachael's promise of African cuisine as by the promise of a real live author. The topic lent itself to a dinner of couscous and vegetable sprigs, accompanied by chicken fried in olive oil and sprinkled with tarragon—all with the host's Italian twist.

The conversation shifted quickly from the rigors of West Africa to talk of "travel" and why people choose to do it. I told them of my experience: "My wife, Janice, and I differ in many ways. I love sleeping under a million stars. She likes sleeping under five, all on the back of the hotel door." I added, "This trip, I'm with a friend, looking to find the now-remote sections of Route 66."

From the end of the dinner table, a lady wearing a knit sweater and jeans said, "Route 66 is legendary—Main Street U.S.A., I've heard."

"It's an antique road, all beaten up, is what I know about it," her seatmate responded.

"What makes a road antique?" asked another.

"Aged, battered, treasured, maybe even priceless. Isn't that it?" The speaker was Anne. "They say there's magic to Route 66."

Rachael said, "You must have seen that Disney movie, *Cars*. It's all about a race car getting lost on Route 66."

Many in the room hadn't seen the movie, so she filled in the storyline. "This cute race car—animated—accidentally gets dropped off the back of a truck that's carrying it across America. Named . . . " She hesitated before it came to her. "Lightning McQueen. He finds himself on the *slow* road, one he knows nothing about. Signs say it's 'Route 66.' He drives into a cartoon town from the 1950s called Radiator Springs—it's in Carburetor County. It's loaded with cars that talk and relic buildings—and no business."

"That's it?" asked Michaela, seated next to me.

"There's more. I've got three kids, and I've seen it three times," added Anne, looking around the table as she stood to pour red wine in my glass. "Like the real Route 66, the movie town's been bypassed by the interstate. Left alone. It's falling down, board by board. Sign by sign."

"Sounds sad," I said. "But that's what we're looking for on our trip. We want to find the places left behind."

"I think there are lots of ghost towns," a dark-haired woman said. "And restoration—places getting attention again. I remember one of the characters in *Cars* saying something like, 'We're a town worth fixing.'"

My heading out on this mythical road meant more to these book club members than my having been to Timbuktu. To them, for whom Route 66 began on their doorstep, the road remained a mystery. It was within reach, but most had traveled it only vicariously, through movies and novels.

Jane, a tall woman smartly dressed in a red blouse, red slacks, and black shoes, poured more red wine for us. "I thought Route 66 was dead, disappeared," she said. "I didn't know it was there to be found. Or that people still cared."

"See *Cars*," Rachael encouraged. "Near the movie's end, the flashy car whines about Route 66, saying that it's just a road, and the smarter one says something like, 'It was much more than that.'"

Those who have driven Route 66 can't wait to recall it and talk about it. "I've been on it, most of it, over the years," said another member. "Never drove it all at once, but I've been to every spot mentioned in that song." She began to sing, "Amarillo, Gallup, New Mexico . . . "

Zeke dropped me off at the W, where I was to meet Peter at midnight. "Don't worry about 66 in this state," Zeke said to reinforce his earlier advice. "The interstate is only as good as its exits. Hit the four-lane and be off. Out. Get beyond the city and into the farmlands."

Shucking my canvas satchel and shoulder pack onto the hotel's marble floor, I was struck by the mezzanine's spaciousness, its balustrades and pillars, and the ceiling's sculpted bas-relief, fashioned in the early 1900s in the city that defined the era. Architect V. H. Vitzthun's beaux arts edifice, intended to debut in 1928 as the Midland Club, was situated in the heart of Chicago's theater district. Like so much of America, those plans were redrawn by the 1929 stock market crash. The times were harsh: suddenly, Phillips Petroleum dropped from $32 a share to $3; wheat lost 75 percent of its price, eventually landing at 33 cents per bushel.

The ensuing Depression and the ragged regrouping of the nation would influence our travels over the coming days. It seemed appropriate that our first night's lodging was in a corollary of those times—a building which, like Route 66 and the people along it, symbolized both success and failure.

I approached the concierge. Peter cornered into view in the luxurious lobby, looking at my wool shirt of checkered browns and reds, sad orange-colored jeans, khaki desert boots, and unkempt hair.

"You look like a logger," he said. Greetings are not Peter's forte.

He'd landed in Chicago an hour earlier, picked up our rental vehicle, signed on as the primary driver, and made his way to the hotel on his very first trip to downtown Chicago. I'd made him promise that the rental car would not come with a computerized map screen or an intrusive GPS guiding system that would ensure drivers always found their way out of a quandary—where's the fun in that? Peter had kept his promise—and had gotten lost driving to the hotel.

We were in a city where jazz lives, breathes, and is talked about as much as baseball—one of the places it calls home. I wanted very much to find a late-night club where the legends of jazz had played in the 1930s.

Chicago in 1935 was more than a railway town, more than the capital of Midwest commerce, more than the eastern terminus of Highway 66; it was the epicenter of jazz. The new music had its stars, the likes of Earl "Fatha" Hines and Louis Armstrong. It also had its up-and-comers, such as the eighteen-year-old pianist and vocalist Nathaniel Adams Coles (he dropped the *s* when he took the name Nat "King" Cole). Cole had been born in Montgomery, Alabama, and was then a twelve-year resident of Chicago's South Side. The area was known as Bronzeville, due to the influx of more than 200,000 blacks between 1910 and 1930 in search of jobs in the industrial powerhouse. Promoters were soon pushing Cole to perform as the "sepia Frank Sinatra" to take advantage of "colored jukeboxes"—feeling that his listening audience and commercial opportunities were limited. Rejecting the suggestion, Cole responded, "I am an American citizen and feel I am entitled to the same rights as any other citizen." It was time for the barriers to come down.

In February 1946, the celebrated Nat King Cole serendipitously met the young songwriter Bobby Troup, and together they gave the world a wonderful road song, forever changing 66's moniker from a "highway" to a "route."

A taxi dropped Peter and me far away from the W, at the Underground Wonder Bar—a recommendation of the W's staff in response to our asking for a jazz club. We slid into slate-backed chairs, took out a map, and started to chart our unplanned journey.

"We'll take every Route 66 detour we can find between here and L.A.," Peter enthused. "That'll add 500 miles of driving, but it'll be worth the rubber."

Nothing had ever come easy to Peter, and he was determined not to let this be a relaxed drive. He had an attitude of exerting influence, which I thought came from contemplating the unpredictability of our days ahead. I shrugged off the lack of a clock and the absence of a plan, but couldn't help noticing his early pangs of separation from a GPS. "We might get lost," he said that evening.

"We can only hope so," I replied.

Overcooked pizza arrived on our small table. The dim room had no need to be well lit; the twenty patrons were there for the music. It was a narrow hall, with the bar forcing a thin walkway until the room split open in front of a six-piece band squeezed into a space that would comfortably accommodate a trio. Luiz Ewerling & A Cor do Brasil jammed into being, leveling our conversation with music so loud that Peter and I had to shout our plans back and forth at one another over the next twenty minutes.

"Road in the morning! Early!" I yelled. "Fellow I met said Illinois is best to get through, so we can hit the real Route 66!"

"Not sure that's true!" Peter yelled back. "I flipped through the guidebook on the plane coming here! There's lots of original route in this state. Let's take our time!"

Suddenly the band's set was done.

"Zeke said it's been moved about and paved over in Illinois," I said, calm now.

"I've got a map book," Peter replied, assured and prepared. "I know where we're going. We'll get off I-55 as soon as we can, and drift south on back roads. I'll drive. Trust me." My heart sank.

"We want to head to Joliet and on a 1930s route to Chenoa, Springfield, and Farmersville." It did sound like Peter knew where he was going, for a change. "Illinois's Route 66 got paved early," he continued. "It's still there—and it's all two-lane and with small towns."

We finished our beers, and the waitress brought us two more.

"No road rules, okay?" I said.

"Right. We swap driving time and take turns navigating," Peter said, establishing Road Rule #1.

"Only way to find the great American meal is to try everything we see," I suggested, and then added Road Rule #2: "We never order the same meal twice."

"Does that go for breakfast?"

"Yup. There are a thousand ways to have eggs."

Peter picked up a slice of pizza, and I pointed at it: "That's our last pizza for the trip."

We'd agreed not to bring any recorded music with us (Road Rule #3). Instead, we decided to pick up road entertainment when it became available, letting the circumstances determine our driving music. I pulled twenty dollars from my wallet and put it in a jar next to the stage, picking up the Ewerling band's "Our Earth" recording. Brazil was irrelevant to Route 66, but tunes are tunes, and we needed to prime our departure next morning.

When Peter squared up the bill with the waitress, he proudly informed her we were about to drive Route 66. Her response was simple, her look far away. Her words rang in my ears the rest of the night: "It's the road of dreams."

Our road trip coincided with a host of economic calamities. America was once again caught up in the financial doldrums; the banking industry went flaccid, and wealthy donors for good causes retreated. It was the worst of times since the Great Depression. Conspicuous consumption became an uber-embarrassment overnight. "Value" took on new meaning as a combination of price, emotion, and perception. Global travel patterns were upended. There seemed no better place to be headed than down the preeminent harbinger of good times and bad: Route 66.

Flying to Chicago, I'd felt unprepared for the trip and not equipped to learn all that I could on the journey. I often equate buying a book with having read it, owning a book with knowing it. So it was that the three Route 66 books I'd acquired pre-trip had sat unopened on the shelf at home in the busy months before our departure. I'd brought two on the flight with me to brush up, as one would cram for an exam.

Fact and fiction—its two stalwarts—define Route 66's reputation. For years, the vast distance that the route crosses was an intimidating expanse of deserts, mountains, and semi-arid lands. It is said that Route 66 overlaps an original and ancient network of trails created by migrating native peoples, but that is only partly true. These patterns were not developed together; nor did the individual pieces of the puzzle cover great distances. They were only isolated segments of what eventually became Route 66. Had they not been overlaid by a famous road, their role would have been considerably less significant; yet they surely did participate in the growth of a nation.

Sustenance would have been the main motivation for the early travelers on these trails, food and survival their objective. Hunting and trade would have led to encounters between various tribes, their individual trails thus becoming linked. Now they could carry out the trading of clay pots for woven baskets and foods from one distant region to another.

These originating peoples then established trade with Mexico's far-flung Aztecs and with natives residing on the Pacific coast, as well as with indigenous interlopers in search of bison. Indian villages expanded to become Indian territories, though the vast land remained largely uninhabited, unexplored. It was a history I wished I knew.

The prospect of both gold and profits from furs had brought Europeans into the territory. Spanish colonists followed their country's explorers north from today's Mexico, bumping into the ambitious French, who were moving south and west from today's Canada to their St. Louis trading post and beyond. Rivers such as the Rio Grande, Canadian, Mississippi, and Missouri became travel routes; explorer campsites became trade outposts.

As Canadian and Mexican explorers continued to trade with the native peoples, the thirteen British colonies on the eastern seaboard looked westward to see an expanse of unsettled land being colonized by countries at war with—or in trade competition with—their mother country; much of it was then connected to either New France or New Spain. After the American Revolution and the formal creation of the United States, the new nation's continental anxiety prompted rapid exploration to exploit those lands.

Rivers, since they always seek the lowest elevation, made the exploration of the West much easier. The river valleys carried paths that became horse pack trails and wagon-train routes. The U.S. Army followed soon after, establishing forts to protect both commerce and settlers. The former thirteen colonies were now an aggressive nation that became colonial itself. From St. Louis, west through the Ozarks and up through Kansas Territory, the Santa Fe Trail led to New Mexico, routing north around Indian Territory, a collection point for displaced tribes.

This westward expansion of America, its acquisition of Spanish and French territories, and wars for statehood laid both the political and geographical course for Route 66. The route's ultimate direction, however, was set by the railways, which would rapidly define the way west. That was the conversation I'd tried to engage Peter in at the noisy nightclub before we left. The band had begun a new set.

"I was talking to a young lady on the plane today. She wanted to know about Route 66 because I was reading a book on it!" I yelled.

"You can read?"

I smiled and continued. "For some reason she only seemed to believe me about the road's history when I told her Route 66 was built beside railway lines!"

Over the din, with the Brazilian music at a crescendo, Peter leaned across the table and shouted, "Then why aren't we taking the train?"

"I feel that tomorrow I'll start to drive through history," Peter said as we left the club. We waved off a taxi and decided to walk. Neither of us knew the way back to the hotel, but we sensed the direction and meandered along the empty sidewalks.

"This is where you should tell me you actually read the Route 66 guidebooks I bought you," I said.

"I meant to," Peter admitted. "I did some reading on the plane coming here. I do know that in a couple of days we'll be in the Ozarks. And . . . the Ozark Trail linked St. Louis to an Oklahoma route west." He sounded informed. I was surprised. "Otherwise we'd bend back north to Kansas City and over that way to Santa Fe instead. It was called the National Old Trail."

"I like the sound of Oklahoma."

"It was called 'Indian Territory,' not Oklahoma," he said. "You've got a lot to learn."

It was 3 AM before we made it back to our rooms at the hotel. That left a couple of hours for shut-eye before we got up and headed out early. Route 66 beckoned.

2

America's Longest Monument

"People promise themselves they'll drive Route 66 one day! It's America's longest monument."
—Chicago pedestrian

I bounced out of bed, threw on the clothes I'd worn the night before, and headed into the W Hotel's lobby, primed for adventure—eleven days of unscheduled road travel! My pre-trip preparations had been brief: how many clothes does one need on a route littered with laundromats? Peter, true to form, arrived freshly shaven, wearing pressed trousers, an ironed shirt, and polished shoes.

In the *route 66* television show (the "r," oddly, is always lowercase for the title), Tod and Buz often stowed their luggage not in but on top of the trunk of their Corvette. Peter and I tried to rent a car just like theirs, even the same color—but decided otherwise when quoted the price. Series star Marty Milner, who played Tod, told *Route 66 Magazine* that "the Corvette was kind of a sand color, because it looked good on black-and-white television. Everyone always assumed it was red."

The car Peter had rented emerged from the parkade, driven by the hotel valet. It was to be our closest travel companion: a silver Mustang with a black canvas top, leather seats to match, and plenty of chrome. It was today's version of the best of the 1960s, with more leg room than a Corvette and not so low to the ground. And it had a trunk: we wouldn't have to lash our luggage onto the back of the car. I tossed in my shapeless canvas bag, looped over with straps and a broken clasp, while Peter gently lowered his factory-fresh black leather suitcase into the trunk. I went to put my shoulder pack in the back seat, but there was only room for a small bag, so I shoved it in the trunk next to Peter's briefcase, jammed beside his suitcase. We'd each brought a sleeping bag for those places where the accommodation was suspect and we chose to sleep *on* the bed rather than *in* it.

Lou Mitchell's Restaurant, on West Jackson, has been the first stop for many a Route 66 traveler. The restaurant's reputation is due to gossip as much as heritage—the rumor that it's good luck to begin one's own journey where others have successfully begun their cross-country drive and the sense that you'd miss a legendary meal if you ate elsewhere. The restaurant's location, two blocks from Route 66's pre-1937 terminus at the corner of Jackson Boulevard and Michigan Avenue, was set in 1923 when the diner, once known as Mitchell's Cupboard, moved here from just down the block—three years before Route 66 was designated as such. Mitchell's has claimed priority as the chosen breakfast stop at the beginning of Route 66 for all westbound trips ever since.

We joined the morning lineup for breakfast. "The pancakes are best," said the elderly waitress, whose green smock was splattered with samples of every item on the menu. She led us through a maze of tables and chairs that were all occupied. The walls displayed modest profiles of Route 66, incorporating photographs and replica signs, and a gift shop offered little in the way of historic paraphernalia. Mitchell's seemed to take the

Route 66 brand for granted. It made little effort to provide its patrons with hard information, relying instead on recognition of the route's name and the hype of their own.

"This place is over eighty-five years old," Peter said as he pulled up the fifties-era chair. "I hope the batter's fresher." When the waitress returned, he asked her what she thought about Route 66.

"Long," she said while pouring his coffee. Then she stopped midway, and tilted her head as though Peter had been the first to ask her opinion. She resumed pouring: "Route 66 almost never gave up being important." With that, she left us.

Six Japanese visitors—three men and three women—were crowded at the table that had been shoved next to ours. They seemed to be students. They'd spread a map of Chicago on their table, anchoring its corners with coffee mugs to plot a walking tour. A younger waitress, looking glamorous and thus quite unlike the restaurant, rushed by with six plates, stopped as she overshot her target, and plunked the plates on top of the students' map. That ended their discussion. One of them asked Peter if he'd take their photograph, and that led to further conversation.

"Wow," they said in unison when Peter mentioned our intended journey. Then one spoke on behalf of the rest. "The whole world knows about Route 66. But how many people get to drive it?"

In my quick assessment of these Japanese "students," I'd overlooked the middle-aged man among them. He said, "I've lived here all my life—born less than a mile away—and I've never been further on old 66 than mid-Illinois. It's beautiful around Elkhart and Williamsville. Not far from here."

One of the women introduced the group. "He's my dad. Our friends are visiting from Japan, but I'm Chicagoan through and through. We'll walk them over to Grant Park, where 66 once began. One day I'd love to drive Route 66 . . . "

My short stack of pancakes sprawled over the plate. "Side order alert," I said as the bacon arrived, reminding Peter and the students that they were in the U.S. of A., where servings often exceed the size of the plate.

Having finished his meal, Peter spent fifteen minutes writing postcards to create envy at home.

"We'll make decent time if you get all your postcards out of the way at the start of the trip," I said.

"This is only the first batch," he said, patting the pile. The one on top featured a photograph of local celebrity Al Capone.

Alphonse "Scarface" Capone lobbied to get Route 66 paved, and fast. He wanted the speedy delivery of his bootlegged liquor and speedy escapes to keep law-enforcement officers at a distance. By 1929, the year in which "Big Al" was eventually convicted of income-tax evasion and sent to prison, Illinois was the first state to have completely paved and signed its portion of what was becoming Route 66. We would be driving on Al Capone's "road of choice."

The young Al Capone morphed from bowling-alley pin-boy to notorious Chicago gangster under the mentorship of "Terrible John" Torrio, a saloon operator, rum runner, and gambling profiteer. Sent to the Windy City from New York in 1919 so that the murder accusations against him would cool down, the twenty-year-old Capone stayed in his adopted town. He arrived with his "Scarface," bearing two razor-slash wounds from a bar fight during his days as a bouncer in the Bronx. He soon learned to quip, "You can go a long way with a smile. You can go farther with a smile and a gun."

Prohibition's ban on manufacturing, transporting, and selling alcohol began under the Volstead Act in 1920 and did not end until 1933. Spurred by the Roaring Twenties and a lively economy, Big Al and his underworld prospered: His take in 1927 alone was estimated at $105 million (when the average U.S. worker was earning $1,358 a year). Speakeasies, distilleries, brothels—name an active vice in Chicago or on upper Route 66 in those times, and the Torrio/Capone team had at least one finger in it and sought to control all of it. Competition was thwarted by bribery and murders carried out by hit men who were well removed from the always-have-an-alibi Capone.

When Capone ventured along Route 66 in the late 1920s, he did so in his bulletproof V-16 Cadillac. Painted green and black, it blended well with Chicago's police cars of the day—if you only glanced at it. Looking more closely, you would see that it was customized with gun cabinets, sported red-and-blue police lights (mounted discreetly behind the grill), and had a police radio.

Before leaving Chicago, one path on today's Route 66 takes you to Cicero, a town now within metro Chicago where the "Big Fellow" and his boys ran a brothel frequented by their boss (who later, perhaps coincidentally, lost his organizational abilities with the onset of syphilitic dementia). In Mitchell, not far south of Cicero, is the Luna Café, where Capone also dropped in, probably not having to rely on the neon cherry being lit up to know whether the Luna's prostitutes were available.

Those profitable times brought fierce business conflicts to the underground economy. George "Bugs" Moran of the North Side Gang was Capone's nemesis. On February 14, 1929, Moran's associates arrived at a garage on Chicago's Clark Street while Bugs watched from across the road. His seven-man crew had been lured there to pick up a load of cheap whiskey. Moran observed four men entering the building behind his outfit. Two of them were dressed in stolen police uniforms.

Inside the garage, there was the sudden pretense of a police raid. The rival Moran contingent surrendered, dropping their guns. Three of them were in chairs and four remained standing, all facing the red brick wall* and anticipating arrest. Instead of handcuffing them, Capone's henchmen (choreographed by Jack "Machine Gun" McGurn) opened fire at their backs. They let loose 150 rounds up and down the seven men. Some victims were hit as many as fifteen times. The bullets pierced them at odd angles as they crumpled to the floor, their hats landing beside them.

The attack, now known as the St. Valentine's Day Massacre, gave Al Capone a national reputation for ruthlessness, a reputation habitually mythologized by the press. It also capped the Chicago public's tolerance for gangland slayings. While Capone was never charged with, let alone convicted of, carrying out those murders, the resulting crackdown on crime and an intense scrutiny of his business dealings led to his eventual imprisonment in 1932—for income-tax evasion. Indeed, Capone had never filed an income tax return, asserting: "This is preposterous. You can't tax illegal income." When convicted, he was given an eleven-year sentence and a $50,000 fine, and the U.S. Treasury Department impounded his treasured 1928 Cadillac. He was off the road.

Capone would have next seen Route 66 in 1934, this time from the window of the railroad coach taking him to California's newly opened prison on Alcatraz Island. It proved to be a facility where he could not manipulate guards, wardens, or fellow prisoners.

---

* As they fired, the gun-wielding gangsters unintentionally repurposed the garage's bricks into American folk art: 414 of the bricks from the bullet-ridden wall—over half of its total number of bricks—were purchased by George Patey in 1967 when the building was demolished to make room for a new development. Each brick was numbered, charted, and then reassembled at Patey's club, the Banjo Palace, in Vancouver, Canada. On February 14, 2012, the eighty-third anniversary of the massacre, the new Mob Museum of Las Vegas opened with the brick collection rebuilt in a diorama among its artifacts.

Inadvertently, one of Capone's legacies was to provide protection for President Franklin Delano Roosevelt after Japan attacked Pearl Harbor on December 7, 1941. Roosevelt had chosen noon the next day as his time to address Congress and encourage the United States to join with its allies by participating in what would become the Second World War.

Fearing an assassination attempt on the president by Japanese or German sympathizers, the Secret Service was unsure how to transport Roosevelt safely from the White House to Congress. They determined that a bulletproof car was needed, but U.S. law prohibited the government of the day from purchasing a car that cost more than $750. There was no chance of acquiring such a vehicle in less than twenty-four hours. Then an agent recalled the existence of an impounded Town Sedan. Overnight, it was cleaned up, lubricated, and moved from the Treasury Department parking lot to the White House.

On the morning of December 8, FDR, speech in hand ("I ask that the Congress declare . . . a state of war . . . between the United States and the Japanese empire"), stepped into a four-and-a-half-ton armored car. One and a half of those tons consisted of bullet-proof metal shielding and inch-thick windows. Popular, refuted myth is the U.S. Secret Service drove the president to Congress in Al Capone's Cadillac.

Eager for the road, Peter and I stepped out of the restaurant into a sunlit day and walked toward our car. We had a full tank of gas, reliable maps, doable timelines, and a confidence born of anticipating paved roads and good signage. Nothing could go wrong. At the street corner, Peter held his map to the breeze and turned it sideways twice in an attempt to orient himself. We stood a hundred paces from our parked Mustang. A well-dressed man, noticing Peter's puzzlement, asked if we needed help. Peter explained that we wanted to find Adams Street, then to connect to the short interstate link to launch our quest on Route 66. "But I can't see where we are on the map."

"First," the man said, as he flipped the map over, "you've been looking at Milwaukee." He was barely suppressing a smile. After showing us the way, he commented wistfully, "You know, you're driving the dream of many of my friends. People promise themselves they'll drive Route 66 one day! It's America's longest monument."

Departures are the sweet spot of travel. The warm autumn morning held nothing but promise. We trimmed back the ragtop, letting it nestle into its holding cave next to the trunk.

With Peter behind the wheel and our seatbelts secured, I shook my head and whispered, "*Mil-wau-kee . . . ?*" Then I shuffled the parking ticket into the glove compartment, hoping Peter hadn't seen me remove it from the windshield. He had. Blasé as usual, he said, "I'll write them later and negotiate forgiveness."

"We split all costs on this trip," I said. "Even your fines."

"Not this one. I'll get us out of it." He said this as someone accustomed to getting his way.

As our convertible crept away from the parking spot on Clinton Street, we crawled through Chicago's streets as the breeze loosened and fluttered leaves from the trees. Peter found Adams. Then, efficiently, we wound through the business district and into residential neighborhoods where the cars conveyed more owner prosperity than the buildings they were parked in front of. We headed out of downtown, bound southwest. Peter gunned the eight cylinders, and we bolted onto the Illinois interstate.

Peter popped his seat farther back and eased his six-foot-four-inch frame, groaning all the while, into an attitude that indicated he'd adapt. "Only 2,445 miles left to go!"

At first we alternated between a black-ink-on-beige map of Illinois, a larger multicolored map of the U.S., and three guidebooks. Our material could not save us from ourselves, and within five miles we missed a turn. It didn't matter; we whisked through the indistinguishable communities of metro Chicago, feeling disappointment at so quickly leaving the eastern terminus of Route 66 and being forced onto I-55. We began to fear that freeways would dominate our trip.

"We need an exit strategy. Let's get off this freeway and head toward Joliet," Peter pleaded. "I read about it last night while waiting for you to get to the hotel. It's on the map. Even you should be able to find it."

He pressed his advice. "Keep the maps handy. There's more than one Route 66. Some towns have two or three different routes through them—66 moved over the years." Although the interstate rules today—rumple-free, smooth, and functional—near it, sometimes out of view entirely, run the remnants of Route 66, a little worse for wear.

There would be daily decisions to make about which version of the route to take, particularly in states like Illinois, where half a century ago, a rapidly increasing population forced the rapid building of roads. Route 66's course shifted as new arteries connected or wove around communities. This could have made our commitment to "find all those forgotten parts" a hollow promise, as we could spend hours circling midsize towns where new routes had emerged within blocks of older ones. My fear was that this questionable premise would simply reaffirm Peter's quirky tenacity.

In Peter's last premeditated move of the trip, he confidently crossed two lanes and took Exit 269. "I memorized that," he said as he pointed us to Joliet on the helpfully named Joliet Road. Where the road narrowed to our single lane, he merged after some hesitation, thus forcing a two-ton truck to brake angrily behind us. Ten minutes later the road briefly became a double lane, but a sign ahead showed it would again narrow to one lane. The trucker that Peter had recently cut off went barreling by, evening the score by cutting in front of us.

"I'll pass him later," Peter snapped.

I've heard that if you took every opportunity to pass other vehicles on a drive from New York to L.A., you'd get there a half hour earlier than if you drove the speed limit and never passed anyone. This didn't seem the best time to inform Peter of that fact.

Initially, reputable Route 66 signs were seldom seen. This scarcity caused us some uncertainty. We sought the signs for reassurance that we hadn't overshot a turnoff, missed an intersection, or mistaken our directions.

It wasn't long before a mock country fair (more a roadside flea market) caught our attention. We parked near the old wooden church (now a community center) that housed it. The aroma of smoking leaves wafted from behind the building and calmed the scene. Although I scrounged around the stalls, I found nothing I wanted. But as I headed for the front door, I saw Peter clutching his new possessions.

"What about this?" he said, holding up a used blue baseball cap—making him the first person ever to ask for my fashion advice. A "Freightliner" insignia was sewn in white letters across the front.

"It looks goofy," I said. "Don't buy it."

"I already have."

"Was it free?"

"No."

"Then you paid too much."

His other hand clutched two CDs he had gleaned from the rubbish. He held them high: *Honky Tonk & Slow Music*, by Johnny Paycheck, in a scraped plastic sleeve; and, to complete the haul, *Country and Western Hits, Volume 2.*

"Are there really enough country and western hits for two volumes?" I asked as I settled into the passenger's seat. "I feel like the trip just got longer." I kicked my feet around the unfolded maps and open guidebooks that cluttered my side of the floor.

A couple of hours into our journey, the Brazilian music had started to wear us down, and Peter had left that CD on a table at the fair. Relief was at hand. Loud and clear, we started with the C&W disc before pulling out of the parking lot. Johnny Cash, Conway Twitty, and Patsy Cline were about to clarify America's longing for simpler times.

Our breakfast had barely been digested by the time we reached Joliet, where we spotted an ice cream parlor boasting taste teases from the 1950s. There was the licorice-banana dip that I ordered, and the awful-looking blueberry-raspberry dip that I asked to be splashed over Peter's ice cream. This did not seem odd in the town that is the birthplace of Dairy Queen, the creator of DQ sundaes, cones, and, eventually, Blizzards.

For years, Dairy Queen's featured novelty was "soft" ice cream, a departure from the harder ice cream that was all one could purchase until the late 1930s. "Grandpa McCullough" and his son, who owned the Homemade Ice Cream Company, specialized in providing three-gallon tubs of handmade ice cream to stores. They discovered that a lower butterfat content and a slightly-less-cold temperature, mixed with a bit of air at the time of serving, produced a tastier product. It was almost as tasty as the flavored milkshakes popular then, and less cumbersome than ice cream soda floats. The trick was to modify a custard machine that could "soft serve" this creation. Once that was done, in 1940, the McCulloughs opened their first shop in Joliet, christening it Dairy Queen because the McCulloughs saw soft ice cream as "a queen among dairy products and the epitome of freshness and wholesomeness." By the end of 1941, ten Dairy Queen establishments graced the roads. Franchising was brought to the world of fast food through the partnership of Grandpa McCullough and the manufacturer of the ice cream machine, and it found its first markets along Route 66. Today, Dairy Queen's original building still stands in Joliet. It is now unused, but there are nearly 6,000 Dairy Queens worldwide.

Even in Dairy Queen's hometown, Peter and I chose a non-DQ roadside oddity as the place to buy our soft ice cream cones. The man behind the counter, seemingly unhappy with serving us, plunged my ice cream cone into an aluminum canister and withdrew it covered with a hideous veneer, shining black. The strange concoction clung to the roof of my mouth the moment I began eating. What else could you expect from a place that featured oversize images of the Blues Brothers atop the building?

"Joliet" Jake Blues, a character portrayed in the 1980 *Blues Brothers* movie by actor John Belushi, drew his nickname from this town. Dan Aykroyd's character, Elwood Blues, was named after the town of Elwood, a little farther down Route 66. An early tension between the Blues Brothers occurs when Jake is released from nearby Joliet Prison and picked up by Elwood, who is driving a battered, secondhand police cruiser instead of the fancy Cadillac they'd owned before Jake's prison sentence. Route 66 was already proving itself to be a source of folklore.

America has its share of oddities. Here on the outskirts of small-town U.S.A., Peter and I began noticing early tributes to the road. The guidebooks promised (or warned) that we'd encounter a variety of shameless promotional efforts, such as junk food places (this ice cream shop, a corn dog palace, a fudge store—all qualified recommendations) or visual quirks (giant this and giant that—a whole series of bloated creations and contraptions designed to lighten travelers' pockets). Peter, oblivious to my aversion, stopped to capture these unnecessary entertainments with his camera, from several angles. ("Hold it! Stop! Back up!" he commanded as if I were driving. I had to remind him, more than once, that he had the wheel.)

Imagine Disneyland stretched over 2,400 miles, with its rides and attractions placed at irregular intervals. It would be the "pretend past" masquerading as today. Let the sun and weather have their way, ignore the maintenance schedule, and return in forty years. I sought a more bona fide storyline from Route 66.

"There's a Route 66 museum in Joliet town," I said. "Let's get us some real road music."

"You don't like mine?" Peter asked. I think he was slightly offended.

"Nice, but they're for another road. We need something that sounds like back-road pavement with cracks in it, that talks about lost homes, lost families, lost towns."

"There you go, talking about 'lost' again," he said. "You make me nervous."

The museum yawned a welcome. Not yet aware of the trail of souvenirs awaiting us on Route 66, we stocked up on the museum's monogrammed pencils and stickers. We made the happy discovery of two CDs loaded with unfamiliar road tunes, including "Tucumcari Tonight" and "We're Heading West" by the Road Crew. I scanned the cover and wanted to play the music right away to get in the mood of one called "Running Down the Mother Road."

Route 66 has its apostles: Drew Knowles, in his *Route 66 Adventure Handbook*, writes in a breezy style, boldfacing the place names and attractions designed to zip the traveler through each town and state, and offering matter-of-fact accounts and concise photographs. Jerry McClanahan and his co-conspirator, illustrator Jim Ross, of the Route 66 map series titled *Here It Is!*, became my most necessary guides. Their single-foldout scans of each state showed all the accessible "old parts" of the route at a glance by using an easy-to-understand overlay of the interstates. Tom Snyder's tall and narrow *Route 66 Traveler's Guide* has a fun introduction by Bobby Troup, wherein Troup says that the last time he saw the ravaged Buick he and his wife had driven on their snowbound trip on Route 66, it was being auctioned off on TV and "the pitchman was saying that it had only been driven by a little old lady in Pasadena." The high priest of the route's pamphleteers is Michael Wallis, author of the substantive *Route 66: The Mother Road*, a compendium of all things Route 66, from tidbits to factoids to portraits of proprietors like the late Lucille Hamons, "the Mother of the Mother Road." She lives on in the Smithsonian Institution's display "America on the Move," where the original sign for her Hamons Court motel and service station has been preserved and is now on view.

Although we were anxious to put some miles on the Mustang, we couldn't resist slouching into the fabricated casings of the 1960s automobiles that graced the museum's foyer. These dream-mobiles faced a movie screen where a documentary was about to begin. I chose the powder-blue Chevrolet while Peter sat in the wing-tipped Cadillac, his arms stretched out toward the dramatic tail lights.

While watching Michael Wallis's video *Route 66 Revisited*, we realized we should have watched it when preparing for the trip. It gave depth to the route while cajoling would-be explorers with a line that stayed with me: "Experience America before we become generic." The current rush toward sameness is a social disappointment. Generations of mass marketers have made retail individuality rare, and the storefronts of one destination's downtown mimic those of almost every other downtown in the country. Would we find that Route 66's back-road economy had forestalled the interest of large companies? Has a neglected road left the "real America" intact? Wallis's documentary encouraged optimism, but the questions stayed with me.

Apparently unencumbered by the issues raised in the film, Peter was soon acquiring gifts for the home crowd, choosing mini-decals and tattoos. The lady behind the counter gave him a free map and asked him to say hi to a friend of hers who was working in another gift shop along 66, in Arizona.

"What do you think makes Route 66 special?" he asked, as though he owed her for the free map.

"It's the characters you meet on the road," she replied. "Paul McCartney drove it, you know. Just a few years ago. Well, he drove parts of it. That's all most people do."

We had begun to understand that many travelers segue onto only parts of the route, avoiding the no-man's lands between the high points. She admired the intentions of our trip: "If you don't read the guidebooks, you'll miss plenty—you might even get lost."

"Not me," piped up Peter. "I've got a natural sense of direction."

We took our trinkets and crossed the parking lot to the Mustang. Peter had an immediate objective: "We're going to the graveyard. William Cornelius Van Horne's buried here. In Joliet."

"Why?"

"That's what I want to find out."

I got in the car beside Peter—train company man, history buff, and born-again photographer. Peter and Van Horne have each built reputations in the railroad trade. The connection moved Peter to say, as we drove, "If I could have dinner with a dead historical figure, I'd choose Van Horne. I thought I knew lots about him, but I never expected to find him here."

We entered Oakwood Cemetery's shaded drive, which was a mile from Joliet's town center. We moved slowly beside many gravestones marking untold stories. Then we saw them. Boulders protected Van Horne's burial site. We gazed on the unexpected memorial. Before us were the remains of a one-time Joliet telegraph runner who rose to oversee the completion of North America's longest railroad. Here lay the Joliet ticket agent who was knighted by Queen Victoria—*Sir* William Cornelius Van Horne—after twice declining the honor. Here rested one of Joliet's favorite sons, a man who became known on the continent as "the king of the railroad."

Peter stammered something as he got out of the car, and soon was solemnly standing before the huge stone monument to the railway superintendent. I noticed that he resembled Van Horne in being "tall and massively built," as well as in having "immense physical energy." Van Horne had left the United States for Canada, and in 1888 became president of the transcontinental Canadian Pacific Railway, Canada's national dream.

"Curious that it was an American who kept Vancouver and Victoria from becoming part of the United States," Peter said. The Canadian government's promise of a railway linking Montreal and Ottawa with the west coast in an all-Canada rail route prevented the young colony of British Columbia from joining the United States—and Van Horne built that railway.

Rail travel opened up North America to tourism. Van Horne pushed passenger rail service across the northern third of America, as the Rock Island Line and the Santa Fe Railway had pulled travelers from Chicago to the Southwest in the late 1800s. Then, as now, there was money to be made—and lost—in the travel business.

Train company promotions from that time defined public perceptions of the West in the continent's central and eastern cities. Van Horne had overseen operations of the Chicago & Alton Railroad and the St. Louis, Kansas City & Northern Railway in the early 1870s. In the boom days of rail travel in the 1890s, it was "the West" that lured easterners in search of easy adventures. Train advertisements featuring Arizona, New Mexico, and California attracted tourists to destinations where the Southern Pacific Railroad wound its way through inhospitable terrain to the territory of the exotic Pueblo Indians, to a land of ranchers not yet transformed into cowboys by Hollywood, and to a West wilder in rumor than in reality.

Hoopla and touristy boosterism by companies like the Atchison, Topeka, and Santa Fe Railway first created—and then reinforced—stereotypes of Native peoples and sold the world on a new place to visit.

The railroads cut swaths horizontally, vertically, and diagonally across the emerging nation's frontier, midwest to southwest. Their poster art depicted teepees for tourists, modifying them into tantalizing lodgings. The railroads shamelessly promoted these portrayals of the land and people—Indian trading posts, Wild West gunfights, over-the-top headdresses, and religious objects refashioned as souvenirs. This creation of false expectations, as much as rifles and six-shooters, shifted the relationship between the "civilized east" and the "Wild West." In their efforts to build a tourist industry, railroad promoters distorted the West's Spanish and Mexican influences and transformed the native peoples' heritage into a marketable commodity. In doing so, their railway depots became tourist towns, and these new tourism destinations demanded constant refashioning to meet the expectations of visitors.

I stood on one of the boulders surrounding Van Horne's gravesite. Peter glared at me. Clearly he considered my position disrespectful. "This guy built the Banff Springs Hotel in the Rocky Mountains," he said, referring to the railway-crafted lodgings. The Canadian railway hotels and their U.S. counterparts, the Harvey Houses, were built beside railroad tracks at key tourist locations.

Peter stared at a giant rock carved from the Rocky Mountains through which Van Horne had built the impossible railway. The marker had been shipped to Joliet by an appreciative Canadian government when Van Horne died in 1915. Not looking up from the dedicated tombstone, Peter quoted Van Horne's famous line, the one that made railways and highways such as Route 66 a success: "If we can't export the scenery, we'll import the tourists."

We left Joliet, passing its McDonald's and Burger King franchises—outposts of the empire that wounded the viability of independent diners across America, leaving their disenfranchised heirs along Route 66. The people who once ran these singular restaurants—moms and pops, families, solo entrepreneurs—would hang out a shingle announcing their specialty. And Route 66 has featured the finest names in roadside diners: Pop Hicks Restaurant, Ted Drewes Frozen Custard, Steiny's Inn, Zella's Café, Dolly's Chili House, and Silva's Saloon all hearken back to those days.

The diner business was relatively simple to get into in the 1930s and 1940s—the grill and stools were readily available, countertops were quick to construct, and produce was easy to find. One could affordably outfit mobile units and move them to new locations as needed. The easy availability of Mom's recipes ensured that most establishments could offer the equivalent of home cooking, and family members provided cheap labor. The aura of good food, good prices, and good surroundings soon became associated with the roadside diner.

Many of these diners later came to offer in-car service, attractive female carhops, push-button intercoms to enable ordering from the parking lot, and snappy building designs—Cadillac-fin roof lines and neon signs.

Not all diners adapted, though, and with the one-size-feeds-all competition that was mushrooming in the 1960s, independent diners were at risk. Most eventually disappeared or were subsumed into the franchise game. The road that once guaranteed individuality began to promise standardized service and similar products wherever one went. Community-based food purveyors became state-wide suppliers and eventually interstate shippers, their success enhanced by Route 66's easy access. When road travelers sought meal security rather than dining adventures, they were rewarded with the familiar signs of franchised restaurants, which promised reliable food and predictable dining. The eight-state conduit, Route 66, was an enabler: Dairy Queen began in Joliet in 1940; Roy Allen & Frank Wright's (A&W) original promotional burger-family-in-fiberglass today watches over Route 66 from a roadside perch in Dillon, Missouri; and Dick and Mac McDonald opened their restaurant in San Bernardino, California, in 1940 (before selling out to their milkshake-machine salesman, Ray Kroc, who was impressed by the number of machines they kept ordering).

This consistency of experience posed a threat to the novelty of travel. Peter and I were headed south and west on Route 66 in search of an America that was still one of a kind. Would we find it? The odds seemed against us.

As we put Joliet behind us, our stereo blared songs from one of the new CDs, *Music from the All-American Highway: The Songs of Route 66*. The disc included an unfamiliar (to us) tune about Route 66 remembrances—"Used to Be," with its woeful words ("There used to be a main street cross the country . . .") and upward beat (then more up, then one more up) that made me want to drive forever on a bumpy road just to keep pace with the tune. And when it was over, there was Jason Eklund's hurried admonition to "Get your kicks on what's left of 66 . . . " Most compelling on that sunny, top-down afternoon was thirty-nine-year-old bandleader Nelson Riddle's arrangement of the *route 66* TV show's theme song. Commissioned in 1960, it soon became ubiquitous. Initiating what was to become a morning rite on our trip, I shoved Riddle's work into the CD player and cranked up the volume for our adopted anthem.

It was a perfect day, a perfect start—there were great lengths of older two-lane to cover—and we went clear from Joliet to Bloomington before being forced to engage I-55 for a spell: The best part of an interstate is its exits. Shortly thereafter, we regained Route 66, and out of respect for the road we replayed all the songs.

In the 1950s, traveling Route 66's directional map had been effortless. Now, it is rougher. We swung around towns, slipped left and right to find map-noted portions of the true 66 ("It's here, I know it's here," Peter would say as he steered, adding, "somewhere") and to learn of their brief claims to fame. In Gardner, the Riviera Roadhouse (destroyed by fire in June 2010) served as a Route 66 stop for Al Capone around 1930, when he was Chicago's public enemy number one. I read more place names, and Peter took each as a prompt to swerve the wheel and search: the early railroad town of Dwight, named for a now-forgotten railroad builder; Odell, with its restored 1940s Standard Oil station, complete with glassed-in gas container as a mantle; and Towanda, the smallest town we would intentionally drive through on our journey, storied in Native lore as "Where we bury our dead." Each of these towns had once hummed with significance, held families who perhaps had dreamed their child would become president of the United States, and erected buildings in the hope of permanency.

Our commitment to drive the old 66 was tested early on. It meant matching two maps and three guidebooks to make sure we didn't overlook anything. That was fine by me, though it cluttered my side of the car when all the materials were open. My lack of loyalty to a single source frustrated Peter; he had winnowed his navigating advisory to one tidy book of maps and directions: Jerry McClanahan's *EZ66 Guide for Travelers*, respected for its broad-coil, easy-to-flatten format and for the authority of its publisher, the National Historic Route 66 Federation.

"We've less chance of getting lost if you'll just use one map," Peter argued.

To keep him quiet, I smoothed my copy of McClanahan and Ross's *Here It Is!* map against the Mustang's dashboard and read their instructions out loud, as fast as I could: "Continue on the I-55 frontage road through Funks Grove to McLean. Entering town, curve right onto Carlisle, left on Main Street, then right onto U.S. 136. Before the railroad tracks, turn left off of U.S. 136 and continue on the I-55 service road. Approaching Atlanta, hook right to follow Arch Street through town. When it reconnects with the frontage road, turn right and continue westbound through Lawndale to Lincoln."

"Sounds pretty clear to me," said Peter.

Zeke's advice to "get out of Illinois quickly" was ill-founded. It had been possible to drive for an entire day with only a brief interstate encounter. Town after town, especially the little town of Atlanta, urged us to pause, kick around on the sidewalks, visit the only shops on earth with their particular names, and avoid the corporate labels that plague the world with their sameness. These towns brought to mind an earlier pace of life, and did so in ways that combined beauty, practicality, and livability. We could again sniff the October aroma of burning leaves.

We were passing near the peaceful town of Pontiac when Peter braked suddenly. "Will you look at that," he said. The road had been empty, except for us, for fifteen minutes. Pulling off the main "old" road, we drove through a shallow ditch, up a grassy hill, and stopped. Before us was a weed-riddled Route 66, with cracks in the pavement going every which way—a deterioration that eventually made way for the "improved" version we'd been driving on, which itself gave way to the interstate.

We shook hands. We'd found what we were looking for: an unused road. It had no purpose; it was impractical to drive. So we drove it. It lasted half a mile, to where it was blocked by a barrier and a sign: ROAD ENDS. It was our first discovery of the original pieces of Route 66.

"I want to find more like this," Peter said. "It goes nowhere and that tells you everything."

This was our first sighting of an abandoned stretch of old Route 66, and we made our way through a shallow ditch and up an embankment to drive where weeds cracked the tired pavement.

I felt oddly at home here, somehow centered and comfortable and not at all a stranger to the setting, though I'd never been near this part of the state.

Back in the car, cruising south, we watched as the sun set. Then Peter decided to find all the ways Route 66's history and alignments wound through the pretty town of Lincoln.

"Hungry?" he asked at long last, knowing I was getting dizzy with his driving, stopping, turning around, and heading down dark roads. "That sign says Blue Dog Inn. Bet we can eat. And find two rooms."

"Fresh paint on the building, cars parked out front, and the lights on inside," I observed. What more could we ask for?

The restaurant, narrow and noisy, had an empty counter with unoccupied stools on the left. The booths on the right were mostly filled with people chuckling, telling stories, and eating. The third booth, down the aisle, was empty. A smiling young waitress came over immediately.

"You look like you'd enjoy a beer," she said. "And then what would you like to eat?"

We swigged Pabst Blue Ribbon from canning jars as soon as she set them down. "The beer's local—well, at least state-local," she said. "Special tonight is grilled pork tenderloin. But I gotta tell you the Philly steak sandwich is awesome."

"One of each," said Peter. "We'll share."

She looked at me and I shrugged, though I hate onions and begged that they be left off my side of the Philly steak.

Our "plan" was to stop wherever the day's end found us and to sort out lodging then. "Any rooms at this inn?" Peter finally asked her, after first questioning where she was born and how long she'd been a waitress.

"Afraid not. Used to be rooms here, but there hasn't been enough business for years. You'll have to head to the interstate exit to find a motel. There're several at the turnoff. That's where the tourists stay." Then she added, wistfully, "The

A man tethered to business protocols, Peter's behavior began to change once on Route 66—sometimes in ways completely understandable, and sometimes in ways less so.

tourists miss the town. Silly, isn't it. They breeze right by us, take a snippet of Route 66 for their memory bank, and keep on the interstate."

Whenever Peter unfolded a map on the table when we ate or on the dashboard when we re-entered the car, he took to humming after Nat King Cole: "If you ever plan to motor west . . . " At dinner he browsed through a brochure listing all the song's destinations in their proper order and featuring a map connecting them. We stared at those check marks—familiar names of unfamiliar places. Peter looked ready to sing with a mouthful of Philly steak. Thankfully, he swallowed.

I turned the brochure so that the words faced me. It's odd how slowly you read when you're trying to sing a song in your mind at a normal pace. I did that, noticing that the words and lineage were true to the way Bobby Troup wrote it out:

If you
Ever plan to
Motor west
Travel my way, take the highway
That's the best
Get your kicks
On Route Sixty-Six!

It winds
From Chicago
To L.A.
More than two thousand miles all the way
Get your kicks
On Route Sixty-Six!

Now it
Goes through Saint Louis
And Joplin, Missouri
And Oklahoma City is mighty pretty
You'll see
Amarillo
Gallup, New Mexico
Flagstaff, Arizona
Don't forget Winona
Kingman, Barstow, San Bernardino

Won't you
Get hip to
This timely tip

When you make that California trip
Get your kicks
On Route Sixty-Six!

"We'll hit 'em all," said Peter. It was as close to a trip plan as he ever offered.

At the motel, I unloaded my rumpled bags after watching Peter carefully lift both his shiny briefcase and his new suitcase out of the trunk. Entering the low-lit lobby a minute behind him, I found him bargaining with a petite lady who was staunchly defending her territory.

"Sixty-eight dollars a room seems a lot," Peter said. "We paid less last night."

"You didn't sleep here last night."

Checkmate, I thought.

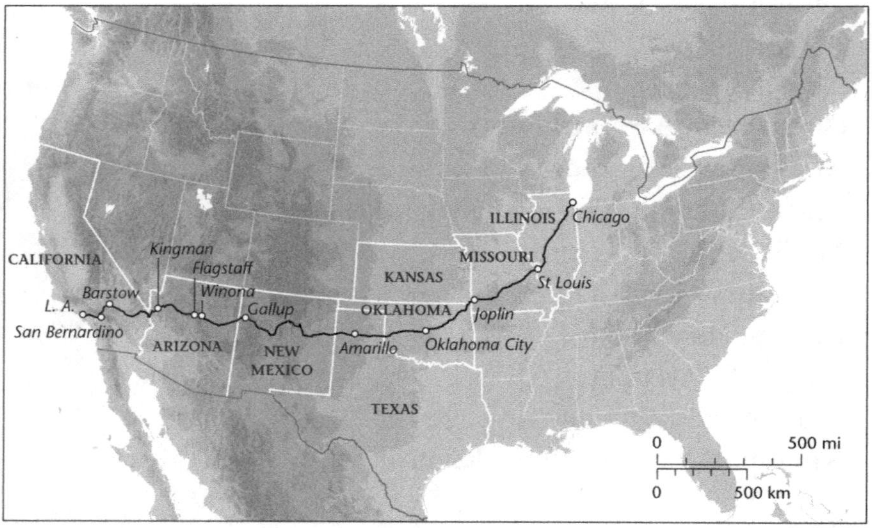

Having in mind these place names on Nat King Cole's and Bobby Troup's lyrical song map from "(Get Your Kicks On) Route 66" was as near as we came to having an itinerary.

I took a key from the counter and wandered up the flight of stairs to my room. The wallpaper was a paisley maze of blues identical to the bedspread, which featured the same design as the sticky carpet. They all bounced off two long mirrors and made my eyes blur. I tossed back the bed covers to break up the sea of blue. They matched the sheets.

3

The Way West

"Route 66 is an opened time capsule."
—Coffee shop customer

Waiting for Peter, I mopped the morning dew from the Mustang's back window with a few paper towels I'd borrowed from the bathroom and shunted my duffle bag into the trunk. I went back into the motor court's canteen, pressed batter into a waiting waffle iron, poured myself a coffee, and walked across the lobby to check out while the waffles cooked. A computer terminal sitting on a desk off to the side winked at me, but I try to avoid being tied to home when traveling. I settled up my room bill and turned around. The computer winked again.

Peter had not given me any reason to believe he'd show up on time, and there were still five minutes to go before our agreed rendezvous. It wouldn't hurt for me to do a quick email check. I logged on. I'd given Peter a rough time about his BlackBerry addiction; "I'd as soon travel with a smoker as with someone addicted to their cellphone," I'd preached. Now, at the terminal, I hurried, wanting to hide my failure of character from Peter.

Up flashed the bank of inbox messages. Scratching at my three days of whiskers, I scanned for anything important enough to open. "Urgent," shouted one, so I clicked. It began with an apology from my office's director of human resources, saying we needed to talk pronto, as a vice-president had given notice that she was leaving the organization. It was Saturday.

Somehow, I would have to phone the two people involved and deal with this matter. I signed out.

I'd barely stood up from the blackened computer screen when Peter appeared. "Off to Abraham Lincoln's hometown today," he announced. "Springfield, Illinois. I'd like to see Abe's monument." He was so caught up in thoughts of Honest Abe that he failed to notice my hand on the computer. I was safe. I picked up the two cooked waffles and offered one to Peter.

Once we were on the road, Peter impulsively decided we'd breakfast at Nora's, an eatery that appeared before us at roadside. There were few symbols of the famous road here—no familiar graphics on the menu, and none on the walls. Not even a poster of Route 66. Photographs of cars and a painting of a drive-in gave the only nod to the past. Although we were cooked for as though we were the morning's 100th hungry customer, we were served with the personal care of the first.

Suddenly, two girls, about eight and ten years old, jumped into the booth next to us. One girl's eyes flicked away when I turned, and the two friends whispered to one another and giggled. I could hear the words "funny accent." The United States is home to hundreds of English dialects, and in some parts of the country variations are noticeable within fewer than 100 miles. To those of any age who are hometown bound, a visitor's voice stands out.

The waitress came over, poured another coffee, and asked where we were headed; Peter explained our journey and asked what she thought of Route 66.

"I heard . . . if you haven't driven Route 66, you haven't seen America."

The older of the two girls asked, "Is that true?"

"We're about to find out," I said.

The younger girl, who had remained silent, now fiddled with what I took to be her school lunch box (even though it was a weekend): a dented metal tin, perhaps handed down from her father that showed a baseball fielder stretching to catch a fly ball. "My dad says it's a blue-collar highway," she pronounced, with confidence, if not understanding.

I said to Peter, "Funny, that. 'Blue-collar highway' is actually a phrase from one of the songs on our discs." I made a note to listen better and try to catch the meaning.

When we were back in the car, Peter, jumping to an implication, said, "Do you see a pattern here?" I didn't. Then he filled me in on his conversation with the waitress. "She's another waitress we've met who is single, a mother, and can't afford to move away."

It once fell to men to be the food servers in restaurants, though in the late 1800s the farther one went west, the less reliable the men were wait staff—railway work and cowpoke jobs paid better, and, it was noted, most food establishments at that time paid little heed to the refined aspects of service.

Enter the Harveys: Fred—of British birth and expectations—and Barbara Sarah, whom Fred met in St. Louis. In 1876, Fred struck a business arrangement with the Atchison, Topeka, and Santa Fe (AT & SF) Railway to be its food provider at railroad stops. The burgeoning number of travelers meant that he could build upon that relationship to service other rail lines, targeting their up-market customers. Steam-driven trains at that time required regular stops to fill their boilers, and it took several hours to travel 100 miles. So there was a real need for frequent food stops in the years before dining cars.

Their experience with restaurants led the Harveys to implement a "waitress preferred" hiring policy that brought many young women—future wives, mothers, and settlers—to its facilities along the railway, which in many places ran beside what would one day become Route 66. Beginning in 1883, the Harveys advertised in Boston, New York, and other eastern cities for "young women, 18 to 30 years of age, of good character, attractive, and intelligent." The implied payoff included an escape from city life, the avoidance of domestic obligations or marriage, and the rare excitement of travel.

Not everyone viewed such a posting as suitable. It was a time when pundits claimed there were "no ladies west of Dodge City and no women west of Albuquerque." But the Harvey approach, assuring chaperoned lodgings, refined working environments, meals, and uniforms, proved a resounding success. In its 100 years of operation, the Harvey Houses firm expanded to a peak of eighty-four restaurants and hotels, ultimately employing an estimated 100,000 single women. In the late 1800s, employees signed a six- to twelve-month contract stipulating up to twelve-hour shifts, aware of the hustling required when that meant four or five trainloads of passengers disembarking every day,

Harvey Houses, restaurants, and hotels promising travelers hearty meals and reliable service sprung up along the railroads and eventually beside Route 66. The Harvey Girls became as famous for their professionalism as were the establishments where they worked.

most days of the week. And they committed to staying single while in the employ of the Harveys.

The "Harvey Girls," however, often had different long-range plans. They set their sights on customers and cowboys. As many as 20,000 Harvey Girls are said to have married men they met through the restaurants. Harvey House became known as the "cupid of the rails," despite the starched, somewhat sexless uniforms that ensured the girls wore white bibs over black dresses that hung close to the floor. Will Rogers quipped that the Harvey Girls "kept the West in food and wives." And, it might be added, in "new settlers"—thousands of their baby boys answered to the name of Harvey, and many others to the name of Fred.

Though speedy service and kitchen efficiency were fundamental to tightly scheduled train service, Harvey Houses were never considered "fast food" outlets. The company does, however, hold the distinction of being America's first restaurant chain. It stressed consistent standards of cleanliness, fine food, fine linen, and fine chinaware—all brought to you by the finest young women in America, particularly as portrayed in the 1946 Academy Award-winning movie musical *The Harvey Girls*, starring Judy Garland and Angela Lansbury.

When Route 66 emerged, the Harvey Houses were still expanding as a chain, and they adapted their locations and menus to suit car travelers as well. Throughout the eight Route 66 states, beginning at Chicago Union Station and including remoter locations such as Ash Fork and Kingman, Harvey Houses became a part of travel on Route 66. La Posada in Winslow, the last Harvey House to be built, opened in 1930. The celebrated El Garces in Needles did not close as a Harvey House until 1949.

And today, the single woman as waitress was the most consistent feature we noticed in Route 66 diners.

Elkhart is a tiny town; 100 families might call it home. Without expecting to find anything other than squat buildings and left behind farm equipment, we were surprised to find the Blue Stem Café. Route 66 was once known as “A Ribbon of Eateries,” and you still travel it anticipating culinary experiences. Despite our recent breakfast, we decided on a sweet dessert. To be honest, I have to admit we stopped so that I could make a phone call.

Peter sipped coffee, spilling a bit of pumpkin-peach muffin down his sleeve as he pulled on a white dowel-backed chair and set his cup on the table.

“This is going to warm the cockles of your heart,” I said.

He raised his left eyebrow and gave me a look that knew somehow I'd screwed up.

“Can I borrow your cellphone?”

I spent the next hour and a half walking the streets of Elkhart, talking on the phone as the town's morning life carried on around me: a mother, with an infant in tow, opening her craft store; a white 1964 Chevrolet cruising down the main street; two boys—darting, hiding, darting—cutting through a lady's yard, behind her back, as she tended her garden. During the long-distance phone conversation, my colleagues and I worked through the amicable departure of the senior executive. Peter circled the town on foot, once, twice, seven times. I circumnavigated the same streets in the opposite direction. It was not possible to avoid his grin each time our paths crossed.

Suddenly, a procession of five combine harvesters paraded down the main street, raising clouds of dust and ending the morning's stillness. I could not hear the voices on my phone for the noise. The lady tending her garden swung around, ran through her fence gate and onto the road, yelling at the parade, “You can't drive here! You can't drive here!” None of the iPod-wearing drivers heard her; none cared.

Abraham Lincoln, born in Kentucky, is buried in Springfield. The city is pleasantly caught in time. The monument to the president is a big tourist draw, a fact that stifled my interest while it piqued Peter's. Fearing swarms of people, I purposely pointed at something away from the directional sign, and Peter at first missed the turnoff. He then piped up, "Hey, I wanted to go there. That's Lincoln's monument."

"You should have said so earlier," I snapped, pretending I hadn't remembered his comment in the motel lobby first thing in the morning.

"Let's go back."

"We're making good time. Speak up more quickly if there's a place you want to go."

"Let's turn around, okay?"

"It's a mile out of our way now." I said.

We drove on in silence, and in the gloom I sensed my error. "Okay, we'll go back."

"Never mind," he sulked. His big frame sagged noticeably. He slowed down the car at the next traffic light.

"It's only a few miles back," I said.

"Nah, let's keep going."

Half an hour later, near Chatham, Peter said, "I really wanted to see the Lincoln Tomb."

"Stop, now," I said. He did, mid-road. The driver behind us honked, pulled beside us, scowled, and drove on, again honking. I looked at Peter. "A little late, don't you think?"

"I'll never be here again."

"Am I going to hear about this the whole trip?"

He thought about that as he started to drive again, making a move to U-turn, but he had a change of heart mid-bend. He straightened out, headed south, and sped up, saying, "I'll probably never see it in my whole life."

"You know what?" I roared. "There's nothing wrong with our relationship that couldn't be cured if you had a five-second pause button. I'd push it right now."

"Ya, well if you'd given me ten seconds to think about the monument, we'd have visited and be done with that."

And so it was that our trip's two most helpful protocols emerged. The Five-Second Pause Button, which could be signaled by either of us when the other person was getting on our nerves. And the Ten-Second Rule, which meant that if you were asked, "Do you want to go there?" you had ten seconds to respond—or to forget about it *forever*.

For Peter, who never gives up on even minor disputes, his driving on was the equivalent of a ceasefire, which of course is itself quite different from détente. The camaraderie between us grew from the mistake I'd made in not stopping. It was a successful error. There was a realization that we needed to do pretty much anything the other traveler asked in order to ensure cordial memories.

"Take a picture," Peter said near Staunton, where we'd pulled over to unbend our knees. He was leaning on the car's hood and was passing his camera to me, no doubt thinking he looked swish.

"Only if you take off that dorky hat," I said.

He withdrew the camera.

We were in Litchfield, at the Route 66 Café, where we'd ordered up chocolate milkshakes. Peter ignored me in favor of penning one-line insights on another dozen postcards. He'd managed to collect images of Route 66 landmarks that I so far had studiously avoided approaching: the giant Muffler Man, a standing-too-tall Abe Lincoln, and the Paul Bunyan giant with companion giant hot dog.

"I think the St. Louis Arch straddles the Mississippi River," Peter mumbled to himself.

"Hmm . . . " I mumbled back, thinking that for two guys who had traveled the globe, how could we not know the Arch's location?

Peter was not one to let the new protocols go untested.

"We should go walk on the Chain of Rocks Bridge. I read that it's reclaimed from the overgrown forest, and you can walk over it," I said.

"Really?" The forty-two-degree-angled bridge had served Route 66 after it was built in 1929. Time passed it by, and it was closed to vehicle traffic in 1968. After a while, Peter said, "Do you want to see it?"

"Sure," I finally responded. "I'd really like to do that."

"You missed the ten seconds," Peter said.

"Huh?"

"I counted. You missed. Like me and Lincoln. You had ten seconds to say yes or no."

We did not turn to see the bridge. We were even.

The 630-foot-high Gateway Arch loomed ahead, the setting sun's rays glancing off it. It was clearly landlocked and within the city's downtown. The stainless-steel structure, built between 1962 and 1965, was intended to symbolize St. Louis's role as a staging area for westward expansion, the gateway to the West. We glided near, but not under, the impressive structure, but my eyes were searching storefronts for a car-rental outlet so that I could get registered and insured to legally drive the rented Mustang. Eventually I persuaded Peter to stop and ask a hotel doorman if there was an agency in the vicinity.

"Head out of town," the doorman advised, looking at his watch and realizing that evening was nigh. "Go north to the airport. It'll be the only one open this time of day."

"We'll get you signed up tomorrow," said Peter.

"Today!" I insisted.

"I'm happy to keep driving," offered Peter.

"I'm not," I said. "Not happy with you driving. Not happy with me not driving. Got it?"

We left the St. Louis airport an hour later, with me insured to drive and anxious for tomorrow's turn at the wheel. Missouri awaited us, unsuspecting.

As Peter and I drove away from St. Louis, the impending darkness and our airport detour meant we would miss the more southern 1926 alignment, where Route 66 meandered through the onetime resort town of Times Beach, nestled in the Ozarks. I had hoped to loop down that way and off I-44 to visit the only named Route 66 Park, which replaced the town.

Times Beach began as a summer paradise promotion in the 1920s—a relatively quick escape from downtown St. Louis, on mostly bad roads, to affordable property: $67.50 for a twenty-by-one-hundred-foot lot. Dozens of families purchased land, built holiday homes (sometimes on stilts, to avoid flooding), and dreamed of a prosperous future, only to have it disrupted by the Great Depression.

This early portion of Route 66 continually struggled to remain a proper road. Lack of funds meant that Times Beach's burgeoning twenty-plus miles of streets remained dirt; they would not be paved even fifty years later. The resulting dusty roads begged for a solution, one that begat a toxic calamity on a scale seldom seen in the United States—making Times Beach a match with Love Canal and the Valley of Drums in the trio of most devastating places for America's environmental clean-up Superfund, in the years before the *Exxon Valdez* and the Gulf of Mexico oil disasters superseded them.

Even after the section of Route 66 that passed through Times Beach was itself paved, the town's streets remained neglected. Summer continued to bring cough-inducing dust.

In 1972, a coalition of residents and businesses persuaded the town council to have their roads sprayed with used engine oil—a not-uncommon practice in rural communities. For four years, the contract went to Russell Bliss, at six cents per gallon.

Bliss was a waste recycler; he had the rigs with which to spray, and he had the oil. And, tragically, he also had a waste disposal contract with the Northeastern Pharmaceutical and Chemical Company (NEPACCO).

A part of NEPACCO's facility, when owned earlier by Hoffman-Taff, had produced Agent Orange defoliant for the U.S. government during the Vietnam War. A large black tank that Hoffman-Taff had used for waste chemical storage remained onsite. Into this tank went the dioxin discards created as a byproduct of NEPACCO's work. Enter Bliss. As Robert Hernan notes in *This Borrowed Earth*, it was found much later that the lethal residue of clay and contaminated water "contained levels of dioxin some 2,000 times higher than the dioxin content in Agent Orange." Bliss mixed NEPACCO's waste into his oil-recycling spray as an extender. At first, the area's increased incidence of disease, defects, and deaths went unnoticed.

Bliss had also been spraying the dust-controlling fluid for the vicinity's horse stables before he received the Times Beach contract. When sixty-two horses died mysteriously in 1971, ranchers, farmers, and residents were alarmed. Eventually the government would share their concern, and in 1979 the Center for Disease Control and Prevention launched an investigation centered on NEPACCO.

The U.S. Environmental Protection Agency (EPA) first visited the near-forgotten Route 66 town in 1982. It was astounded at the dioxin levels in the local soil—100 times the hazard level—and in 1983, it bought the square-mile enclave of Times Beach for $32 million. It was the first such buyout in U.S. history.

Under the headline "Times Beach, Mo., Votes Itself Out of Existence," the *New York Times* proclaimed on April 3, 1985: "The dioxin-contaminated town of Times Beach officially ceased to exist today when its aldermen voted unanimously to disincorporate."

The federal government quarantined the site while evacuating the few dozen people remaining of the onetime 2,240 residents. The former townsite was locked down by barricades and gates for a dozen years. Given the national media coverage and the panic associated with the toxic threat, the evacuees were unwelcome almost everywhere they went.

Due to a lack of applicable laws and the absence of hazardous-waste disposal regulations, NEPACCO could not be successfully sued. Bliss was never convicted of any crime and claimed ignorance of the chemical time bomb he had spread.

An enormous effort was made to decontaminate Times Beach, culminating in 1996–97. Buildings were dismantled and homes razed, but one building was left standing: an old roadhouse, opened in 1935 as the Bridgehead Inn. A massive incinerator was erected onsite to deal with over 265,000 tons of soil from the town and twenty-eight other eastern Missouri locations, capping twenty years of reaction to what was called "the awful contamination."

In 1999, the incinerator having been disassembled and moved away, having received the EPA's "all clear," and after federal spending of $200 million on clean-up, the State of Missouri created the 419-acre Route 66 Park. Today, a beautiful paved road goes through the park and passes Steiny's Inn, formerly the Bridgehead Inn and today a visitor center. The road crosses a picturesque bridge over the waters of the Meramec River, a bridge recently declared unsafe for automobiles as well as cyclists or walkers. This Route 66 alignment is the road that once brought visitors and residents home to Times Beach and later helped evacuate them.

"What do you think of Route 66?" Peter asked a fellow restaurant patron, who responded, "There's a lot of junk disguised as charm." Skeletons of cars and truck carcasses often hide in fields or sit across the road from boarded-up motor courts, complementing the legend of Route 66.

There are as many ways to leave St. Louis on Route 66 as there are flavors of milkshake. Initially we missed them all. Having fancied the more southern of the two main corridors, we now found ourselves on Manchester Road by accident. We were approaching a road not shown on our maps, yet seemingly one that could connect us with where we wanted to be. Peter took it, at my suggestion. As we realized my miscalculation, we agreed to reset course for Gray Summit.

Peter said, "Let me count the days to your next mistake."

"Whole days?"

"Hours."

On Missouri 100 (aka Route 66 before 1932), we drove past bright lights, milling people, and a sign for Silky Custard, not sure where we were on the map. We turned around for a treat.

With a cup of custard in my hand, I saw my whiskers reflected in the diner's window: my hair was frizzed and wind-split in a dozen directions, many of them upwards. Peter snapped a picture and emailed it to my sons before I could grab the camera and delete the embarrassment.

"Your friend Abe Lincoln wrote, 'A man can't raise himself up by pulling another down,'" I said without much hope. Peter remained unashamed and unrepentant. He took another picture.

Charged with sugar energy, we left what we thought to be Gray Summit in search of St. Clair, my map indicating it as a possible place to stay over for the night. Peter, partially remembering an early reading of his guidebook, said, "There's a motel in Cuba, Missouri, called the Wagon Wheel. Let's head there instead."

Peter and I are both good at making decisions. It is having a *choice* that confounds us. For some unexplained reason, and driving at sixty miles an hour, he then unilaterally cancelled the Cuba mission and announced, "I'm taking us to the town of Union." Union did not show on my map.

In the dark, hunkered over the steering wheel, Peter glared down the road, looking for any designation that matched what I, as navigator, read out to him. To ensure that we had a chance at accuracy, I alternated between two guidebooks and an unfolded map.

I have a propensity to be wrong when navigating. Peter had identified this trait early on in our trip, and as a result became overconfident about his own decisions. It showed in his sternness, his stubbornness, and his unwillingness to listen to me. These attributes brought us to the saga of Highway 50.

"What you say isn't what I see," he said.

"We're looking for Highway 44," I reminded him. "When we get there, we're cruising 66 right next to it."

"I'm not seeing 44," he said. And to my surprise, he announced, "I'm looking for Highway 50."

"Then you won't see 66."

"You're not being helpful," he snapped. "Sixty-six is the way west. We'll find it by finding Highway 50."

I poked on an interior light to check the map.

"There's an idea," Peter said. "Use a light to actually see your map."

Between my reading, his hunches, and our haggling, we cobbled together an agreement on which route to take. And then, ignoring it, Peter arbitrarily turned off the main drive onto a spur road and up through a motel's portico. He rolled down his window, stopping where a short-haired blond girl in a smeared cook's smock sat on a boulder. She was happily smoking away her coffee break.

"Do you work here?" Peter asked, ever the conversationalist. Without waiting for a reply, he announced: "My friend here has got us lost. We're looking for Highway 50 because we're driving Route 66."

"Neat," she said, and I was not sure whether she meant that it was neat that we were lost, neat that we were looking for Highway 50, neat that we were driving Route 66.

"Any directions to St. Clair?" I asked through Peter's window, thinking we should still head that way.

"Back, over there." She waved her cigarette at the intersection she'd known since childhood. "Cross over. Quick left. Road ends. Then take a right." She said something else, but Peter had already thanked her as the car rolled forward out of earshot. We were on our way again, with loads of confidence and partial directions.

Peter made a right turn, found a dead end, and got the "crossover" partially right—merely out of sequence. It got us on to a road that was not the busy highway we'd exited. Peter knew in his heart he was headed in the right direction the moment he saw a nearby sign that said Highway 50.

"Fifty?" I asked. "Fifty? You're not serious."

"That's it. I knew that would be it. I saw the map earlier. I'm sure. If you'd only let me take the turnoff three miles back, we'd already have connected to Highway 50. This is it. We're home free. Relax." The night's drive started to get progressively darker, if that was possible.

"Do you think . . . ?" I began.

"*No*, this is it. I wanted Highway 50. I'm finding Highway 50. Route 66, here we come."

We drove for quite a while, skimming over the shadowy hills roller-coaster style, encountering only three sets of oncoming headlights. No one else was driving on our side of the road.

"It'd be nice to see a Route 66 sign for confirmation," I said.

"We're okay. We're on the right road." Peter's mule-headedness was something to behold.

"Still, anything saying 'Route 66' might be encouraging," I said.

"Then play one of the songs."

The lack of crossroads was a concern to me, but not to Peter. The occasionally seen houses, set well back from the road, fit with Peter's idea of what Route 66 looked like in the dark, so we continued driving west on the mystery road.

In a feeble effort to explain why we were not lost, Peter said, "Missouri has lousy Route 66 signage."

"Either they have lousy signage and we're on it," I countered, "or it has great signage somewhere else."

The car interior went silent.

I tried to find where we might be on the map, but it was hopeless. The two street signs we did see bore no resemblance to any mention in the guidebooks or on the maps before me. I tossed them back on the floor, trampled them with my feet, and tilted my seat back. "Wake me when it's over."

Nearly an hour into Peter's chosen route and his frozen-custard-mindset, we saw commercial lights—a sign that someone might be around and might be able to recommend accommodation. We both jumped out of the car, Peter clutching his favorite guidebook, and me flapping a large map in the breeze. We burst into the convenience store, banging the door against a potato-chip stand.

Startled, the lady behind the counter was on the defensive. Peter disarmed her with a boisterous laugh as I spread the map over the counter between her and me. I traced my finger along the line designated Highway 44 and its parallel sections noted as Route 66 to show her where we wanted to be. I said, as casually as I could, "Can you show us where we are on this route?"

Peter looked down at the sheet of roads as she used her finger to push mine out of the way and then turned the map around so it faced her. She turned it again.

"You're not on this map," she said, looking directly at me as though I was a fool.

"Huh?"

"You're not there. You're here!" And she moved her finger to the emptiest part of our page, off the map altogether and well onto the empty counter. "You're way up here!"

"Hmm," I said, trying not to look at Peter, who was trying hard not to look at me. "Well then. Where's the next connector road to get us W-A-Y D-O-W-N T-H-E-R-E AND BACK ON TO ROUTE 66?"

"There is none," she said. "None at all. If that's where you want to get, you have to drive back where you came from. It's only an hour."

Outside, in the fresh air, I laughed so hard I could barely breathe. I gulped for air and swallowed my sentence. Eventually, I inhaled the cold air slowly and shouted at a sheepish Peter, "If you EVER mention Highway 50 again . . . "

We backtracked.

Into the silence I pushed our one unheard music disc, *More Songs of Route 66*. The back-cover blurb prompted me through the selections to a song I'd read about before the trip and had been surprised to find in Peter's museum-bought collection from Joliet. Troubadours Woody Guthrie and Pete Seeger once wrote a song that had remained unrecorded until recently. Here was a Steve James rendition to capture Peter's repentant mood: *66 Highway Blues.*

There is a two-story motel in St. Clair, Missouri, displaying the name Budget Lodge. St. Clair had once been named Traveler's Repose—the name was changed when civic leaders felt it implied a "lasting rest" rather than an overnight visit. As I dragged my rucksack through the glass front doors, Peter's loud laugh bounced off the walls as he responded to a comment I did not hear. He was entrenched in room-rate negotiations with Tom, the night manager who'd seen it all, heard it all.

"Sixty dollars," Peter offered into the fray.

"Sixty-nine," Tom countered, not moving. I sensed that his feet were braced to hold his ground.

"What was your rate when you opened in 1990?" asked Peter.

"Fifty-nine dollars," said Tom.

"Great, we'll take that."

"I don't have any of those rooms left," said Tom.

I realized that, to Peter, it was the hunt, not the catch. He could not resist taking a business guy's swing at making a game of it whenever coinage was involved. What counted to him was the sport of banter and the chance of a win, however insignificant the monetary victory.

We returned to the front desk after dropping our luggage in our rooms. I asked Peter if his room smelled. "A little," he said. "Why?"

"Nothing," I said. "Mine doesn't."

Tom recommended the Pizza Shack for dinner, sending us back to the highway. "Cross over. Quick left." I got really nervous hearing those directions again.

"Good food?" I asked.

"Only place open," he said.

Two couples, seated separately, greeted us before the owner did. "You look like travelers," said a man in his mid-twenties, swigging from a bottle of beer. His lady friend, perhaps ten years his senior, raised a glass of wine our way in a hesitant toast. Mark, the owner, hovered and then offered to order for us, and left.

The couples jump-started the conversation, telling us of their own travels, swapping place names like Scrabble squares. "New York, New Orleans," said one woman.

"Minneapolis, Denver," said the other couple's man. They continued to list several places—all in the United States.

"Ever been to Mexico?" asked Peter.

"No, but I thought about it."

"Canada?"

The man with the beer lifted its nose to his lips and gulped, putting the bottle down as though the resulting burp had helped him think. He said, "I've been to Toronto." His eyes had turned to the television above the bar, where the University of Missouri Tigers were fighting the Texas Longhorns in a highly contested football game. The home team had given up a touchdown.

The foursome felt our trip was special. The man said, "Route 66, end to end, really? You must be great travelers."

"*Fortunate* travelers," Peter replied as Mark, the shack's owner, set down two hefty all-meat meals before us and brought more draft.

Mark stepped into the conversation. "Why do you travel so much?"

"Maybe you travel to learn who you are," Peter said. The man across from me looked at the foam on his beer. Whatever he saw there ended our conversation. I wondered at Peter's off-handed remark. What would he be looking to learn from his own travels? We hadn't talked about that, and now I took his phrase to be a telling one.

Peter's work has owned him, instead of the other way around. He's had decades of dedication to the business of building business, and some of life's false joys got in the way of truer ones. Being away from those obligations and the daily rigors of work had seemed an easier shift for him than I'd have predicted. His chosen topic, more often than not, was the road ahead—and not as a figure of speech. Was there something about Route 66 that was breaking the mold for him?

When the meals were done, Mark cleaned away the plates. Peter pulled a brown envelope from his pack. It held an assortment of Route 66 postcard images: the Jesse James Wax Museum, the Garden Way Motel. Then, declaring, "We should go here tomorrow," he held up one promoting the Meramec Caverns.

He bought dinner. I offered to split the cost.

"In twenty years, life will have evened the two of us out," he said, shrugging off my contribution. So began our twenty-year plan of not being conscious of who paid for what trip costs, waiting for reconciliation two decades away.

Texas scored a big touchdown in the football game, making the final score 56–31. A man slammed his beer mug down on the bar in disappointment. Mark started up a blender to quell a chorus of home-fan anger, and within minutes he came by our table with an autumn treat. He placed two small dessert glasses in front of us, on the house: "Here's a pumpkin-pie shooter."

4

The National Old Trails Road

"My men folks have left me stuck in the mud all my life."

—Missouri farm wife, 1912

My Missouri morning broke happily—I was the driver that day. Up early, again skipping a shave, but having showered, I packed my gear in the trunk and took the driver's seat.

It was drizzly and damp as I sat alone in the car, warming it up. I let the wipers clear the front window.

For the first time Peter showed up unshaven, though on track in once more being half an hour later than my hoped-for starting time. He slunk into the passenger's seat—where he thought I should be sitting. "Missouri was one of the first states to pave the route. And it was just as quick to replace much of the route with Highway 44."

"You mean Highway 50?"

"You're beautiful to be with," he said.

"Each new day is a fresh chance to try and get it right," I said.

Peter picked the guidebooks up from where I'd left them on the car's floor, arranged them in order of size, then placed three of them in the glove compartment. As I drove, he chose one spread-open-on-the-floor map after another, folded them and put two in the passenger door's side pouch; the rest went in the glove compartment.

I thought he was sulking a bit because he wasn't driving. Then I realized there was genuine disappointment in his voice when he said Missouri had a lot of great driving, but "few 66 dead ends."

So I asked, "What's your preoccupation with dead ends?"

"Once they weren't dead ends. People designed them, built them, drove on them, had happy thoughts. Probably believed they would go on forever."

"And . . . ?"

"And . . . and we shouldn't ignore that every part of Route 66 was once part of someone's dream."

Holding open the remaining map, he pointed out the zigzag pattern of Route 66's alternating between north of Highway 44, then south and back again, thankfully seldom merging with the interstate. "You've got three hundred miles of Route 66 to drive. Joplin for dinner?"

As the rain started to fall, we rededicated ourselves to seeking out parts of the road not easily traveled. "First," Peter chuckled, "remember these directions and we'll be fine." He read rapidly from the page in front of him, bettering the performance I'd given the day before: "Take the outer road into Sullivan. Past the city park, turn right on Elmont, then left at the outer road and continue through St. Cloud, Bourbon, Cuba, and Fanning to St. James. Turn right in St. James at the junction with MO68 (Jefferson), cross I-44, then turn west again on the out road. After eight and a half miles . . . "

"Makes sense to me," I said.

"Sure," he laughed. "Clear as mud to you."

I swung into traffic, cutting off a BMW that had showed up as if from nowhere. It honked, curved around us, and screamed down the road.

"Slow down," Peter advised.

I sped up.

Beginning in Rolla—and for the next 115 miles, until Missouri's Springfield—Route 66 overlapped the path taken by Cherokee Indians in the winter of 1838–39 on their 1,000-mile forced migration from the state of Georgia to Indian Territory, now in the state of Oklahoma. Known as the Trail of Tears, it reshaped the United States.

The Trail of Tears began on Cherokee ancient lands, located in northwestern Georgia and portions of neighboring Tennessee, North Carolina, and Alabama. The Cherokee were the last of five Indian nations in that vicinity to face expulsion from their traditional territories. The first to be relocated were the Choctaw, in 1831, followed by the Seminole (1832), the Creek (1834), and the Chickasaw (1837). The final indignity was the expulsion of the Cherokee in 1838. In all, more than 60,000 Americans—including a number of African-American slaves "owned" by the Cherokee—were involuntarily moved.

Their trek took them through Tennessee, the western part of Kentucky, the southern tip of Illinois, and then Missouri, where it went straight across the state to present-day Springfield and headed southwest to Indian Territory, a vast allotment in which the five tribes were systematically relocated in separate jurisdictions. The Cherokee were placed in the north.

Measures to move the Cherokee had first been contemplated when Georgia's immigrant population boomed in the early 1800s, putting pressure on the Indians to make room for the newcomers. Both willingly and unwillingly, they ceded parcels of their fertile land to the U.S. government, the Georgia state government, settlers, and businessmen—all anxious to acquire the eventual 25 million acres. Then, with word of a gold strike in the mountains of Georgia in the summer of 1829, the United States experienced its first gold rush. The push to get the Indians out of the way began in earnest. The U.S. government proceeded to steal land from the Cherokee through intimidation, manipulation, and the Indian Relocation Act of 1830.

Andrew Jackson's presidency is characterized by his betrayal of the Indians' rights. He presented it otherwise: Warning them of cultural extinction and the continued erosion of their lands should they stay in the southeastern U.S., Jackson offered them "an ample district west of the Mississippi, and without the limits of any State or Territory now formed . . . " He assured them that, "There they may be secured in the enjoyment of governments of their own choice, subject to no other control from the United States than such as may be necessary to preserve peace on the frontier and between the several tribes."

A three-term congressman from Tennessee vigorously opposed the Indian Removal Act. Davy Crockett was forty-four years old when he bitterly split with his fellow Democrat and fellow Tennessean, President Jackson, over what he called "a wicked, unjust measure."

The belligerent Jackson, whom the Cherokee called "Sharp Knife" for his tactics, told them the relocation "would serve as a reminder of the humanity and justice of this government."

The bill brought national controversy, passing Congress in a 102–97 vote in which the contrarian Crockett's "nay" reverberated widely. "Let the cost to myself be what it might," he said. He was confident that it was the moral and right decision: "I would sooner be honestly and politically damned than hypocritically immortalized." His actions cost him the 1832 election. Defeated, Davy Crockett left Tennessee to start a new, albeit brief, life in Texas.

The Indian Removal Act was quickly signed into law by President Jackson, and in 1831 the U.S. Supreme Court refused to hear the Indians' legal case to keep their land, ruling that the Cherokee were not a sovereign nation, and, by implication, neither were the other independent nation groups—not the Choctaw, the Seminole, the Creek, nor the Chickasaw. The U.S. government immediately began displacing the natives from their lands and moving them west to (then) undesirable land. However, in 1832, the Cherokee successfully established autonomous-nation status in a separate Supreme Court case, delaying Jackson's plans and launching a treaty-ratification process that was deeply flawed; the native leaders who signed the contentious Treaty of New Echota were eventually assassinated by their own people for doing so.

The Cherokee nation's four-month walk to their new home began in the autumn of 1838. They were force-marched west by the U.S. Army, accompanied by covered supply wagons. The movement of 15,000 healthy Native Americans continued as the pleasant fall weather turned to rain, then sleet, then snow, then ice. Throughout the harsh winter of 1839, their 1,000-mile exodus became rife with disease, malnutrition, and hypothermia. At one point, the natives were given blankets previously used in a hospital's smallpox ward, another reason for them to be shunned by white people en route. Four thousand Cherokee perished before reaching Indian Territory.

"Winners write history," we are told. So it was that for decades school books and popular histories frequently called U.S. cavalry "wins" *victories*, and referred to the occasions when the Indians prevailed as *massacres*. It is not at all a subtle point. Similarly, for over a century Andrew Jackson's "exchange" of land was portrayed as a benevolent act by a caring government. There was precious little explanation of the Cherokees' ancestral farms being won by settlers engaging in whites-only land lotteries; less was told of the plunder and the scorched-earth approach to clearing away any visible reminders of the exiled Indian nations.

The Trail of Tears forged a path, one-tenth of which was eventually covered by Route 66, the highway that almost always went where others had gone before. Tsalagi, the Cherokee language, refers to this migrant route as *Nunna daul Isunyi*, "The trail where they cried."

Oklahoma gained statehood in 1907, but not before the descendants of the resettled nations tried to protect their continually shrinking land base by petitioning for the Indian Territory to become a separate state of the Union. The petition was rejected by Congress. If the native peoples had been successful, Route 66 in the next state ahead on our drive would now pass through the state of Sequoyah.

Max D. Standley's painting portrays the Cherokee nation's tragic trek in 1838 along what became known as the "Trail of Tears," following their forced removal from traditional homelands and their transition to Indian Territory in what today is Oklahoma. Portions of their journey's path eventually became part of Route 66.

Through the whipping windshield wipers, we saw the first of many barn sides covered with faded advertisements. In the 1930s, entrepreneurs had paid farmers to let them paint promotional billboards barn-wide and rafter-high. Eventually they were replaced by special-purpose advertising billboards. Despite President Lyndon Johnson's 1965 Highway Beautification Act, which was aimed in part at eradicating the billboards, still they crop up. Here they alert travelers to the Missouri's Meramec Caves, a holdover from the glory days of family vacations, and they remain popular. "They used to tag bumpers with paper ads while the car owners were in the caves," I said to Peter. "So they claim to have invented bumper stickers. Do you want to go there?"

It failed the Ten-Second Rule.

Route 66 is an expression of America's romance with the personal vehicle. America's automobile ingenuity in the 1890s built on the success of Herr Benz in Germany in 1888 and that of Monsieur Peugeot in France in 1891—accomplishments that would soon be overshadowed by automobile giants such as Cadillac and Ford, and by a pan-American road. By the turn of the century, 11,000 automobiles were on the road in the United States, and seventy-five companies manufactured them (among these the reliable Maytag, later of washing-machine fame). Such was the popularity of cars that the American Automobile Association (AAA) was created in 1902, at the Chicago Automobile Show, to bring a national presence to lobbying for road improvements and to encourage motor touring. The AAA's early mandate was "to promote a transcontinental road."

America's road system in the first two decades of the twentieth century was a puzzle. ("Guess which road we're on?") Many of its disconnected segments were short and for personal use only. These "roads" had begun as bicycle trails or farm-to-farm buggy paths. Developed by private auto clubs, they were named on a whim, with no regard for where they might one day lead or with which other roads they might connect.

Relatively new state roads, constructed to get goods to market, frequently intersected with these private roads and often led to the duplication of numeric designations and names. The resulting confusion, occurring during a time of rapid population growth and urban expansion, left Manifest Destiny without a reliable road map.

Eventually though, despite the mayhem, through-state and state-to-state roads became the avenues of trade and travel, connecting the eastern United States with the West. Vying for transcontinental recognition, the proponents and users of each emerging route competed against the others for prominence and prosperity, lobbying for state and federal funds and improvement contracts—and courting the towns and cities that stood to benefit from their proposed course.

The personal ownership of automobiles continued to increase, and automobile travel was becoming a feature of the American landscape. Trunks became a common feature on cars, and vehicles were given larger gas tanks. Long-distance car travel had arrived.

An Ocean to Ocean Highway Association, as much an emotional pitch as a road-building endeavor, was formed in 1911. It was that era's defining vision, equivalent to President John F. Kennedy's later vision of landing a man on the moon. Forging this trail literally, politically, and physically were influential groups such as the Good Roads Organization (representing bicycle users—at this time numbering in the millions), the Women's National Trail Association, and the Old Trail Association. Mail carriers were strong advocates of a national road system.

In 1912, a convention of community leaders and politicians had been held in Kansas City to choose the attendees' preferred route to California. The resulting National Old Trails Road

(N.O.T.), hinged to New York, was tagged "The Broadway of America," though it really began in Washington, D.C. It would continue to St. Louis, then to Kansas City, Wichita, and Denver, where it would head south to Salt Lake City and continue to Santa Fe—essentially following the original 1825 Santa Fe Trail from St. Louis to Santa Fe—and then continue to Los Angeles. This decision made the termination of the "Ocean to Ocean" movement likely, as the proposed N.O.T. would follow the convention's suggestion to parallel the Santa Fe Railway route from Albuquerque into Arizona and Flagstaff-Kingman, and onto Barstow and California.*

With the National Highway Association being formed in 1912, the N.O.T. gaining ground, and the Lincoln Highway on the verge of its formation in 1914, the "Ocean to Ocean" organization became redundant, and that association terminated its existence with its second annual meeting in April 1913.

The highway that would become Route 66 also owed much to the dynamic Ozark Trail network and its promotional association. The Ozark Trail Association was flexible enough to incorporate Missouri and Oklahoma—and eventually Texas and half of New Mexico—into an alternative route proposal between St. Louis and the West. Originating in the resort of Monte Ne, in the northwest corner of Arkansas, the Ozark Trail provided a loose connection of wagon roads and motor routes between St. Louis, Springfield, and Tulsa, and beyond.

In 1915, the National Old Trails route became the first road to rightly claim transcontinental status. The next year President Woodrow Wilson signed the Federal Aid Road Act, allowing the nation to embark on schemes that, by 1926, led to the creation of the National Highway System.

---

* The one technical exception being that the N.O.T., like the original Santa Fe Trail, would pass through the city of Santa Fe, whereas the railway never did. The Santa Fe Railway served its namesake city with a spur line from nearby Lamy, which was on the rail line.

From all of these schemes, the National Highway System's best-known artery—later tagged as the world's most famous highway—emerged from a patchwork of links. Including portions of the Pontiac Trail between Chicago and St. Louis, and parts of Boon's Lick Road to Kansas and the Ozark Trail from St. Louis to Tulsa, a ragtag group of routes (under the auspices of an expanded Ozark Trail) went from Oklahoma City into New Mexico on the Beale Wagon Road, and on to Santa Fe, where it absorbed the National Old Trail en route to Los Angeles. By 1926, that collection of roads would be substantially defined on paper—and ready for designation as Highway 66.

A dismal Missouri sky hung over the day. Peter pointed rather than spoke and guided us through the County J exit and south until his map work had us start west along County Z and on to a dead-end patch of 66.

"There's a place called Arlington," announced Peter. "No one goes there anymore, so I think we should." It was an easy drive along old two-lane and often within sight of the freeway. Eventually, though, it curved into the trees, became quiet, and led to the near-ghost-town of Arlington. Tom Snyder's *Traveler's Guide* calls this a "real old-road treat." Nevertheless, this worthy drive over the Little Piney River and into history is missed by nearly all Route 66 travelers. We shrugged off the eeriness of this isolated place, parked the Mustang, and walked the town's silent streets. Travel is sometimes an antidote to ignorance, and here the lesson was clear: what was, isn't; what is, won't be.

We backtracked along the road we'd driven, learning along the way that this portion of historic Route 66 has confused researchers with a maze of "alignments" both south and north of the interstate.

"Your affection for dead ends is a little unsettling," I said to Peter, as he held up the map to show me that we had crossed over the freeway and placed ourselves on a short access road.

"Watch for John's Modern Cabins," he said. "They were built when the route was new." On our right, overgrown by tall trees and hidden behind bushy shrubs, were John's collapsed wooden shelters, fronted by a lonely sign, presumably trying to say "Vacant." In my pre-trip mindset I'd assumed we'd stay most nights in motor courts like this—refurbished, of course. Yet they were not easily found when our time came to bunk down each night.

Again, we retraced Route 66 in order to go forward and drove through Hooker Cut, a stretch steeped in ghoulish traffic history from the 1930s. Many fatalities were attributed to its untamed curves, poor sightlines, rough surfacing, and narrow passage hewn through the ridge—all early dangers that were magnified by untrained drivers. The combination of those factors contributed to the section's reputation as "Bloody 66."

At a dip in the road, we swayed left and drove to a stretch where the original 66 struggled over an iron bridge built in 1923 at the Devil's Elbow, a name coined by loggers in their frustration with the Big Piney River bend's log jams. We stopped and got out of the car for a walk. Orange and red leaves matted at our feet, held together by the glue of rain. I tried to kick some high to hear them rustle. They flew in clumps.

The story of Route 66 has many beginnings and many advocates, but no story is more important than that of Cyrus Avery, an Oklahoman whose early endeavors need to be recounted while we're driving in Missouri. The route was blazed with false starts and political ambitions by dreamers and schemers and ne'er-do-wells. Avery was one of the dreamers. The passionate

There are many derelict motor courts remaining along Route 66, and some have found themselves protectively registered in America's Most Endangered Historic Places, a listing compiled by the National Trust for Historic Preservation. For others, it was too late.

speechmaker was the new road's first believer, an energetic builder, and its most enthusiastic ambassador.

"I challenge anyone to show a road of equal length that traverses more scenery," Avery proclaimed at rallies. His dark hair framed a slender, confident face. In public he wore a round-collared shirt, modest tie, wool vest, and matching suit. Avery joined forces with the Ozark Trail Association when he attended the organization's founding conference in July 1913. His early reputation at such gatherings was as a renegade who spoke confidently and eagerly forged common ground with allies.

Avery's eye was always on improved roadways through his own state of Oklahoma, but he knew he had to begin by working with routes originating elsewhere. With the shared objective of better transportation corridors, these promoters cobbled together a scheme built on existing land routes, such as the Old Wire Road and the Albert Pike Trail. Avery believed that these fragments could be joined into a cross-country road. His vision was built on practical considerations. He advocated connectivity, continuity, and clarity in signage on what was going to be "one of the greatest traffic lines in the United States."

Avery was involved in oil, real estate, and coal mining—all industries reliant on access roads. He called Tulsa home, and that fact drove his efforts to have the multi-state highway pass from Missouri through Tulsa as well as Oklahoma City, the state capital. Meanwhile, competing interests in Washington, D.C., Kentucky, and other states fought to have the route bypass Oklahoma entirely, looping instead to the south—or, north, via Kansas-Colorado-Utah, then Nevada, and on to California. Avery countered their plans by demonstrating that his national corridor meant both less snow and fewer miles through the desert.

Appointed Tulsa county commissioner, Avery drew attention to neighboring Missouri and its roads—superior to Oklahoma's both in extent and in quality. Wearing an additional hat as director of the Tulsa Automobile Club, he lured the 1914 Ozark Trail convention to Tulsa. As host of the successful event, Avery's stature as a "good roads" advocate was enhanced, and he was given positions of influence among the nation's road-building decision-makers.

Avery explained Oklahoma's challenge well: "The fact that transcontinental railways have for the most part missed the state, because it was so long Indian Territory, has also helped turn travel to other states." That situation needed to be rectified—a new highway route could not be solely based on where railways had run.

At the 1916 meeting of the Ozark Trail Association in Oklahoma City, Avery proposed an extension to Amarillo, Texas, and then on to Santa Fe, New Mexico, where it would reconnect with the National Old Trails road into California. That configuration proved a commendable detour from the "all N.O.T." route. It became an erstwhile competitor to the Lincoln Highway and presaged the "diagonal highway" that in time would outshine them both.

By the early 1920s, Avery was at the forefront of the move to merge roads and tourism, in hopes of raising the revenues of one to help further the other. Of course, this also helped his own new business—the Old English Inn and Service Station, seven miles out of Tulsa, at the conveniently named Avery's Corner.

In 1923, Avery, now Oklahoma's highway commissioner, made it his job to improve conditions on the state's muddy and poorly maintained roads. The following year was the beginning of a two-year quest for him and his associates: to create the country's highways system, recommending to the federal government existing routes that should be designated "national" and therefore ought to receive federal funds for their upgrading. He termed it "laying out, coordinating, and establishing a system of highways with markers and directional signs." This planning of arteries by Avery and a small group of advisers to the federal secretary of agriculture was extremely controversial, nowhere more so than in Avery's efforts to ensure his home state's and hometown's inclusion on the list.

The first agreement among the planners of this nationwide approach was in identifying a series of east-west highways to be intersected by a grid of north-south highways. Avery's pet project (eventually Route 66) remained an aberration: The route's diagonal slide across the nation made its consideration by Congress less likely than their approval of the more "logical" horizontal and vertical highways.

Across the nation, there were still more than 250 uncoordinated, and generally conflicting, trail-naming programs. Avery wanted to eliminate existing trail organization signs—those tied to private roads and automobile-club designations. In their place, he lobbied for interstate signs to be "adopted in order that the traveling public could get from one community to the other without getting lost."

In an apparently simple solution, the committee members agreed to abandon "names" in favor of numbers. Major north-south arteries from the Canadian border to the Mexican border would end in the numbers one or five, the sequence starting in the east. Complete east-west routes—from the Atlantic to the Pacific—would end in zero, starting with Highway 10 in the north and working south. It was thought that the public would understand that odd-numbered designations ran one way, and even numbers the other. A motorist on a numbered road in the middle of nowhere would now actually have an inkling of where the road was heading. That's when Cyrus Avery embarked on gaining acceptance for his Chicago-to-L.A. route as "Highway 60." The effort pitted him against Kentucky for that designation, as well as

Cyrus Avery, the "Father of Route 66," believed that bicycle paths, auto club roads, and fragments of existing streetways could be joined into a cross-country route, and his 1926 pavement politics reset the course of travel, trade, and tourism in America.

against those advocating for "Highway 62." His eventual failure in this would lead to his greatest success.

Peter and I doglegged a bit around portions of Route 66. Following his favorite guidebook, we started down an uncertain road. He motioned for me to pull over in the settlement of Bourbon when he saw the Circle Inn Malt Shop.

"Anyone for breakfast?" he asked.

Entering this tired café, which seemed to have existed since the dawn of pancakes, I realized this was the "elsewhere" that others wished they were able to visit, a place where they could disappear in a time warp.

The waitress tipped coffee into our cups and placed a glass of milk beside the packages of sugar that were resting in a saucer.

Peter asked her name.

"Sheila," she replied, noncommittally.

"Sheila, how far is it to Cuba? We're headed there."

"Oh, I think it's twenty miles. Never been there myself."

"Never?" Peter's face squinted in disbelief. "It's only twenty miles!"

"I'm not much for going west," she said, not at all defensively. "Never had any reason to. I've been twenty miles east, though."

"Never?" Peter seemed incredulous.

She swung on him. "Never had any reason to," she insisted, looking at him directly.

A stout man on a stool behind me had apparently overheard our conversation. He jumped in to salvage the waitress's dignity. "Take a woman like her—" he paused, pointing to our waitress, "—away from *the route*," the man suggested, "and you take away the soul of Route 66."

Where the hell did *that* come from? I thought.

We were driving through Springfield, Missouri, which marks the beginning of one of the longest sections of the original Route

Peter gradually developed a penchant for exploring abandoned Route 66 buildings, a curiosity that matched his dedication to finding "all the old parts" of the road itself.

66 available to today's driver: Hall Town to Paris Springs to Carthage to Joplin, all the way to Oklahoma City, resplendent with mothballed auto courts and shuttered service stations. We crossed a steeple bridge to catch a glimpse of history: the Springfield courthouse, an elegant building, site of an often overlooked turning point in the history of modern travel—and we missed finding it.

The steps of the courthouse witnessed the meeting of the three fatigued and frustrated men who *named* Route 66. On April 30, 1926, two Oklahomans clambered up those steps to meet with a Missourian and resolve a heated dispute about the number to be assigned to their hard-fought-for national road.

The gregarious, high-collared, and sometimes high-handed Cyrus Avery had driven from his home in Tulsa with his abettor, the diligent John M. Page, Oklahoma's chief highway engineer. Missouri's highway commissioner, B. H. Piepmeier, arrived separately, anticipating a contentious deliberation.

Avery and Piepmeier had fought for "60" to identify the entire road from Chicago to Los Angeles, wanting the "0" status because it indicated a major route. Piepmeier agreed with this, though his Missouri would not be dropped from alternative national routes as easily as Oklahoma would.

Kentucky fought back, claiming prior use of "60" and invoking the "rule" that a west coast terminus in Los Angeles needed a corresponding east coast terminus. This resulted in Kentucky's proposed start of Highway 60 in Newport News, Virginia. The Kentuckians proposed Virginia-Kentucky-California and tossed Avery and Piepmeier a bone, suggesting that the Oklahoma City to Chicago leg could become an offshoot tagged "60 North."

Avery was insulted by the offer; besides, Oklahoma had already presumptuously printed sixty thousand brochures showing Highway 60 going through the state, and had begun erecting Highway 60 road signs along its state road. This bickering drew wide attention, and Avery sensed that Congress might rule against not only his chosen route number, but his chosen route, as well.

When Avery, Page, and Piepmeier huddled over the map table that afternoon, they knew they were not the victors in the battle for highway numbers. They disliked the patronizing proposal that Oklahoma City-Tulsa-Chicago become "60 North," appended onto a national corridor as an afterthought. They scanned U.S. maps showing all the other numbers bearing the approval of the federal authorities. They connived at how best to avoid the secondary-trunk status being foisted on them. The national grid's guidelines left them few choices.

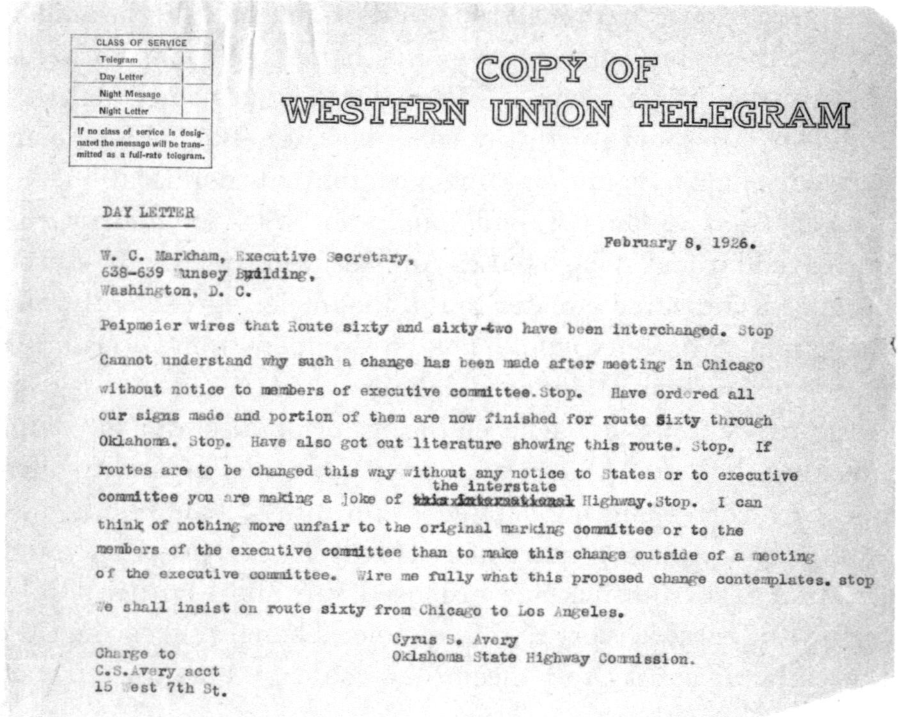

CLASS OF SERVICE	
Telegram	
Day Letter	
Night Message	
Night Letter	

If no class of service is designated the message will be transmitted as a full-rate telegram.

COPY OF
WESTERN UNION TELEGRAM

DAY LETTER

February 8, 1926.

W. C. Markham, Executive Secretary,
638-639 Munsey Building,
Washington, D. C.

Peipmeier wires that Route sixty and sixty-two have been interchanged. Stop Cannot understand why such a change has been made after meeting in Chicago without notice to members of executive committee. Stop. Have ordered all our signs made and portion of them are now finished for route Sixty through Oklahoma. Stop. Have also got out literature showing this route. Stop. If routes are to be changed this way without any notice to States or to executive committee you are making a joke of ~~this International~~ the interstate Highway. Stop. I can think of nothing more unfair to the original marking committee or to the members of the executive committee than to make this change outside of a meeting of the executive committee. Wire me fully what this proposed change contemplates. stop We shall insist on route sixty from Chicago to Los Angeles.

Cyrus S. Avery
Oklahoma State Highway Commission.

Charge to
C.S. Avery acct
15 West 7th St.

This telegram from February 8, 1926, conveys the frustration of state highway officials Cyrus Avery (Oklahoma) and B. H. Piepmeier (Missouri) to W. C. Markham (executive secretary with the American Association of State Highway Officials) and chastises him for not supporting their new highway's designation as "60" (eventually it became "66"). Note the telegraph vernacular of "Stop" to indicate the punctuation of a "period," which coincidentally seems to accent their emotional request that the federal agency reverse its decision.

Page peered over the cartography while Avery and Piepmeier talked of their dwindling options: They must move away from "60," but were too far north to use "70." And "64" was already assigned between Arkansas and New Mexico. Highway 62 promoters had cross-country ambitions for their road to become another strategic artery, bypassing Tulsa, though the number 62 was rumored as a default designation for the Avery-Piepmeier proposal.

Tapping the map, Page was the first to identify "66" as a possibility. Its alliteration, looping graphic, and synchronicity made it attractive. Piepmeier, an earnest, methodical man, saw the logic; Avery sensed the inevitability. The two men sprang into action, rushing to send a telegram to federal decision-maker Chief Thomas H. MacDonald, affirming, "We prefer sixty-six to sixty-two."

That summer, the Public Roads Bureau Division of Design confirmed Avery's request: "The route from Chicago to Los Angeles will be given number 66." Springfield had earned recognition as the birthplace of Route 66 when, on November 11, 1926, Congress approved the overall highway grid and numbering system, including Route 66. Let the mapmaking begin!

With the acceptance of "66," the Oklahoman Avery and Missourian Piepmeier kept their states from being marginalized by other highways. They did, however, suffer some embarrassment for their rash earlier decision: "As for the 'US 60' shields, we will have to junk them," Avery admitted.

Avery secured 415 miles of the new route within Oklahoma—more miles than any other state (405 of those miles still exist, for those willing to search for them). Route 66 would form 2,400 miles of what soon became an 80,000 mile network of federal highways.

Having served as a midwife in the birth of Route 66, Avery turned to new activities: getting the entire roadway paved and promoting its use. He initiated the U.S. 66 Association, to include all eight states—yet the organization never saw fit to elect him as president, though he came to be known as the "Father of Route 66." Avery worried about highways 30 and 40 as competition and embarked on aggressive promotional activities to establish Route 66 as the preferred road for travel and transport. He confidently christened it "The Main Street of America," a slogan that is still in vogue.

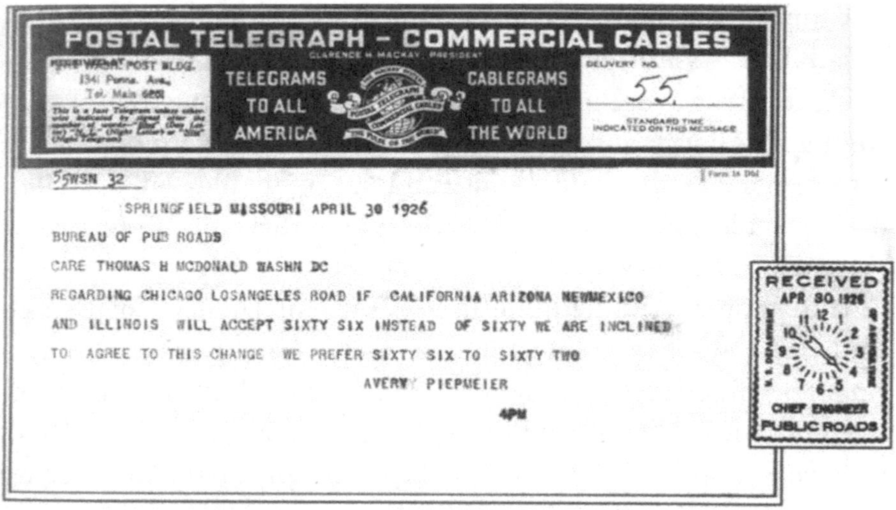
POSTAL TELEGRAPH – COMMERCIAL CABLES

TELEGRAMS TO ALL AMERICA — CABLEGRAMS TO ALL THE WORLD

DELIVERY NO. 55

55WSN 32

SPRINGFIELD MISSOURI APRIL 30 1926

BUREAU OF PUB ROADS

CARE THOMAS H MCDONALD WASHN DC

REGARDING CHICAGO LOSANGELES ROAD IF CALIFORNIA ARIZONA NEWMEXICO AND ILLINOIS WILL ACCEPT SIXTY SIX INSTEAD OF SIXTY WE ARE INCLINED TO AGREE TO THIS CHANGE WE PREFER SIXTY SIX TO SIXTY TWO

AVERY PIEPMEIER

4PM

RECEIVED APR 30 1926 CHIEF ENGINEER PUBLIC ROADS

This telegram from April 30, 1926, secured "sixty-six" as the designation for the thoroughfare envisioned by Oklahoma's Avery and Missouri's Piepmeier, and offered their acceptance of "Highway 66" to name their preferred routing from Chicago to Los Angeles, ensuring a major route would pass through their two states.

The progress of Route 66 was seldom smooth. The number-one responsibility of the route's architects was to ensure that all its component roads were consistently passable—they were, after all, now part of a major thoroughfare. After its birth in 1926, the route had to wait twelve years before its entire length was either paved with asphalt, protected with boards, or covered in cement.

Route 66 in eastern Missouri today delivers open stretches, little traffic, and a few surprises. As the road improved in the 1920s and 1930s, service stations sprung up to support the increased number of vehicles—all with small fuel tanks and needing frequent mechanical attention. Such locations came to be called "gasoline alleys."

One of the sweetest places on Route 66 is the Gay Parita Sinclair Station, owned by amateur historian and raconteur Gary Turner, who treats everyone as if they were his first guest. Part restoration and part replica, his gas station harks back to prosperous Route 66 days—it was established in 1930 and named for the then proprietor's wife. For today's traveler, it has been spruced up with white paint, red-and-green trimmings, and clean gravel.

Peter and I were hopping out of the car when the side-building's screen door opened. A man, more hefty than rotund, made his way with some effort down the rock path, where we looked at his creation.

"Glad you stopped," he said. "Got things to show you."

"We've got the time," said Peter, shaking his hand.

From its inception in 1926, Route 66 frequently shifted its course from one street-way to another and moved its alignment within and around towns as its routing sought new commercial opportunities. It often left behind remnants of a once-proud road that would be ignored for evermore.

The man started walking over to the large garage, built of rocks, turning to look back at us twice, to make sure we followed. "I'm Gary, and I'm the owner. Would you look at this truck . . . folks love to see it on the route." The doorway was truck-wide and truck-tall so that his vintage rig could back in.

Peter asked him about Route 66.

"First, let me get you guys a root beer." With that, Gary went to a beige-enameled fridge, opened its thick door, and held up three brown bottles. "See the labels?"

The label showed "Route 66" as the brand, bottled in Wilmington, Illinois. Gary twist-curled each bottle open and passed two over to us. I leaned against his truck while Peter pulled up a slat-backed chair. We relaxed in the garage, Gary propped on a carpenter's bench in front of a work table and rolling a cigarette.

Peter prodded Gary again, sounding like a cub reporter. "What do you think is the most important thing about Route 66?"

Gary lit his cigarette and glanced sideways to ensure he was out of sight of the house and thus spared his wife's reprimand. Exhaling, he became reflective. "I've thought about this. Route 66 is a journey, I think—a journey through time and history."

Peter put down his camera. Gary, puffing on his cigarette, continued. "It crosses eight states, but we don't see state lines. We're all one family—the family of Route 66."

"Like America?" I said.

"Not like America now," he replied. "Used to be. Maybe." He was thoughtful, but not hesitant. "People seem willing to take a democratic stand for this country. America's had a rough patch. Hell, we're not perfect. Besides, we've had a bad run of it. It'll be good again."

"Are you a Democrat or a Republican?" asked Peter.

Gary leaned back on the table and let go a puff of cinder-colored smoke.

"You probably know Will Rogers's line that 'I'm not a member of any organized political party. I'm a Democrat.' Well, me, too.

Those folks aren't perfect, none are, but they're my type, they're this road's type. 'Course, the Republicans did provide funding to let the heritage get preserved . . . "

Car tires crunched the gravel outside, and in pulled a siren-red 1958 Chevrolet Impala, white canvas top down. Shiny chrome emphasized the car's sleekness and its oversized white-walls had not a speck of dirt on them. The car had recently been polished and dusted; what didn't glisten wasn't worth looking at. As we approached, the driver and his passenger got out—all smiles, as though their car had finally found a gas station to match its own Route 66 DNA.

"Engine a 283?" asked Gary, almost singing his presumption that this model had everything that was standard then.

"348 Turbo Thrust," the driver replied, smiling proudly at the novelty.

For a brief five minutes, America shone before us in a rearview mirror. America's safe harbor is the 1950s. Today, revisionist history portrays the decade as an extended period of national innocence, an era when everything seemed possible and nothing hampered the nation's well-being. Naive? Of course. Accurate? Of course not. But we left those facts alone. It was immensely satisfying to ignore the present and spend a few minutes immersed in contemplating a glowing past.

Gary went into the station, turned on his radio, and soon the garage's speakers blared Impala driver Buddy Holly's 1958 hit "It's So Easy." The re-creation of that decade's emotions disarms even cynical people. "My station would have been here to service your car when it was new," Gary told the owner. The juxtaposition of this remodeled car and this revived vestige of Route 66 made the best of America momentarily believable.

"Swing your car around." Gary motioned to the two visitors, circling his left arm in the air and pointing to the bygone era's gas pumps with his right. "Drive back under there, and I'll take your picture." He took the camera from the Chevrolet's passenger, and primed the photograph by giving the men a flag to hold. They unfurled the banner between them, letting it catch the wind. It fluttered, revealing a Route 66 shield in the center bordered with each of the eight transit states' smaller crests. The visitors' erect posture said more about America and Americans in their element than if they'd held the star-spangled banner itself.

Then Gary sent us on our way, encouraging us to visit his daughter's restaurant several miles down Route 66 and with firm directions to a "historical" village. Neither suggestion fit in with our plans or interests, but Gary did set us straight on a curved road.

"I'll tell you what most people miss," he said. "And you'll miss it, too, if you don't pay attention."

We'd have overlooked the turnoff for an oft-ignored fragment of 66. "A friend of mine is restoring the Phillips 66 station. These parts used to have lots of gas stations and car repair shops. Cars

in the 1930s and 1940s used to break down regularly. They weren't that '58 Chevy, let alone your Mustang—it doesn't need any attention."

Gary's guidance got us on to a two-mile stretch of road that most guidebooks ignore. Halfway up the curve of the original route was a right-hand pullout, where Gary's friend's project stood proudly in the middle of nowhere—a renewed Phillips station. The service station no longer had any practical use. The metal roof showed signs of the building's long decline, but otherwise the stone structure was freshly scrubbed. It bore a recent coat of white paint on the doors and window covers, not to attract customers, but as an expression of the affection of its new proprietor.

Phillips 66 stations were of a squat design, which made them not only unique, but also difficult to use for other purposes than pumping gas. When the design was first introduced, it conveyed expectations of pleasant surroundings and service at a time when most gas stations were eyesores and tended to regard customers suspiciously. Phillips went whole hog, hiring traveling registered nurses to check on their stations' cleanliness and serve as travel information officers for drivers.

Peter walked a circle around the service station, fussing with his camera, trying to capture the serenity and bleakness of the Phillips image with a black-and-white photograph. Perhaps he thought that would ease any confusion of this facility's orange sign with black lettering versus the later corporate logo's red, white, and black. And here, nicely, the pumps were the traditional orange as well, which was the dominant color of the stations from the name's inception until 1959. Returning to our car, he asked, "I wonder if Route 66 was named after the gas?"

(previous page) Route 66 evolved from animal trails to native footpaths to explorers' routes, later followed by covered wagons and railways. Eventually it became a roadbed for rickety cars and tentative trucks, followed by sleek vehicles of chrome, glistening paint, and finned taillights. It now offers samplings of each at museums and restored businesses.

Phillips 66 became fortuitously synonymous with Route 66—a co-branding illusion that resonates even today. The association was unintentional.

Earlier in the twentieth century, oil-rich Oklahoma was the center of oil refining and the headquarters for the many companies that were trying to market new petroleum products. In the fall of 1927, a Model T shot along Route 66 not far from Tulsa. Its tank held a new gasoline, as-yet unnamed. At the wheel was Salty Sawtell of the Phillips Company; beside him sat the clever John Kane, a manager at the company.

"This car goes like sixty," said Kane, attributing it to the "new gas."

"Sixty-nothing," said Sawtell, pointing to what the speedometer showed. "We're doing sixty-six!"

Within weeks, the gasoline's name was launched, and soon after the corporate logo was redesigned from a circle to a shield. The synergy of Phillips 66 with Route 66 became an optical, as well as thematic, match. The oil company's association with an emerging national symbol proved propitious.

Peter continued to snap photographs randomly as we drove, whether or not they were needed. Now we were approaching a dilapidated trailer park shrouded behind trees. It was on a parallel frontage road, once itself a part of Route 66, now overgrown with weeds. We were unsure if local authorities had shunted the homes out of sight or if government inspectors wanted to ignore them. A frightful lack of attention had been paid to the site's attractiveness—or suitability for building permits. This was obvious from the road at thirty miles an hour and confirmed by Peter's shout to "Slow down, back up, look what we're missing!" His eye for sad subjects was as unerring as it was unnerving.

I reversed and parked on loose rock. Prickly weeds and brush clung to wooden posts that supported a drive-through, drive-under portico. The former service station's roof, now sagging, was pitched slightly on one side. Gutter moss crept over the shingles, thinning as it neared the peak of the roof. The structure was clearly losing its battle against gravity and climate.

As we got out of the car, a man appeared in the doorway of a weather-beaten house 200 yards away. He stared at us with a caretaker's interest as I walked to the storefront. Peter aimed his camera at some orphaned signs. The front door's once-stylish lettering announced CORDELE WILSON BOOKSELLER. I tried turning the doorknob. It was locked. I stood back. Bullet holes decorated the door and shrapnel was embedded in the frame.

I peered in the window. Shelves lined the walls and formed aisles throughout the store. Most of them held hardcover books. One shelf leaned against the counter where it had fallen—or had been pushed. Half its contents lay spilled on the floor, dust jackets curled, book spines cracked. Bits of insulation had fallen through the broken ceiling and formed a layer of chunky yellow snow over the books on the floor.

A shelf full of paperbacks leaned against the back wall. Their multi-colored spines had faded to beige and become wrinkled. Hardcover books protected with clear plastic wrappings glinted in the daylight. They were irresistible. I wanted to see the riches inside.

Hoping the door was stuck rather than locked, I put my shoulder to it. It was secured with a bolt that might stop a thief for seven seconds. Walking to the side of the building, I found a teetering fence whose slats had been kicked out in several sections. I entered between an erect fence post and two broken boards, then withdrew my foot from an unsteady board. It bared its nails at me as a guard dog would its teeth. I decided that if the front door was locked, the back one would be, too. It was not open for my business.

Peter had walked over to meet the caretaker in a display of innocence. The heavyset man carried a rifle, and his gait was awkward as he approached Peter, narrowing the gap between them and making for a better aim should he decide to use his gun.

His T-shirt looked as if it had come from a tent-and-awning shop, and he looked terribly uncomfortable. Stopping by a fire in a pit, he signaled Peter to come closer. I left the bookstore to join them, in hopes that the man had a key and would be willing to let us in.

"This is Robert," Peter said when I approached, as though they were old chums. "He lives here. He's fifty-seven." Once more, Peter had elicited telling details from a stranger within a minute of meeting him. "He watches over the place."

"Have for years," said Robert. "Got out of that war in Vietnam and got this bloat on my chest and a little pension, but not enough medical support, so this is where I live with my fourth wife who left me, but the kids come by when football's on TV and we visit before they go back to the city to have their dinner 'cuz I don't cook much because of this." He pointed to something that was trying to poke through his shirt; a cyst. He grinned at me. "I saw you looking in the bookstore. It's closed."

"When will it open?" I asked.

"The kid who owns it is the son of the man who used to own all these acres and died and gave it to him, and the guy wanted to make the gas station from 1940 into a bookstore years ago and brought all the stuff in and set the shelving up and bought a truckload of books from a vendor, but never showed here enough to keep it open so no patrons, no regulars, and things fell apart with the rest of the man's land that nobody cares about and that's why it's run down."

"Okay." I breathed for him and for myself. I risked another short question, knowing it might bring a further barrage that might burst his heart. "Got a key?"

"Only one with a key is the kid and he's never here except once in a while when he needs money and comes by to take a book out and sell it to a collector, so they must be volumes worth something 'cuz he does that and seems to get cash and then goes about whatever he goes about in town miles from here and doesn't show up again because he's not his father."

"You enjoy being the caretaker?" Peter asked.

"No. Job fell to me. I'm the longest one of us to live around here," he waved at the trees, the expanse of ill-kept land and shoddy buildings. "'Cuz the back places have move-ins and move-outs all the time and need fixin' up, but I'm not doing that 'cuz I don't get paid to do that and they leave when it gets messy and the new renters take over and shift the last tenant's garbage to a pile outside in the yard and let the places almost fall down in their filth."

He shook our hands as we left. "If I did have a key, I'd let you in. It was supposed to be the best bookstore on Route 66—once."

We neared Joplin, Missouri, our morning's stated destination for dinner. But we pushed on. It was getting dark and Peter was antsy.

"Let's stay in Kansas tonight. We should sleep at least one night in every state, especially Kansas—'Home on the Range' is the state's official song," he said. "Keep going."

Kansas was the first state to have its portion of Route 66 completely shunned by the interstate. But Route 66's original course touched on Kansas, and that was the route we wanted. The state had fed Route 66 with its own immigrants, and its own travelers, despite being the shortest link among the Route 66 states. Peter guided me off Joplin's Rangeline Road and westward, seemingly away from civilization. The buildings, the towns, even the jilted history nearly all petered out as Route 66 headed toward Kansas.

A hundred yards before entering the new state, we found Paddock Liquors housed in a building where once a filling station thrived as part of the state-line clubs and services for prohibition-wrought residents of Kansas in the 1920s and 1930s. Those days (and nights), we thought, were over. We walked past the dormant gravity pumps and poked around. Paddock was sheathed in defensive grills and metal girding to protect the sales person, fridges full of beer, and shelves of whiskey. “Don’t be thinking I’ll buy anything here,” said Peter. “It feels like a bootlegger’s nest.”

Leaving Missouri was less of a ritual than we’d anticipated. A pavement bump—a concrete hump intended to separate one state’s claim from another’s—was charming, in a way: The road narrowed to become a mere driveway, the brush beside the road closed in with the evening’s darkness, and then a sign confirmed the presence of the state line. It was over. We were in Kansas, on a bit of land that, for a dozen miles, brags of being Route 66.

The stretch of road where we now traveled, unencumbered and unthreatened, was once closed by a union strike that blocked travelers and goods. The year was 1935.

The town of Galena, Kansas, named for the lead ore that sometimes holds silver and is itself of great commercial use, has declined since its days of grandeur, when prospects for growth seemed limitless. At the close of the 1920s, the community thought it had it all. Now, as then, the mine’s tailings—piles of slag known as “chat”—pepper the landscape. The area has earned the name “Hell’s Half Acre,” and that sounds like a remarkably small patch of ground compared with the miles of post-mining hazards that the designation represents.

Here, miners pitched their efforts against Eagle-Picher Mining & Smelting Company management as the boom years of the 1920s ended. The layoffs began, a strike ensued, and, given the dearth of jobs, it was not surprising that many union members wanted to return to work. A Blue Card Union emerged, formed by workers who were trying to break the strike. Bloody battles were fought between the rival unions. Scab workers came into the mix, and the violence heightened. Eventually the Blue Card Union was proven to be “company-directed” and disbanded. But not before further incidents of violence.

In 1935, Route 66 was blocked for three days by "angry rebs" led by the powerful John L. Lewis, head of the United Mine Workers. Eventually Route 66 was reopened. But it took many years for the tension to dissipate.

On April 11, 1937, nine men were shot and one was killed while protesting the efforts of union organizers, their assailants lost in the crowd. The spray of bullets brought them down in front of the offices of the International Union of Mine, Mill, and Smelter Workers in Galena.

Using the car's interior light, Peter found the desired page in the guidebook. "Little Brick Inn at Baxter Springs sounds quaint. I'll bet there's a restaurant with home cooking. We're in for great wine, an amazing dinner, and good conversation."

"We've talked all day," I said. "What's left that you want to say?"

"Relax. This'll be a night to remember. We're in Kansas now—'Wizard of Oz' country. I've never been in Kansas." This meant he'd never been to Baxter Springs. If he had, we might not have missed the signs. We cruised into the unsuspecting town, passing deserted sidewalks, empty storefronts, and closed shops.

"There's the hotel." I said this with a tone of assurance because we had driven nearly through the entire town.

"There's only one hotel in town. Must be it," Peter agreed. We pulled in.

At the counter, I stood by as Peter negotiated our room rates down from $52 to $49 a night. I heard the exchange: "I'm the manager, and that's our policy."

Then Peter said, "Okay, I respect that. I'm the consumer, and here's my policy."

The manager caved.

"Brilliant," I said. "You've saved us a lot of money. We are now ahead in the game by the equivalent of a cup of coffee."

"Each," he countered. "Think of it," he said, and I sensed a lesson coming my way. "The first night in Chicago, we stayed in a classy hotel—but your son got us a deal through his friend for rooms at $150. The next night I got the price to $65, even though the night manager didn't want to go that low. Last night, in Missouri, we knocked the price down to $62 a room. Tonight I got it to $49. Do you see a trend?"

"I can't wait till tomorrow," I said. "I'll bring my sleeping bag."

"It's not the money," Peter said. "It's the sport."

We got the keys to our rooms, and the night clerk walked with us to make sure the rooms were suitable. Mine was a freezer. Shivering, even with my jacket on, I dropped my bags and left right away. I wondered if the room temperature was a tactic to combat an offensive odor, perhaps coming from a dead animal. The clerk promised to fix it—the temperature—and assured me that the room would be warm by the time we returned from dinner.

Outside, we got into the Mustang and backed up. "Nice to have the rooms. If we didn't stay here, we'd miss a night in Kansas and be across the Oklahoma state line for accommodation."

"Yup," said Peter. "Let's have dinner, then come back to the Baxter Inn."

"Baxter Inn?"

"Yes. Read the sign."

I stared at the sign: "4-Less Baxter Inn."

We looked at one another.

"It's not the Little Brick Inn!" he said.

"We booked into the wrong place!"

Rather fast, we drove down Baxter Spring's main street, Route 66, looking for the Little Brick Inn. Surely, with a name like that, it would have Kansas enchantment. We felt that was where we would find our "real" rooms and then weasel out of our Baxter Inn obligations. "I'll even let them keep the money we paid," said Peter.

Back among the darkened stores and shuttered shops, we found the intersection where the guidebook promised the Little Brick Inn. And we found the inn. The café below the "inn" was closed. Its promise of nut-crusted catfish for dinner was not to be realized. A typed sign taped to the door indicated the three-story building no longer provided accommodation. We stepped back from this restored-brick bank building, the site of an 1876 visit by Jesse James and his gang's prompt withdrawal of $2,900 in cash.

We drove on a ways and stopped beside a restaurant that had a dozen cars parked nearby. Peter checked it out. "Not tonight. Looks to me like it's part of a restaurant chain. No novelty in that. And! They told me it's Sunday. They aren't allowed to sell liquor."

"Okay, let's go to the gas station store and get a six-pack of beer."

Peter hustled out at the convenience store, returning to the car with news: "The beer's locked up behind a wire cage. Wanna drive back to Missouri?"

It began to dawn on me why Kansas might be the only state not mentioned in Bobby Troup's song.

Only a brightly lit drive-in restaurant, a buzzing pizza place, and the predictable Kentucky Fried Chicken were open. We opted for carhop service. At Sonic Burgers, the chicken burger and ranch fries made for the best dinner in town, which is not to overpraise it. There was limited competition. A chocolate milkshake, eaten with a spoon, accounted for half the price and three-quarters of the enjoyment.

We sat in the car at the drive-in with nothing to do and four hours to do it before bedtime. "Want to go to church?" I asked.

"Church?"

"It might be the only thing open." My culture is Christian, but I don't practice.

"I read somewhere that this part of Route 66 is the 'knuckle of the Bible belt,'" Peter said.

"I think that's *buckle*."

We circled town a few times to see if a church was open; perhaps we could join a hymn-sing. Not finding that diversion, we tried to find *any* entertainment. But we were too late for any action. We returned the Mustang to the motel.

As we walked across an empty Route 66 to stretch our legs, we found a cavernous parking lot. In its corner was a Walmart—among the vanguard of outlets often seen as belittling Main Street character where it appears and a cathedral of consumerism. An employee was locking the front door. There went the last option for a Sunday night time-killer.

The parking lot was empty. This being a trusting town, Walmart had left its garden furniture display intact and unlocked. We walked through it, stepping over wooden skids of fertilizer and around plastic shrub pots. We took two wooden lawn chairs, set them side by side, and sat down as the store's lights dimmed. It was time for a cigarette or a pipe, but I'd given up my pipe. I missed it terribly. Though Peter and I earlier seemed all talked out for the day, we now talked more, sitting in the Walmart parking lot with grazing land behind us, the animals snuggled in for the night, and the Baxter Inn's lights fading in the distance, across Route 66.

All I'd ever heard of Baxter Springs before this trip was that Mickey Mantle had played notch-above-sandlot baseball here on the Whiz Kids of Baxter Springs for three years as part of the Ban Johnson Amateur Baseball League. He called such places "flyspeck" towns. While preparing for Route 66 I'd reread part of Mantle's autobiography, *The Mick*, realizing that it was in this town where a baseball scout from New York first asked him, "How would you like to play for the Yankees?"

In 1951, Mantle's first season with the Yankees, the nineteen-year-old slumped; the pressure to perform and his lack of maturity affected his hitting and fielding, and he was returned to the minor leagues. Suffering from frayed nerves, he phoned his father one night after a poor game to say his baseball days were over.

"I'm not hitting, Dad. I just can't play anymore. I can't . . . "

"Mutt" Mantle jumped in the family car in Commerce, Oklahoma, headed on to Route 66, and made the five-hour drive to where Mickey was staying. The elder Mantle arrived at a lonely hotel room and heard his teenage son's anguish: "I'm telling you it's no use, and that's all there is to it."

The Oklahoma father started to throw Mickey's socks and shirts into a bag. "Yer a quitter. I'm taking you home. You can go to work in the mines."

Mickey Mantle suddenly saw himself as the young boy full of promise on a baseball field in Baxter Springs, on that summer day when his father had rushed through a throng of fans to congratulate his son on a game-winning swing. The memory of that scene jolted Mantle out of self-pity. "Dad . . . give me another chance," he said. "I'll try, honest, I will."

The next season, Mickey Mantle replaced Joe DiMaggio at center field for the Yankees, the team for which he would eventually hit 536 home runs and play in twenty All-Star games.

God bless Baxter Springs.

"I'm sure there's value in being here," Peter said, shifting his lawn chair, scraping it on the ground of Walmart's deserted parking lot. "I'm just not sure what it is."

"Perspective?" I slowly emerged from my Mickey Mantle musings, knowing they would return in the morning when we drove through his hometown over the state line in Oklahoma. "We've no responsibilities here. And we've no set time to show up anywhere. No one we know even has a clue where we are right now."

"Or would believe it," Peter said, pointing to a metal swing set, a plastic picnic table, and an empty concrete water fountain displaying a fake deer.

Peter seemed happy to be on this trip, away from his surefooted approach in business and now, daily, looking forward to the unexpected. Two weeks is a lot of time to share with mostly one other person, and his doubts about being with me never seemed far from the surface. That day we'd tramped around the grounds of a hollowed-out motor court that once radiated pride of place for its owners and was a refuge for travelers; today, disinherited. Peter had walked down the crumbling sidewalk to the last unit, and, when he was returning, I'd spooked him as I came out of a unit's doorway. "Why would you go in there?" he asked.

"Why would you not?" I replied.

He ended up poking around the empty lodgings, creating his own interpretations of the peeling wallpaper ("must have made a family smile when they first put it up") and slumping roof beams ("place hasn't been used in decades"), saying that he felt as though he were on a walk of memories, and that some of the people who'd stayed there never really left.

I mentioned this recollection to him as we sat on our uncomfortable chairs in Walmart's low-lit shadow. He shrugged it off as having been a moody moment.

So I said: "We've got pretty much everything one could hope for—right here. It's perfect."

A car farted in the distance.

"Perfect," Peter echoed.

"They're rich people—they have land, a legendary highway, fast food restaurants, and a quaint-but-closed bed and breakfast."

"And a quaint-but-closed-non-alcohol-serving restaurant," he said.

"Oh come on. Don't be maudlin. What more would you want?"

"Let me count my wants," he said.

"Seriously," I said. "I'll bet folks live here because they're happy here. I've read that the richest man is the one who needs the least. That'd make 'em rich here."

It was Peter's turn to look around at the setting. He lifted and turned his chair while sitting in it, to get a better look at how far the emptiness stretched. A front chair leg bent under

Peter's weight as he landed, and it made him lean forward. "I think I can see Oklahoma over there."

"That's tomorrow's drive," I said. "And it's your turn behind the wheel." He viewed the prospect with mixed feelings, I thought. If he was driving, it meant that I was navigating—and no good would come of that.

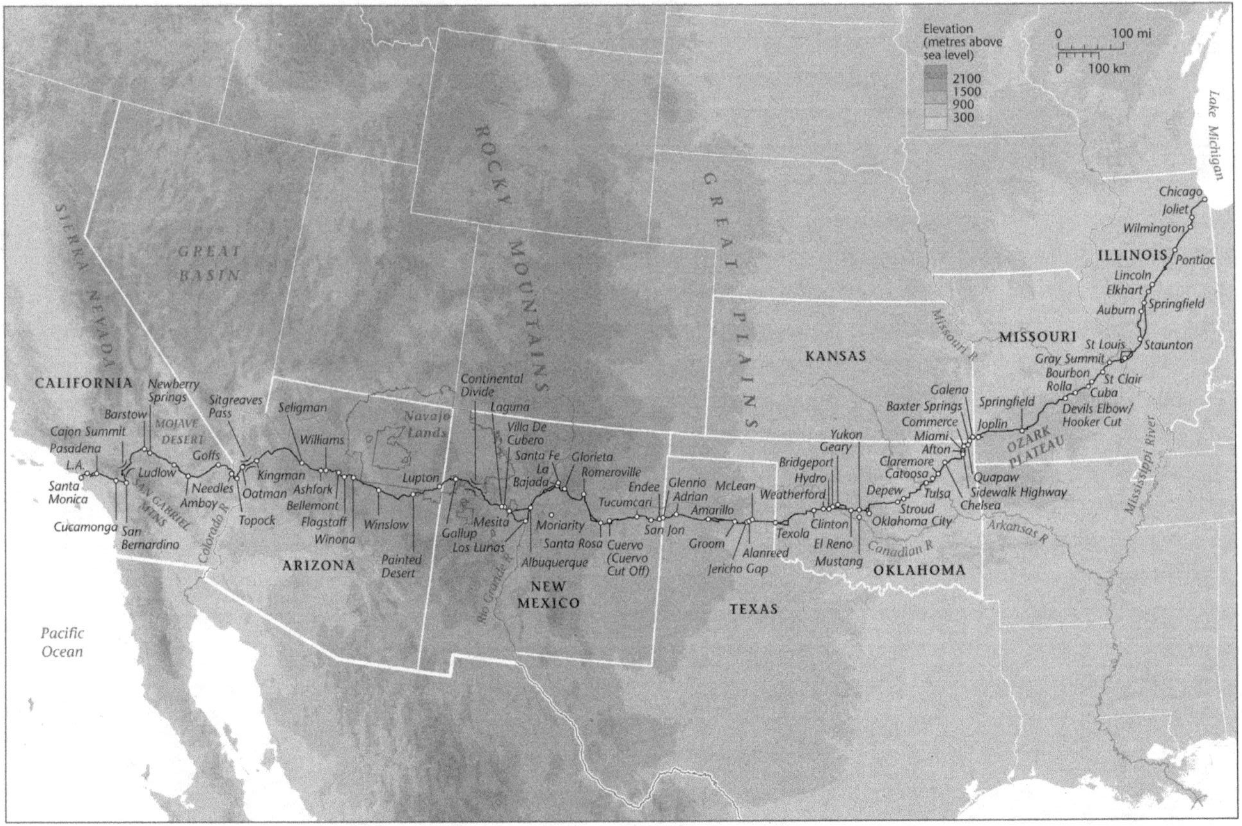

Rick and Peter's route: Although five interstates have now bypassed, intersected, and dismantled Route 66, today one can still find and drive on almost 90 percent of the legendary road—but it takes hopscotch effort, dedication, and a patient compass.

5

The Will Rogers Highway

"A country has got to be based on settlers, not grafters."

—Will Rogers

Peter looked at the odometer as he started the engine. "We've traveled 800 miles so far. Today we begin the 400 miles of Oklahoma's Route 66 . . . once we get out of Kansas." He smiled at my envy: He was at the wheel, in the state with the most of 66 left to explore. We headed to Afton under a sky where blue fought with gray—the gray dominating—where the route begins a more southwesterly meander across grazing lands and becomes the road of "have-nots."

Within a few miles, we crossed the state line and noticed the road was now designated as the Will Rogers Highway, after the man who earned the respect of even cynics and the admiration of those who favored clever diplomacy over bully tactics. Movie star, national newspaper and radio columnist, and rodeo personality—this was his homeland. His widely read observations about politics and his country were the witty insights of an everyday American. Here in Oklahoma the highway's name reminded travelers of a native son; elsewhere, the renaming didn't really take hold, and the reference was infrequent.

We slipped off the pavement near Quapaw, into Hemi's Cafe.

"Deedee's Chess Pie is what you'll want," the waitress said as she wiped the tops of salt shakers to pass the time. "Unless you missed breakfast, and then we'll fill ya up with cakes and eggs."

"Pie sounds great," answered Peter. "What's in it?"

"You'll see."

It was presumed that we wanted Deedee's Chess Pie as dessert, and we were encouraged to order pork cutlets for breakfast. They arrived, served with brown-rimmed eggs that had been fried in the same pan. The plate barely had room for the potatoes, grated thin by a scraper and flipped on both sides. It brought their color to a shining brown, in line with that of the cutlets and singed egg whites.

"This might be the great American meal," Peter said, mopping up the streaming egg with a slice of Wonder Bread.

Our coffee was refilled by a tall girl in a sleeveless black blouse, a short matching skirt, and light-green apron. Peter asked her why she lived on Route 66. She replied, "It's 2,000 miles of 'Don't look back.'"

Peter pressed, as he can do when he's unhappy with a person's response: "But what's so special about Route 66?"

And the twisted corner of her mouth, though not used, implied to me, but not to him: *If you have to ask the question, I'm not sure you'd understand the answer.*

When we had no room left in our stomachs, Deedee's Chess Pie arrived. The waitress placed the slices before us, ensuring that the conversation ended. Strips of dough were laid criss-cross over a piping-hot filling of peaches.

Peter, not always one to know when the other person has ended a conversation, asked the waitress how many visitors they had in a year.

"Oh, hundreds."

"How many of them are driving Route 66?"

"Well, all of them, I'd guess. That's our address."

Peter realized he'd better get to the point. "How many people are driving Route 66 all the way to California?"

"I'd say thousands of people each year hit a part of Route 66. They believe they're seeing all of it. They don't. It goes on forever, you know."

We left Quapaw, ready for a longish drive, but first I wanted us to cruise my childhood hero's hometown: Commerce, Oklahoma.

The golden era of baseball spanned the early 1950s to the mid-1960s. For five of those years I played Little League, where seven- to twelve-year-olds wore jerseys named after Major League baseball teams—the Braves, the Dodgers, the Red Sox, the Cubs, the Cardinals, and, top of the heap, the Yankees. The coach rotated our positions, though I frequently played catcher or shortstop. Any boy positioned in the outfield wanted to be Willie Mays or Mickey Mantle. One year, when the manager handed out the team shirts, mine sported a seven—Mickey Mantle's number. I asked to play center field.

Mickey Mantle grew up on Route 66. He came from Commerce, though he claimed he was born "in Indian Territory, the Cherokee Nation." The son of a semi-pro ballplayer, his childhood was shaped by the game. "Mom cut my toddler clothes down from Dad's baseball uniforms."

Mantle was born in 1931, at a time when Oklahoma was defeated by the Great Depression and his father's baseball career had waned. His father became a miner, an employee of the Eagle-Picher Zinc and Lead Company. In his growing son, he noticed athletic gifts, talents that could take him away from tunnels and hard-rock mining. A ball and glove were never far away during their father-son evenings, and batting practice was mandatory. When baseball scouts first came to Oklahoma to watch this teenager, they saw an error-prone infielder who swung a swift and accurate bat, and who could switch hit—left or right—with unusual strength. And he ran bullet-fast to first base. They wrote about this "slugger" and signed the seventeen-year-old into the farm teams of the New York Yankee organization, first in the Kansas-Oklahoma-Missouri League and then to play for Joplin in the Western Association. One summer day, Mantle's coach pulled him aside as the team bus motored along Route 66. He said, "Mick, the Yankees are bringing you up the day our season ends."

The Route 66 farm boy shot to notoriety as center fielder for the Yankees. He was known more for his batting than for

In 1952, New York Yankees' Mickey Mantle is shown in front of his parents' home with his sixteen-year-old twin brothers Ray (left) and Roy the day after his twenty-first birthday. Mantle was born, raised, and baseball-trained on Route 66. He exuded confidence, leadership, and everything American until his body weakened, his fame was tarnished, and many people stopped caring—not unlike the highway he called home. (*Photograph © Bettmann/CORBIS*)

his catching, hitting a remarkable 300-plus average year after year. It was his accurate throws from center field, and his "next to Babe Ruth" consistency with home runs, that gave him solid fame. That reliability and the hitting of over forty (then over fifty) home runs in a single season (more than once) made him the idol of ballpark boys—just about every backyard and city park in North America and beyond.

For twelve World Series, sandlots in the United States, Mexico, Cuba, Canada, Puerto Rico, and Japan heard shouts of youngsters pretending to be "Mickey" at bat, or "Mickey" grabbing a fly ball. I was one of them, and now I felt both an eagerness to get out of the car and a reticence to do so as Peter drove down the main street of Commerce. The sign hanging over this part of Route 66 announced that we were driving on Mickey Mantle Way. We slowed as we passed a baseball park, its outfield fence inviting for home-run hitters. Our guidebook claimed that Mickey Mantle had played here as a youngster. In my mind, America's Main Street needed no further credentials.

The Mantle era of baseball occurred at the same time that Route 66 exemplified much that was right with America. And no one played stronger baseball, or better embodied a winner, than the kid from Commerce. At his peak, Mantle made a prescient remark about the nation's high times: "I guess you could say I'm what this country is all about."

In the good years, "the Commerce Comet" was hailed as "the symbol of a confident and untroubled nation." But Mantle wrecked himself, physically and mentally, in the years after his stardom peaked. Alcoholism further depleted a body that had endured fifteen serious injuries. Mantle admitted he was "a walking poster boy for the orthopedic industry." But like his nation, Mantle was flawed, not doomed.

Fighting cancer in the mid-1990s, he hit a slump. Then he received a donated liver, a reprieve, and a further chance at recovery. "I got another time at bat," he said. The seasoned campaigner was once more going for the fences.

When he was dying in the summer of 1995, Mantle said, "If I'd known I was gonna live this long, I'd have taken better care of myself." I wondered, as we drove along the section of Route 66 named for him and watched the evident economic collapse of the storefronts, if he'd have given the same advice to his country.

One of the few ambitions I had in traveling on Route 66 was to drive on the Sidewalk Highway, a piece of road that was a triumph of logic over politics. When in 1926 community leaders started lobbying for government funds to pave a much-traveled sixteen-mile stretch of Route 66 near Miami, Oklahoma, they were at first denied money, then promised funding, and finally provided with insufficient funding for the job. They cajoled a perplexed crew of builders to address the quandary of placing pavement all the way, or pavement part of the way, and contrived a solution: if there were adequate funds to fully pave the eight miles of a two-lane Route 66, then that equaled sixteen miles—double the distance, *if* only one lane was paved the entire way. The resulting nine-foot-wide hardtop (eight feet of it paved properly, with lesser-grade pavement for the borders that extended it to nine feet wide) exemplified pavement politics at its most surreal.

Although we slowed the Mustang south of Miami on a post-1937 section of Route 66, watching for the turnoff to the Sidewalk Highway, we missed it, seeing the turnoff only as we passed. Driving on one of the last sections of Route 66 in Oklahoma to be paved required a detour from the fragment of Route 66 we were on. Peter slipped the car into reverse, cautiously backed up, and pulled onto the Sidewalk Highway. Then he stopped, got out, and threw me the keys. "I know this means something to you," he said. I gratefully shifted to settle over behind the wheel.

This road seemed not to know what it wanted to be. Though it was two lanes wide, only the center had been paved. The rest, on either side, was rough dirt with smatterings of small rocks. Half a mile away, a harvester pulled off the field and into the oncoming lane. It bounced our way, raising dust, trying not to dodge potholes or challenge us for the right of way. I pulled over to the side of the road, lowering the roof.

"Why are you stopping?" Peter asked.

"Let's get out and stroll 'the sidewalk.'"

We stood near the car as the tractor slowed. The driver's eyes, set in a suntanned face, blinked beneath his bandana. He acknowledged our reassuring waves and seemed to appreciate that we were city bumpkins, enraptured by what he passed every day. Assured that we didn't need his help, he turned his concentration to avoid hitting our Mustang. In keeping with the road's tradition of sharing what little pavement there was, I had parked so that our two left wheels were on the pavement and our two right wheels were on the dirt shoulder. The tractor drove likewise, part on and part off the pavement.

In the cracked cement in front of us was a Route 66 shield, its paint faded, but proud. "I feel . . . " Peter began, standing over the emblem with his camera. He ended his phrase with a shrug, not knowing what more to say. I stood back to let him be. Then he said, "I feel this moment alone was worth coming for."

We walked a quarter of a mile. The fields were vast and indifferent to our presence. Not talking, we stopped, turned, and strolled back.

I sensed Peter's distance from home was having an effect on him. His banter remained quick, but the times between conversation were stretching, as though the changing vistas brought on fresh thoughts that he'd rather digest than share. He hadn't spent much time in the company of people who lived close to the earth and here they, or their markings, were everywhere and unavoidable.

What remains of Route 66 today are frequently dirty dead ends, sometimes impassable; more often, though, they are wonderful, lonely drives with hidden marvels like the "Sidewalk Highway."

Our Mustang, top down, glistened as we approached. We climbed up and over its doors and slipped into our seats. Peter pushed Nelson Riddle's CD into the player, keeping the band's horns and high piano notes at low volume, and we cruised away, saying nothing.

The road curved, remaining a sidewalk-of-a-road until it gave up even that pretension, slipped into full-time dirt, and seemed to join the fields. Finally we drove off the peculiar section of Route 66 that had been formally ignored in 1970. We were now in Afton.

At a gas station, I checked tire pressure and washed the windshield. Peter returned from a grocery store with cheese corn and water to find me hanging two DayGlo dingle dice from the mirror. Each was about three inches square, silk-screened a distasteful yellow, featuring unappealing large dots. They were made of a material you'd keep well away from flame. Thinking them a nice addition to our vehicle, I said, "I thought these colors were to your taste."

He cringed.

"You could use these. A man's car has to be what he is not," I insisted. "And these are classy and wild."

So began our shifting of the dingle dice—they went up the moment Peter left me alone in the car; they came down as soon as he got behind the wheel.

Car travel on back roads is travel at its best. Sometimes, though, we drove through a land that was untidy. One cannot ignore intellectually stimulating junk such as metal-braced signs that barely cling to their rivets. This stretch of rural Route 66 was like a long drive through a bad part of town: Although it was visually distracting, it carried an unexplainable spell.

Peter's thoughts had ricocheted elsewhere. "Has it ever struck you that Route 66 goes between two of the continent's greatest cities . . . separated by quite a few mediocre ones?"

I replied, I hoped, more kindly. "Chicago and L.A. are terrific places, but the country between them holds more real people than either of those cities."

"Maybe—those people who still live here. Look at the landscape. Homes are sparse, and the farms are mechanized."

"The interstate gets blamed for bypassing and depressing communities, I know. But maybe there are other reasons for their decline," I said.

"Are they a relevant part of America anymore?"

"Of course," I said, feeling defensive.

Then Peter made a point that was at the heart of Route 66's decline: "It used to take ninety people working the land to feed 100 people in this nation. It'd be similar for Europe. Now it takes one and a half people on the land to feed 100 people in the cities."

Peter, the historian-turned-navigator, routed us over an iron bridge that was part of the original Route 66 in 1926. We put gravel behind us and set our sights for pretty Claremore, noting the now more frequent Will Rogers Highway signs. This town was Rogers's home for years and the place in which he planned to retire. The dream was tragically cut short by an airplane crash and Rogers's death in 1935. Cynthia and Bobby Troup traveled through here in 1946, and they stopped at the then-new Will Rogers Memorial. I mentioned this to Peter, half-hoping for him to bite, but it failed the Ten-Second Rule. We drove on, erroneously thinking that a differently-located Will Rogers Museum awaited us.

It was on this path that Will Rogers rode his boyhood horse, the cream-colored Comanche. Rogers was part Cherokee on both his mother's and his father's side, and his birthplace of nearby Oologah was part of Indian Territory. He took deep pride in being "a citizen of the Cherokee Nation" that joined in forming Oklahoma as the forty-sixth state in 1907, when Will was twenty-eight years old.

Will's storytelling formed the basis of his comedic talent and launched his vaudeville acting career, which eventually resulted in him starring in silent movies. Then came success in "talkies," a move to California, and his recognition as the "honorary mayor" of Beverly Hills. By 1933, Will Rogers was the top male box-office draw in the United States.

As the most widely read newspaper writer of his time, he regularly pilloried elected officials in his columns. "People often ask me, 'Will, where do you get your jokes?' I tell 'em, 'Well, I watch government and report the facts. That is all I do, and I don't even find it necessary to exaggerate.'"

Rogers's reputation was built on self-described "common-sense philosophies," which seem as pertinent today as when he spoke of them in the 1920s. He saw bankers, for example, in unkind terms, noting the effects of their mortgage loans and the difficulties banks created for the noble borrower. "A country has got to be based on settlers, not grafters."

And his internationalism, honed after three trips around the world, echoes today, nearly eighty years later: "It will take America fifteen years steady taking

Will Rogers headed out from Oklahoma on Route 66 as a twenty-nine-year-old entertainer, rodeo roper, and comedian, eventually becoming America's most beloved journalist, actor, and adventurer.

care of our own business and letting everybody else's alone to get us back to where everybody speaks to us again."

We'd made a mistake. Claremore's Memorial was part of Will Rogers Memorial Museum. We backtracked. Peter and I separated soon after entering the museum's atrium. Each of us wanted time alone to absorb this man's America and America's take on this man. I soon came upon a room covered with the faded front pages of newspapers. From around the world, they told of Rogers's shocking death.

The author, movie star, journalist, broadcaster, and adventurer was an early fan of air travel, whether flying with companion Charles Lindbergh or on fledgling airlines. His close friend was fellow Oklahoman Wiley Post, the first pilot to make a solo trip around the world. Together they charted a 1935 flight from Seattle to Alaska, and from there the duo planned to fly over the North Pole to Russia, envisioning a profitable mail route. Post prepared a modified plane fitted with floats, since the men would be flying over vast expanses of open water. When the appropriate floats could not be delivered to Seattle on time, Post installed alternative pontoons, which experts later speculated were "nose-heavy."

On a cold and foggy April 16, 1935, Wiley Post and the fifty-five-year-old Will Rogers crashed in their single-engine aircraft near Point Barrow, Alaska. Both men died when their plane hit the frigid waters of the Arctic Ocean and flipped over.

Radio stations in many parts of the country went silent for thirty minutes out of respect for their most quoted broadcaster. Over New York, airplanes towed black banners.

I left the room after watching newsreels from those days, walked across to a different display and spent five minutes watching Will Rogers in clips of his funny movie roles. I couldn't laugh. I'd come across the story of his death out of sequence with the days he spent making the world feel happy.

The Texas Centennial Committee moved first to tie the man with the highway. In 1936, it advocated that Route 66's full length be known as the Will Rogers Highway "to honor the man whose humor had lifted the spirits of the nation in hard times."

At an August 1938 gathering in Amarillo, chosen because it was convenient for delegates, the designation "Will Rogers Highway" became semi-official. This was done partly as a remembrance, and partly to draw attention to the still-struggling highway. The new name was not meant to replace "Route 66," but only to enhance its appeal as the "shortest, smoothest, 'seeingest,' road between the Great Lakes and the Pacific Ocean."

Bronze markers were erected near state lines in 1952. They today appear at various intervals, and the designation seems incomplete. In 1953, coincident with Warner Brothers' release of *The Story of Will Rogers*, a caravan sponsored by the Ford Motor Company traversed the route. The procession ended at Palisades Park, overlooking the Pacific Ocean, where a dedication ceremony was held under the auspices of the Main Street of America Association. The event was one part adulation, and one part movie promotion.

Writer Irvin Cobb penned words of praise on Route 66's coincident designation as the Will Rogers Highway, saying it "wings in its curving course across more than half the continent . . . it parallels the track of pioneers . . . to travel this road is to travel with the vanished yesterdays . . . a testimonial to the undying spirit of one who made the whole world laugh."

Peter and I met near the museum bookstore and silently nodded to each other. We walked out of the lovely stone building, dropped our contributions into the box for donations, and did not converse for a while. I started up the Mustang, opened the ragtop roof, and we drove silently until geography and the guidebook demanded that navigator and driver talk.

Peter and I had come off another one-lane bridge he wanted to see, a detour he'd arbitrarily directed us on to, traveling on the course Route 66 ventured from 1926 into the 1950s. Reaching a semi-modern section coming into Catoosa, we were making good speed when the road became part of the town's main thoroughfare. We had two lanes to ourselves. I was at the wheel. Peter watched for a Route 66 sign that would confirm his navigation skills. Seeing the shield, he proudly pointed to it, announcing, "Comfort sign." Ignoring him, I switched sharply from the outer lane to the inside lane, to curbside, slowing down.

"*Wha-a-at* are you doing?"

"We have a welcoming committee," I said, looking in the rearview mirror.

Peter glanced over his shoulder to see blue and red lights flashing right behind us. Then we heard the whoop of the police siren. He exhaled, "Mary, Mother of Murphy . . . "

The sheriff's black-and-white stopped right behind us. A sturdy, hatless man got out and approached our vehicle. He was my age, though in better shape, and exhibited the confidence that makes a driver's flippancy cave quickly.

He approached our vehicle cautiously, and from behind me said, "Good morning. You almost missed stopping in our lovely town."

The feeling of guilt is useless and has not extended the life of one person even half an hour, but it does have its time and place. "Officer, I think I might have been speeding."

"I think so, too," he said, standing behind my car door, where he had a full view of me and Peter because the convertible top was down. I was into my fifth unshaven day, and I grow an unattractive, scruffy-looking beard. My hair had been tossed high by the wind, and I noticed in the mirror that it had a two-inch peak off-center. My face beamed orange from sunburn, and my eyes were bloodshot. Peter had two days of stubble on parts of his face and was wearing that silly hat backwards. His self-conscious smile was a poorly timed smirk that looked like a toothless grin.

"We're driving all of Route 66," I said. "From Chicago to L.A.," I added, hoping the words would ring a bell. "And I guess I got a little excited about being here in Catoosa. I *am* sorry." My backup philosophy is that it is never too early to start sucking up.

"I imagine your loved ones would like to see you both return safely," the officer replied, implying that neither of us should be this far from home alone. "And the way you were driving, that might not happen."

"Yes sir."

"Now, I'm doing my job if I send you along your way on Route 66 with a clear message not to speed." He bent inches from my face, locking eyes with me. "Does that make sense to you?"

"Yes, Sir."

"Good," he said. "You look old enough to understand."

Recognizing an opportunity, Peter asked the officer, "Could I take a photograph of you giving my buddy a ticket? Would that be okay?" He had removed his baseball cap. It revealed a jumble of snow-white, hat-head hair.

"I'm not going to give your friend here a ticket."

The mood shifted to calm. Peter got out of the car and prepared his camera. I got out and stood in front of the Mustang beside the officer. He exuded competence. Peter put the camera on video and captured the policeman lecturing me: "If you want to get home to your loved ones, drive more carefully."

As we stood beside each other, the officer whispered to me, "I'd better get back to work, before the chief comes by and finds me talking with you instead of giving you a ticket."

I looked at his shirt's insignia. It read *Chief*. And I saw his epaulet, which was tagged with a silver pin that said *Chief*. He noticed my doing that, and he knew that I knew. Then Catoosa's police chief, Raymond Rodgers, sent his two out-of-town visitors on their way to safely complete their quest on Route 66.

Route 66 continues to offer giant-this, giant-that to kids and easily amused adults, one of whom I was traveling with. These leftover amusements from the nifty fifties may be the last suspicious charms of that era to disappear. We were approaching the giant Blue Whale, in the style of the Giant Penguin and Giant Turtle. We drove on; neither of us had to invoke the Ten-Second Rule.

You cannot weave through Tulsa on a single Route 66—there are too many versions. Each iteration reflects the city's growth—attempts to keep Route 66 running near commercially important spots as well as to curve a bit away from the traffic hassles of downtown. On entering Tulsa, we were soon on a pre-1932 road, enhanced with a new topping. We looped on it and crossed back over it to have a closer look at the route's buildings, some dating from the 1920s. This gave us another opportunity to look at the impressive Blue Dome gas station before dumping us in a street of tired commercial buildings. On East 11th we spotted a diner and a sign's promise of cobbler and coffee. It was not yet lunchtime, but we chose to sample what one travel guide called "vintage American road fare."

I stopped in front of a parking spot located between two cars and began to reverse into it, when a police truck stopped right behind me. Looking in my rear-view mirror, I didn't move. I couldn't move. They'd blocked me. Peter's irritation at my stalling – his nose was still in the guidebook—prompted him to say, "Any . . . time . . . now . . . "

"I'm waiting for the jerk behind us to clear away," I said, watching through the back window and offering no further explanation.

Peter looked behind us, saw the impatient police officer, and glared at me. "You can't even *park* without drawing attention from the cops." He gritted his teeth as I nudged forward and motioned the driver to swing around me in the room I'd made. Then I curved the Mustang a little too quickly backward into the open space, my rear wheel bumping up and over the curb and slamming down to make a perfect parallel with the walkway.

"Nice," said Peter. "Ugly, but nice."

The diner was decked out as a Route 66 scrapbook. Route 66 signs—stolen or borrowed from their one-time practical use—were everywhere, as were photographs of the once-popular road. Here, one was skimming history rather than understanding it; rubbing against facts instead of seeing them.

"My name's Brenda," said a happy-looking young lady, the stains on her smock indicating that it was the end of her shift. "Cobbler's best at this time of day. Those guys—" she nodded her head to the left "—are having it. Always do."

Two men in overalls, their hands in need of washing, sat in the booth behind us. Both had their heads and cups cocked her way, waiting for coffee. She left us and went to them. One of them asked her how she was feeling. She answered, "Fine. Life is good. I'm going to trade my husband in for a Chevy truck."

She returned to top up our coffee before it had barely been sipped. "Did I tell you the cobbler's best?" she said. "I meant to."

"We'll have it," declared Peter.

Peter was in form, trying to glean local views about the road we'd come to call our own five days into driving. The waitress ignored his questions and went to serve others, looking at Peter over her shoulder with squinting eyes.

I was beginning to see Peter's inquisitiveness and repetitive questions as inevitable at each encounter, as though he was researching a personal database about the road trip. And I resolved not to interrupt it.

I was convinced that Peter's map interpretation skills had put us on the wrong road—again. He got me to turn around a block, twice, and drive on a secondary road that he claimed was once Route 66. Then he got us back onto what I still thought was a wrong road, but a Route 66 sign stood proudly by the roadside, prompting his "Comfort sign!" comment—again.

Roughly thirty miles south of where we now drove, in the town of Okemah, Oklahoma (in a county with the lovely name of Okfuskee), one of America's great songwriters was born. And although the story of this troubadour and his Route 66 alliance is more rightly told as rooted in Texas, I hoped to find Woody Guthrie's music available in the vicinity. But that was not to be. I reconciled this by poking a disc into the radio's stereo and replaying Nite Tribe's rendition of his classic Oklahoma Hills: "Way down yonder in the Indian Nation/Ride my pony round the reservation . . . "

This portion of the road could claim to be part of Route 66 only from 1926 to 1928. The road was true to the terrain, dropping us into the little town of Depew. The wide main street had the look of harvest time in America, the midday clearing skies warmed the meadows, and the air was rich with the smell of freshly mowed crops. Though not busy, the street had some activity: Two kids were punching each other's shoulders on a bench outside the general store. The buildings had resisted the ages with fresh coats of paint over tired timbers.

We had intended to cruise through this one-time cotton town, one-time oil-boom town, but then we noticed a shop under a sign announcing "Crafts." We felt a need to improve our music selection—we were more than tired of the discs we had heard and reheard. Peter, who could not carry a tune in a bucket, was beginning to know most of the words, and I had had enough of that. This store might be a promising source of fresh music, and it just might have my sought-after Woody Guthrie selection. I hoped to find a CD containing a song I'd read about at the Will Rogers Museum. In a 1940 recording session, Woody Guthrie spontaneously created a song welding together the route's two names, his "Sixty-Six highway" and the "Will Rogers Road." To the limits of his vision, the singer sees "jalopies" of desperate migrants, and asks Rogers, "Can you think up a joke, Will, for all o'these folks/From New Yorker town down to Lost Angeles?"

We walked across the empty road into the store. Three women stood chatting in front of the counter. They turned to greet us as we entered.

"Do you sell music?" I asked.

"Not at all. There's a store in the next town that can help you. That's where you should head."

"Well . . . her husband plays music," said the tallest of the women, pointing to one of the others. "She says he's back in town, but we don't believe her."

They giggled at this comment, in tones far younger than their years would indicate, and one offered: "He's released a new recording." She looked at the musician's wife. "Don't you have a copy of it?"

"We'll take it, whatever it is," I said.

The woman went out to a black pickup truck and rummaged about in the passenger seat, returning with Dub Shelton's CD *The Other Side of Grace*.

"Thank you," Peter said as he took the disc. On its cover was a denim-shirted man sporting a goatee and wearing a white hat with a black band. Peter passed it over to me, and I glanced down the play list to see "Lord You Hit the Spot with Me" and "Heaven's on My Mind."

"You wanted new music, Peter. And we've got new music." Given the area's religious fervor, its high per capita church attendance, and its collective faith that good always wins out against evil, it should not have surprised us to find that theme reflected in the available music. We paid the woman for the disc.

Seeing our interest, the tall woman said, "You might find a disc or two at Spangler's store. We'll walk over with you." All three of them walked out of their shop, leaving the door open, to accompany us across the street.

George was leaning hopefully on the cash register when we opened his screen door and entered to the smell of dry goods and a hint of mold. He greeted us and immediately dismissed any idea of music. "There's a store in the next town that can help you."

We were about to leave when Peter turned and complimented George and the ladies. "You have a wonderful town here. Seems safe. Pretty homes. You're lucky."

"Except for the murder," said the tall one, looking thinner with the statement.

"The murder . . . ?"

"A few years ago. National news. A man killed an older couple right up the street. The white house. They came home from church one day," said the shortest woman, whom I'd thought was shy.

"There's nothing worse than being in the wrong place at the wrong time," said George.

"And they couldn't find the killer for a month," said the tall woman, sounding a little anxious. Standing erect, she turned to pass on the narrative to the others, as one would a stage line.

The stouter woman continued, "The terrible man was spying on his girlfriend across the street. That's what we heard. He broke into the house while the old folks were at a prayer meeting. He wanted to get a better view of his girlfriend. He was upstairs when the couple got home from church. We don't know what happened next. He killed them."

"There's nothing worse . . . " George began again.

The third woman joined in to reminisce about their community's month of national notoriety. She pointed toward the murder house, then away from the crime scene to a location across town as though she were a tour guide. "The murderer hid in the church over there for a month. Everyone looked everywhere—well, the police did. We all kept inside. A murder like that never happened here before."

"Rattled us," said George.

"It broke our hearts," said the short woman. "It's not supposed to be this way out here, random and all that—innocence, and all that."

"The murderer hid in the church," the tall woman repeated. "Folks went there on Sundays, of course. They went every Sunday for a whole month while he was hiding out there, unseen."

The shorter woman said, "When they found him there, he stole a car and escaped down Route 66."

Here, in the heart of nobody-does-nobody-harm country, small-town America had been confronted with the horror of murder and its aftermath.

October 2003 brought a beautiful autumn to Depew. Trees traded their summer green for the comfort of yellows and reds and warm oranges. The coziness of fall wrapped itself around the town's 564 residents.

Maple trees shaded a verandah-fronted house, as if protecting it. Their calm assurance of easy transition to another season was part of a pattern for the home's owners, A.J. and Patsy Cantrell, happy in their sixth decade of marriage and with three grown daughters who had moved away. Life for the Cantrells was about church and neighbors, as he coped with emphysema and diabetes and she with heart disease and a slow loss of vision.

Across the street lived one of their children's schoolteachers, John Wright, and his wife, Carla. There were rumors that the Wrights' daughter, Kathy, was estranged from her abusive boyfriend, Scott Eizember; indeed, that she had obtained a restraining order against him, and that he was later arrested for breaking into her Tulsa apartment after she'd left. While the man was in jail, Kathy had begun to reassemble her life. It was good to see her and her sixteen-year-old son, Tyler, back in Depew with her parents.

Eizember left jail one day that autumn, having posted a bond no one anticipated, and made his way to Depew. He knew of the house directly across from his ex-girlfriend's parents' place. Those front windows would provide him with the perfect vantage point from which to spy on the Wright house, to watch and wait for Kathy to appear. There were matters for him and her to address—things to talk about, to resolve.

Eizember pried his way into the unoccupied Cantrell home some time past noon. There he found a .410 shotgun and shells in a closet. He proceeded to load the gun. The intruder surprised A.J. and Patsy when they returned that afternoon. The shocked A.J. was cuffed about the face with the blunt end of his own gun. At seventy-six years of age, the retired sign painter was no match for his six-foot-tall, forty-two-year-old assailant. His head was battered, and he fell to the floor, dying. As Patsy tried to escape, a shotgun blast hit her back, propelling the seventy-year-old to her death in the family home, on the floor where her kids once played.

Eizember dragged the slain couple to the bathroom, laying Patsy's body on top of her husband's. He kicked their Chihuahua dog so hard that the blow dislodged her eye. With the bodies out of his way and the tiny dog cowering near them, Eizember watched the neighbors' place impatiently, leaving bloody handprints on the Cantrells' curtains as he waited for Kathy to appear. When Kathy's mother, Carla Wright, and son, Tyler, arrived, Eizember waited a while and then made his move. He stormed in their front door, startling Tyler, and demanded to know where Kathy was. Frightened, the youngster turned to run away. Eizember levelled A.J.'s gun and fired, felling the boy.

Carla Wright screamed from the kitchen, where she was baking treats for her Sunday school class. Eizember entered and beat her with his shotgun. She managed to escape outside and ran across to the Cantrells' house in search of help. No one answered her cries.

A stunned and fear-filled Tyler pushed himself up from the floor and hobbled out the back door into a pickup truck. Fumbling with his keys, he started the engine. Before he could flee, Eizember leapt onto the back of the pickup. Tyler drove away, swerving to dislodge his attacker from the truck. Eizember fired through the rear window, hitting the astonished teenager in the shoulder. The truck veered and crashed at the Depew football field, where two teams were in the middle of a game. Tyler's grandfather, John Wright, was at the microphone as the game's play-by-play announcer.

Eizember fled the football field and commandeered a car ride for seven miles, eventually disappearing into the thick forest near Depew, in a picturesque area known as Creek County.

This devout small town was changed forever when A.J.'s lifeless body was found and the details of Patsy's violent death were made public, as the critically wounded Tyler lay recovering in a hospital bed.

An extensive manhunt began for Eizember, including "shoulder-to-shoulder sweeps through the dense woods." At one point, he was sought by nearly two hundred police officers and state troopers, with search planes swooping overhead. As weeks went by without a trace of Eizember coming to light, a public plea for assistance was made on the television show *America's Most Wanted.*

It was November 23 before anyone again saw the suspect. In Depew's First Methodist Church annex there is a pantry and a closet with access to an unoccupied attic—a warren and a hideout. The church had offered friendship to Eizember when he had arrived in Depew a year before. It was here that he had met John Wright mowing the church lawn. He claimed he was bicycling Route 66 to raise funds for the families of victims of 9/11. Wright had befriended him and had eventually introduced him to his daughter, Kathy.

Now, a year later, on a fateful November morning, a regular helper at the church's food bank went to the former parsonage to get supplies for a needy family. The elderly woman sorted her clutch of keys to find the one for the pantry, and opened the door. And there stood Eizember, staring out at the startled woman. He held a .380 handgun he had stolen in a home burglary. The frightened woman bolted from the church, leaving her keys in the pantry door. She tripped and broke her ankle, but managed to limp to safety. The wanted man took her keys, found her car, and headed out on Route 66 in search of escape routes.

It is an American road tradition as old as the Model T to slow down when passing a stranded motorist, to ensure the traveler is safe. Thus, when Eizember's stolen Toyota sputtered and ran out of gas in Arkansas, 200 miles from Depew, he was rescued by a well-meaning Dr. Samuel Peebles and his wife, Suzanne, who were heading home. The physician and his nurse wife, both in their fifties, had made it their lives' vocation to help people. Their roadside offer to a clean-cut stranger who appeared injured was a Good Samaritan gesture, in keeping with their philosophy. They let Eizember get into their van and promised to drop him off at a nearby corner store so that he could use its phone. As they neared the store, he pulled out his gun and demanded that they keep driving.

"I'm already gonna be on death row in Oklahoma," their captor told them, rejecting the couple's plea to take their vehicle in exchange for their freedom. "I wouldn't hesitate in killing you."

For 300 more miles, the trio traveled together in the minivan, Dr. Peebles driving through Arkansas and down into Texas as the felon talked of heading to Mexico. At their requested washroom stop, while one hostage used the facilities, Eizember kept the other at gunpoint. The Peebles had no idea who their passenger was, but they believed his threat to shoot them. When Eizember used Suzanne's cellphone in an attempt to call his ex-girlfriend, authorities became aware that the Peebles were in harm's way and attempted to notify their family in an unsuccessful effort to locate them quickly.

The doctor and his wife traveled with a concealed revolver in the driver's side door in case of emergency. At their second bathroom break, unnoticed by their kidnapper, Dr. Peebles was able to retrieve the gun and tuck it in his jacket. When they stopped farther down the road that evening, he walked away from the van, boldly pulled his pistol and fired it at Eizember eight times. When the chamber was empty, four bullets had hit Eizember in the chest. The impact enraged the younger man more than it hampered him. He charged and grabbed the weapon, and slapped Peebles's own gun across the doctor's brow, whipping it back and forth until the older man crumpled to the ground. Then the murderer-turned-kidnapper jumped back in the minivan and sped away.

Thirty-seven days after he had killed the Cantrells in Depew, a bleeding man was pulled over to the side of a road by police. A grocery store clerk had called 911 to report that a man with gunshot wounds and a weapon had been in their store. The story of who he was, of the double slaying and of the kidnapping, took time to piece together. The confusion began with Eizember's statement to police that he had been shot at random by a passing motorist.

Depew was not rid of Scott Eizember's spell when the double-murder suspect sped away. He had not only violated their sense of small-town safety, he would also continue to haunt them. In Oklahoma City, five days before Eizember was scheduled to go on trial in El Reno for the first-degree murder of her parents, Linda Cantrell was killed by a gunshot from a man she'd met at the auction of her parent's estate in Depew.

Peter and I drove out of the serene town of Depew and into the sunshine. Surely the law of averages, if not of God, would ensure that the town would not experience wickedness like those murders again.

To forestall further evil, I pushed the new religious music CD into the stereo, tapped forward to track five, and dedicated one of Shelton's songs to Peter: "No More Wrong Roads." Miles down the road, as our savior disc ran out of inspiration, we entered Stroud, Oklahoma. The town was initially disappointing, but then we saw the Rock Café. The eatery, which had opened in 1939, had long had a reputation as a food fan's citadel. But Peter was on a different mission.

"There," he said, pointing. We parked at the side of the road, where a sign indicated the location of Sugartime Music. "That'll be where we find more discs for sure."

The front entrance of the music store was almost bereft of merchandise. Sheet music lay in piles on a table, and song booklets were available in a spindly wire rack. A single guitar sat on a wide shelf, knee-high, and a wooden desk blocked off a large portion of the room.

"Hello," Peter called out, to no response. Uninvited, he started down a hallway while I went out in the street to see if there was another music store nearby. When I reentered Sugartime Music, I'd lost sight of Peter. But his voice booms, and in small spaces it reverberates. I found him at the end of the hallway chatting with a black woman accompanied by a boy and a girl, who remained mute. They were discussing a recording with a white man who was sitting behind a control panel in a music studio. At the top of a pegboard wall, above a window and almost touching at the ceiling, was a photograph of Joe Cocker.

"I'm Joe Navrath," the man said. "This is my recording studio. Glad you came by."

"We're looking for music to buy."

"Not here. There's a store in the next town that can help you."

He continued discussing an upcoming recording with the woman, knowing he had us as an audience. "I've written this.

It's called 'There's More to Christmas than Santa Claus,' and these children have the absolute right voices to accompany me on the recording." He played a chorus from the song on his electric keyboard and asked the kids to sing, which neither of them did. He played it again, looking at Peter and me this time. I feared Peter would break into song, but he held back.

Joe played one more chorus, singing solo. Then the woman and her two kids made as if to leave, and Joe rose to go with them. They accompanied us outside where I noticed a tattered flag, white nylon with a Route 66 symbol wrapped in its folds. It was attached to an inch-thick metal post that had been cemented into the sidewalk. Many years of splashing from passing cars had stained it, and the wind had worn its edges to tears and threads.

"Would you sell me that flag, Joe?" I asked.

"It's in pretty bad shape. Twenty dollars," Joe replied.

"Ten bucks," Peter offered.

"I'll need pliers to get these rusty bolts loose," I said, presuming Peter would close the purchase. "One of my sons collects flags," I explained. "The flags need to come with a story about how they've been found. This one's unusual. Got pliers, or a wrench?"

"It's a mess," Peter said to me as Joe disappeared inside.

"It's a beauty," I said. "Torn, dirty and bolted to a post on Route 66. Sean will love it."

Joe, who had looked taller when he was seated, returned from his shop with a crescent wrench. "Tell you what," he said. "Fifteen dollars for the flag, and I'll give you this music." He handed Peter a CD from his studio, *Looking*, by Joe Navrath. "I wrote the songs."

"Done," I said, and wrenched the nuts loose. The little boy caught the filthy flag after the first bolt gave way, and it furled into his arms. He kept gathering the falling banner to his chest, dirtying his shirt. When it was free, he and I did the Boy Scout flag fold—we each held an end taut: folded in the lengthwise half, folded in the short half, and continued to alternate folding until the size matched that of a pocketbook.

Peter paid Joe with the twenty-dollar bill I'd handed him.

Meanwhile, things were not so rosy for the boy's mother. Popping her car's hood, she said, "It's leaking." She took a jug from her trunk and began pouring water into the radiator.

"If you ask a service station, they can add a radiator repair liquid," Peter advised. "It'll likely stop that leak. Not much money."

"I don't have *much money*," she replied softly.

Peter gave her *my* five dollars' change, which he had got from Joe.

"You are a very thoughtful man," she told Peter.

As we drove away, Peter pushed Joe's CD into place. "Here's track four," he said. "It should be your theme song: 'How Can I Go Wrong?'"

Peter was driving again. He had delivered us onto a gravel-pitted mile-long stretch coming out of Stroud, where a pre-Route 66 track had been incorporated into the new road when it was mapped in 1926. And eventually we got onto paved road.

We had never intended to drive by W. H. Odor's "round barn" of Arcadia enough times for it to be re-restored. This landmark is the largest round barn in America (a category that has a limited number of contenders). It was built from bur oak in 1898 in an effort to cope with winter's assault, especially from snow. Too many rectangular barns had been crushed in the harsh encounters between weather and wood. Perched on a rise, the round barn had the air of a watchtower.

This is an easily accessible attraction, whose location is well publicized by every piece of promotional material. Instead, Peter sought a 1928 segment of Route 66 that showed on only one of our maps. The text hinted that "one mile can be accessed." Success means different things to Peter in different situations, but it always relates back to tenacity—often it is doing something that others find difficult, or winning an argument against logic because he won't let go and wears down his opponent. Here, success to Peter meant finding what they called "hidden Hiwassee Road." I was navigating in pursuit of this notch on our self-made checklist of obscure Route 66 pieces when we overshot the Round Barn by heading west, at my insistence that, "It'll be right up here." Then, determining we'd gone too far, I suggested that we backtrack past the Round Barn, retrace our way through the low land on what was also a true portion of Route 66.

"Keep your eyes peeled," I said, suggesting a turn that didn't quite agree with the map, which itself didn't show us where the "hidden" road was located. I had a hunch we were close. "The entrance has to be near here."

We missed it.

Peter turned the Mustang around and headed west again, toward and past the Round Barn, which was when he observed something about my incompetence as a guide, though we were on his chosen path.

"Gotta be back where we were," I said, picking up the one unopened guidebook from the floor, which I again used as a library. "Sorry 'bout that. It's avoiding us."

"Us?" Peter asked. *"Us?"*

"Oh, did *you* see it then?"

"Us!" he acknowledged.

Peter turned on intuition and headed up a hill for two miles. Even I could tell that we were off target. He made a U-turn and retraced our course. I switched guidebooks again to get an option. It led us down a private drive. Finally, in frustration, we stopped as the rain began. In the falling darkness we compared all our available resources. Peter flipped on the car's interior light.

"Do roads hide when you navigate?" he said.

"No. We seem to have more challenging pieces to find when I'm doing this job."

That elusive stub of Route 66 was as tidily tucked away as any we'd find. Not even mentioned in most writings, it had two oblique access points off the main flow of Route 66 traffic. Even when they had been found, they seemed invisible. As with many short spots on Route 66, this pavement was now a local road: residents only, please. Passersby were not encouraged by signs. Not that we were unwanted; we were not invited.

We drove it twice without seeing any other cars or signage. It is now tightly treed, and it narrows at either end where it meets the main road. It oozed the trappings of an exclusive neighborhood, having homes nestled well back from the road, manicured entrances, and yards with lots of elbow room. The attempt to keep this slice of historic Route 66 obscure (an ode to preservation) has been successful.

We opted to steer around the brightness emanating from the Oklahoma City's buildings, keeping an eye out for signs that would direct us to Warr Acres, Bethany, even Texola.

As dusk settled in, Peter revived his earlier thinking about the town of Yukon and its widely written about and much-photographed neon sign that marks the Yukon Motel. "It'll be an honest Route 66 stay," Peter encouraged, knowing that we both hankered for a heritage motor court. "Let's head there."

When we got to Yukon, drizzle hung in the air. It caused a low cloud to clamp around the grain elevators, one of which was painted with a sign, YUKON'S BEST FLOUR. A strobe light show aimed at the elevators was about to begin. There was no other activity in the town. A cluster of photographers was grouped on a street corner, their cameras propped on tripods and pointed at the Best Flour elevator in anticipation. I presumed that Peter wanted to stop for no other reason than that he needed a grain elevator photograph in his snapshot collection.

He was out of the car and down at the corner before I realized there was no need to plug coins in the parking meter at this hour. I pocketed my change and caught up when he'd already asked enough questions to fill me in: "It's a photography class. Bob here is the teacher. No light show tonight. Too cloudy."

"Did you ask him where the Yukon Motel is?" I said this to remind him of the one thing he was supposed to do.

Each night, Peter would look over at the meager motor court I pointed out with serious interest, and he'd mutter, "I'd prefer a Fairmont hotel, please." And then we'd drive on to find more options, always seeking the authentic balanced with the practical.

He turned to Bob and said, "Where's the Yukon Motel?"

"Gone," was the quick reply. "New owners. Took down the beautiful sign, too. The neon still worked! A shame."

"Is there any other place here to stay?" Peter asked, not wanting to aid the motel's new owners, who had shucked history in favor of modern pretensions.

"Yup. One," said Bob. Then, he asked, "You riding hogs?"

"We've got a car."

"That's better. If you were riding bikes, I'd tell you to put 'em in the room with you at night. That way they won't get stolen."

A girl student, pert, dark-haired, and confident, intervened. "Go to Mustang, it's only twelve miles from here. Lots of places to stay. Garth Brooks is from there, but they don't do much to tell you that. Down there two miles," she added, pointing west. "Left at a stop light. Five miles south. Right again. A few miles. Can't miss it."

"It's the other way, Mary," said Bob, looking unsure of why he was so self-assured. "Back toward Bethany. You'd have come through there. South maybe ten minutes, if not that many miles. *Then*," he emphasized this, looking into the glinting eyes of his student, "you head right—that'll be west—and go until you see lights."

Mary was not put off. "I've lived here all my life. Quickest is *that* way." She turned, pointing her breasts like headlamps.

"Nope," said Bob. He led us into his street-corner studio, unfolded a map, and outlined in a flash where we were. It was too fast for me to get it, but Peter grasped the gist of where we might be and where we might be headed, and Bob traced a line on the map that mimicked his earlier directions. Peter kept nodding. I recognized that nod, and it drove a wedge into my gut.

Bob's final words were, "If you see Lake Overholser, you've gone too far."

Peter now exuded the same air of confidence as had Bob, which was the same air of confidence as that of the differing

Mary, which meant that one of them had misplaced confidence. I was now alone with that person.

I had voted to go with Mary's emphatic body language; Peter opted to follow Bob's sketch. I deferred. He got behind the wheel, determined to drive. We found the promised traffic light, but I took little comfort from that, as one such light had been promised at either end of town. We made a southward turn off Route 66 and drove in the dark into the more dark, where street signs seldom appeared, and with no resemblance to those on our map. This did not deter Peter.

He guided the car's thinking, tapping the Mustang's dash and saying, "Good work." I felt redundant. With the car receiving such personal reinforcement, my hesitations seemed out of place.

It wasn't long before we found the "then-you've-gone-too-far" lake. Such a bold marker could not be missed. It could, however, be misunderstood. And we found a road with the name Overholser. It was not quite where or what we wanted. Peter ignored such inconveniences. He drove. And drove. As in any relationship, there are times to go silent in hopes of a favorable outcome. Eventually we found ourselves back on the road where we'd begun.

Peter said, "Brilliant. It's like you got us to circle the lake."

"Me . . . ? Me . . . ?"

We were both sure that our desired direction now was north. Shared assumptions on direction have gotten lots of males temporarily lost (think Lewis and Clark). When a lit sign hovered over a gas station, I thought we were in luck, and said, "Pull over," with the implication that Peter should get out and ask for directions. He did.

He left the door ajar and the motor running as if he were in a getaway car, and I watched through the station's window as he talked animatedly with the clerk, his hands flailing and pointing. I could see, if not hear, Peter's braying laugh. When he hopped back in the car, I uttered a meaningful "So?" He did not respond.

We had driven well down the road in silence when, even in the dark, I could see that Peter was puzzled by something. I asked, "What direction did the clerk say it was to Mustang?"

"He didn't actually say . . . "

"What do you mean, 'He didn't actually' . . . ?"

"I believe this way is north. You believe it's north. So I simply asked him if we were headed north."

"What?"

"He said *yes*. So, I'm sure if we keep going this way . . . "

"You mean you didn't ask him which way to Mustang?"

"I really didn't see any reason to. I'm sure it's north."

"One should never miss the opportunity to be lost on Route 66," I said.

Peter refused to be rushed. We saw a freeway in the distance, which could have solved our problems. We even saw the hint of an on-ramp. Such luxuries were not for Peter-of-the-moment. "There's a bridge to cross," he said. "I saw it on the map. It'll get us to that road the photographer mentioned, and from there we're home free."

It started to rain.

A car headed down a side road. For reasons that escaped me, this event buoyed Peter's confidence. "Let's follow him." We did. Then the other car turned off the road and disappeared into the night.

Slowly, we nosed ahead in the dark and found a steel bridge looming as a shadow before us, the wind swinging trees near its girders, increasing the darkness. The bridge looked rickety. Peter informed me of something he'd gleaned from his gas station conversation: "This bridge closes in a year. It's from 1924."

"We got here just in time."

"I'm sure it's maintained," he said.

He stopped on the brink of the bridge. We nudged forward, crossed dark, wind-whipped water, heard creaks, and felt the wavering of the bridge, and as soon as we were off it, Peter turned right on the first road—because it was there.

A colleague in the tourism industry says, "With today's technology, ours will be the last generation on earth to know what it's like to be lost." And Peter will be the last of the last.

Coming up through a construction site, we found a motel near the spot where the freeway and our dirt road converged. As I dropped my bags in front of the check-in counter, I heard Peter say in a cheery voice, as confident as it was loud, "We're traveling Route 66. Haven't had to pay over $50 for a room so far. Does that match your rate?"

I picked up my bags, grabbed one of the keys on the counter and took my gear to another room-of-sameness. A physical connection to the early days of motoring was evading us when it came to accommodations. We sought variety; the wanderlust of early travelers was fed as much by the individuality of motor court decor as by the stark differences between the diners' offerings.

When I returned, Peter had gone to his room to download the day's photographs onto his hard drive and to write postcards—dispatches from the front line of travel. Though I'd let my two sons and my wife know that I was absent-with-leave and would be out of touch for nearly two weeks, Peter had emailed all three of them pictures from the road *every night!*

I needed a walk. The skips of rain were refreshing, and I strolled for half an hour in the chilly October night. When I returned to the motel, the lobby was empty, quiet. I dropped into a stuffed armchair and sighed. No one else was around. Suddenly, a lady emerged from a closet. She tidied up around the place with a long-handled whisk brush. No dust pan. She was American-large, one of those attractive women whose circumstances, eating habits, or metabolism super-sized her.

She noticed me watching her, and I became self-conscious.

"What brought you here?" she asked.

"We're driving Route 66," I blurted as she swept under my feet, perhaps to thwart my stare. "All of it."

"You mean *all of it*?" she chided. "Lots of folks think they do *all of it* and don't do but the highlights, the easy-to-drive spreads." She stared back, testing me. She looked to be cut from the same cloth as Roseanne Barr, albeit from a larger pattern.

I smiled and wondered whether she, too, visually gauged those she met. What was she thinking of me? That I was John Goodman, and that I should be outside exercising my body rather than lounging here, wasting her (and my) time?

"Yup. All of it," I insisted. "We've been hitting all the places shown in one guidebook, and neglected in the others."

"I was a truck driver for years. Up. Down. Saw it *all*. On weekends, my husband and I would head out and visit those places you think are mysteries. And more."

"Why don't they mark it better? *The route*, I mean."

"Me? I'd say that every state should have fifty more posted signs. You know—showing 'Historic Route 66,' those shields."

"That'd be welcome," I could only agree.

"What it'd do is make the whole route a living landmark." She swept dust and tramped-in dirt into a corner across from me, propped the broom against a door jamb and started all over the floor again, this time with a wet mop.

"Add fifty more emblems painted white on the pavement, too," she said, wiping the floor more quickly as she talked. "Fifty of them per state. Nobody steals those ones! It'd be easy to send a crew to spray Route 66 decals every five miles. They're great to see. Reminds you where you are."

She stopped and leaned on the mop handle. I realized it'd been cut short to match her height. She'd been at this job a while.

"Talkin' like this makes me want to get back on *the route*," she said. "I think I'm going to take my old man for a ride."

"You only live once," I offered.

"And if you do it right," she said, "once will be enough."

6

The Mother Road

"If only I could do this book properly it would be one of the really fine books and a truly American book."
—John Steinbeck

Along Route 66 today are hundreds of dilapidated signs, tilting at imagined winds. Each was once the proud rigging for a neon poster advertising a motor court, a gas station, or a coffee shop offering homemade apple pie. Although these signs provide the visitor with no current information, they are one of the reasons people seek this road. They are a museum of what once was. Elsewhere they'd be seen as junk, to be removed behind a high fence on the edge of town. But their teetering presence keeps the visitors coming.

"Not much prosperity here," Peter observed.

We were still in Oklahoma.

"Seems the people here don't measure their self-worth by their net worth," I said. That much seemed apparent from our trip so far.

It was our sixth day on the road, and we looked forward to the coming six. We wanted to head out on the one-time Chisholm Trail, more recently known hereabouts as Route 66.

Throughout much of Oklahoma, Route 66's aura of nostalgia has been aided by a modest-to-poor economy. Stronger markets would have brought more commercial activity, and rapid progress would have caused derelict buildings to be moved or razed. Here, you can watch the crumbling of buildings that were once hoped to last forever.

"It's amazing that sign still stands," Peter said while taking a photograph of a barely readable billboard that advised drivers "Watch Your Curves! Eat More Beef."

Apparently I wasn't watching my curves. "Slow down!" Peter exclaimed as I turned too sharply on to a street in the town of El Reno. "Stop. Back up." I'd heard that before—he'd missed taking a photograph of another faded sign. Bent steel wrapped itself around the sign and held it aloft, reading JOBE'S. As I slowly reversed, Peter leaned out the car window to frame the photo and noticed that Jobe's was open for breakfast.

"Whaddaya think?" he asked. "Hungry?"

We parked in a lot that had once offered car-hop service. Peter opened the screen door, and we walked into the hub of hospitality—off-white linoleum table tops, rimmed with lackluster chrome, and bordered on both sides by bench seats upholstered with creased black vinyl. White stuffing poked through some of the creases.

"Not from here, are you?" The older man in the booth across from ours was looking straight at us. His pewter hair looked recently cut, and he wore a coat with a high ridge even though it was warm inside. He looked away, raised a cream-colored mug to his mouth, grimaced at how hot its contents were, and held it away from his face to let the steam settle. "Where're you from?"

Before we could answer, he continued. "Not seeing as many travelers as we once did here on 66."

"We're driving all of the *old* road," said Peter, looking around for a coffee server.

The man seemed content to hear that, but said nothing. Peter pointed at me, introducing us. "Rick." Then, "Peter."

"Homer Snudpick," said the man, finally sipping from his cup. (I swear this is true.)

"Coffee!" said a voice from the kitchen. It was a statement, not a query. "Robert" was next, as the proprietor pointed two full mugs toward himself, stated his name, and placed them on our table. Returning to the kitchen, he stayed within sight—an open kitchen was part of the setup.

"This was a motor court once," Homer explained. "Right here used to be the office. It was made into a restaurant, if you want to call it that, years ago."

The front door slapped open, and a tall pole of a man wearing a baseball cap ducked under the door jamb as he walked in. His blue hat proclaimed in white letters: OKLAHOMA MILITARY ACADEMY—ALUMNI. He walked straight over to the coffee pot, picked it up, walked over to Homer, and refilled his cup.

"How are ya, Homer?"

"Well, I got outta bed this morning."

The man poured more coffee into Peter's cup and a slip of it into mine, though I hadn't sipped any. Setting his own mug on the table, he filled it before placing the pot back on the warmer. "Gene," he said by way of self-introduction. He sat down across from Homer and began to rock back and forth slightly.

I looked through the scattered blinds that blocked my part of the café's window. Four of the vertical slats bumped and curled at the window ledge, showing gaps where they bulged open. Across the narrow pavement of Route 66 was Phillip's Motel, left to contemplate its past. I let the blinds close. I moved the Skippy peanut butter jar to the side of the table and picked up a tattered menu that was decorated with coffee-cup rings. I browsed the offerings.

"You'll love the pancakes," Gene said. "I've traveled over all these United States of ours, and I live here because of Robert's pancakes." He laughed at his own joke. "Have 'em."

Robert shrugged in the background, performing his part of the tag-team sales effort, and Peter nodded to order on behalf of both of us. Soon we heard sizzling on the griddle.

Homer opened up, perhaps because Gene had mentioned travel. "I was in the Philippines. Wounded. End of World War Two. Shrapnel up and down me."

"Well," Gene injected, "you couldn't stay home from *that* war."

"Oh, I went all right," Homer replied. "Happy to leave the farm. I wanted to get away from that pitchfork."

A shoulder nudged the restaurant door open, and in walked an elderly man with a shaven head and a golf shirt labeled *Salida*. "Mornin'," he said to everyone and the walls, reaching for the coffee pot as soon as he entered. He walked over to refill Homer's cup, spilled a little into Gene's, then turned to our table and poured more coffee into Peter's and mine.

"Welcome to the crossroads of the nation," he said. "Route 66 and Highway 81 meet here."

We stretched into a series of handshakes and offered our names.

"Gene," he responded. He also sat down across from Homer.

"You still pickin' tomatoes?" he asked the other Gene. Without waiting for an answer he said, "I like cucumber. My wife likes onions. Wife, she cuts 'em all up and puts 'em all in a bowl of vinegar. Stirs 'em up. We sit at the table, bowl between us." He demonstrated to us the bowl's location with his hands, like a coach outlining a sporting match. "She eats the onions. I eat the cucumbers."

Robert came out from behind the stove with two Melmac plates of tall-stack flapjacks. He placed them in front of Peter and me, and then went to get the knives and forks. When he returned, he moved the Skippy peanut butter into the center of the table, as though we should smooth it on our flapjacks, which I did. I used my fork to cut a wedge of the offering and ate the best mouthful of pancake I've ever tasted. Peter did the same, also forgoing butter and syrup. Smiling, he looked over at me as if to say, "Who'd have thought?"

The diner door popped open again. A man held it ajar with his hip as he looked behind himself, as if second-guessing his entry.

"Morning, Gene," chorused Gene, Gene, and Homer. (I am not making this up.)

The latest arrival, Gene-three, looked our way and smiled beneath his Frontier Chevron cap. Seeing Robert, he waved. Then he picked up the coffee pot and walked toward Peter and me. Pouring fresh coffee for us, he said, "Travelers? Well, you're in the zone. Oklahoma! You're at the heart of Route 66."

After Gene-three had refilled the cups of the other retirees, he put the pot back on the warmer. Robert looked at Peter and grinned, "Place runs itself."

"We're happy to see you," said Gene-two. "*The route*," he tossed a sideways glance out the misted window, "has been there over eighty years. You're traveling the right way. Better 'n Interstate 40."

The three Genes and Homer talked among themselves as we ate. Soon Homer turned to us to address the economy. "No boom here. Never. So no bust. We struggle like we've always done."

"This is the best place on earth," added Gene-two. "Army took me to Germany. I've lived in other states. Came back here to live now. See my final days." He frowned—or was it a smile?

"I used to run the seed-and-feed," Gene-one told us. "Got to be too much. Not always good. Inconsistent. So I bought the bowling alley." He nodded to himself, affirming how he'd found financial stability in a farming community. "Then I sold it."

A man in a red-green-blue plaid shirt and with a spotty morning shave suddenly stood up behind a low corner wall, where he'd been eating his breakfast unnoticed, and started to yammer. "Got to get the load moved. Damn prices rising all the time. Used to be twelve dollars plus a dime. Now, it's twenty dollars plus a dime." He hurriedly refilled our coffees without spilling a drop, replaced the pot on the heating coil and left the diner in a huff.

Homer rose and stepped between our tables to shake our hands. "Road's wet," he said. "Lots of rain last night. You drive carefully. Come back one day." And he was gone.

"So . . . " said Gene-one. "How were the pancakes? Was I right?"

We both had our mouths full, so Peter nodded convincingly. As I washed down the last bit of grilled batter with coffee, I asked Robert-the-cook, "What's your secret?"

He shook his head, as though letting me in on the recipe would compromise national security. I prodded. "There's something . . . unusual. Did you tip brandy into it?"

"Ha. No. The truth is, it's vanilla. But," and he accented this by wiping both hands on his beige slacks, "it's not the vanilla you buy at the store. It's the vanilla syrup that I'm supposed to use in milkshakes."

Gene-one smiled. Gene-two smiled. Gene-three smiled.

Peter and I went to the cash register to pay our bill, but Robert waved us off. "Homer bought your breakfast."

It was near here in the 1930s that a thirty-four-year-old writer conceived his major work, a novel in which Oklahoma was a corner of the larger canvas. That book would portray dispossessed people heading west in the Dust Bowl exodus, traveling on Highway 66, "the main migrant road . . . waving gently up and down on the map . . . over the red lands and the gray lands, twisting up into the mountains . . . "

In 1937, Californian John Ernst Steinbeck was courting celebrity with the sales and reviews of his novel *Tortilla Flat*. He and his wife, Carol, returning from a European trip, had recently arrived in Chicago—where they purchased a Victory

Red 1936 Chevrolet, a stylish sedan with a steep-nose chrome grill—likely a showroom car being cleared to make way for next year's models. The Steinbecks left for a late-summer drive on what the author termed the "long concrete path."

They traveled west on Route 66 with a road map that later provided the place names and reminders for the fictional account of the Joad family's voyage. In his journal, Steinbeck wrote of seeing people and cars "panting across the country." Later legend would make much of this trip's role in the writing of *The Grapes of Wrath*, describing it as part of the author's preparations and, at its core, a study trip. Various biographers stated that Steinbeck specifically wanted to retrace the route where, only a few years earlier, migrants had shifted west to where they'd heard there was no Depression: California. Some writers noted, incorrectly, that Steinbeck had lived and moved with a migrant family on their journey, portraying them as the Joad family in his eventual book. It was not that way at all. It was a vacation for John and his wife of six years; Carol would later say that their travels were without "conscious effort to do any research for his book along the way to California."

Steinbeck never returned to Oklahoma after reaching the coast. In California, he spent several weeks doing research for his writing, research that resulted in over half of the novel being set in the state of California. It was there, while on several magazine assignments, that he visited the migrant shanty-towns, as well as the more tolerable government camps. And where, en route, he says he "saw people starve to death . . . they dropped dead."

Though he visited Oklahoma only once, Steinbeck chose to emphasize the "Okies" image over those of the "Arkies" and "Texacanos," all derogatory designations used by California border guards and employers to describe the oversupply of workers offering cheap labor. He wrote of the migrants' fractured quests, their broken cars and unraveled hopes, and of the "scarred earth" they left behind, the squalor of squatter camps and the dismal chances of success.

In *The Grapes of Wrath*, Steinbeck wrote:

> 66 is the path of a people in flight, refugees from dust and shrinking land, from the thunder of tractors and shrinking ownership, from the desert's slow northward invasion, from the twisting winds that howl up out of Texas, from the floods that bring no richness to the land and steal what little richness is there. From all of these the people are in flight, and they come into 66 from the tributary side roads, from the wagon tracks and the rutted country roads. 66 is the mother road, the road of flight.

The factual backbone of the novel grew from seven articles commissioned by the *San Francisco News* to portray the migrants' hardships and their distraught circumstances. Steinbeck had earlier written a magazine article about migrants, with "their pitiful household goods," traveling in "rattletrap cars." The series, "The Harvest Gypsies," appeared in 1936. Collected later into a pamphlet, the thesis was emboldened with a new title: *Their Blood is Strong*, in which Steinbeck wrote: "Thousands of them are crossing the borders in ancient rattling automobiles, destitute and hungry and homeless" and of the migrants

John Steinbeck, author of *The Grapes of Wrath*, gave Route 66 its most famous moniker, "The Mother Road." He once wrote: "A book is like a man—clever and dull, brave and cowardly, beautiful and ugly."

"having used up every resource to get here, even to selling of the poor blankets and utensils and tools on the way to buy gasoline." Gasoline was twelve cents a gallon.

Steinbeck began working on a book-length manuscript around this time, using the working title *The Oklahomans*. He claimed the draft was intentionally destroyed in the fall of 1936.

Carol Steinbeck, poet and gardener, became her husband's first reader through her typing of a manuscript that he scrawled longhand in a green ledger. As she transcribed her husband's 200,000 words, she offered editorial suggestions, sought clarifications, and provided encouragement. She also gave the novel its title, from "The Battle Hymn of the Republic" by Julia Ward Howe. The words appear in the first verse: "Mine eyes have seen the glory of the coming of the Lord; He is trampling out the vintage where the grapes of wrath are stored . . ." The book's English-language title translated into foreign-edition titles such as *Angry Grapes* in Germany and *Rage of Grapes* in Japan. These translations (perhaps even their titles) and the subsequent movie based on the book created an international mystique for Route 66.

A simple telling of the novel goes like this. It is Oklahoma, 1930. A young man, Tom Joad, returns home from the Oklahoma State Penitentiary, where he's been imprisoned for four years for killing a man in a beer brawl. Near the family farm Tom meets Jim Casy, a disenchanted preacher who is no longer in the fold, though he'd once baptized the baby Tom. Together they discover the Joad family's abandoned farm, the house of broken windows and swirls of prophetic dust. Tom soon finds his family at his uncle's tenant farm. They have received a notice from the landlord to move on from there, too. The banks are without compassion, and the landowners are empowered with new financing to purchase Caterpillar tractors that can efficiently plant and harvest consolidated farms. The story plays out against the harshness of the elements—zero precipitation, stunted crops, severe winds, and dust storms that are "blowin' the land away . . . "

The entire Joad family—Tom's strong Ma and steady Pa, faltering Grandpa and spitting Grandma, and siblings Noah, Al, Winfield, and Ruthie—are as emotionally tethered to the jalopy truck as are their tied-down family possessions. They have "no place to live but on the road."

Steinbeck then introduces Tom's sister, Rosasharn (Rose of Sharon), and her husband, Connie. They, too, are passengers. Her pregnancy and eventual loss of their baby provide the novel with a controversial summation in which she uses her breast milk, meant for her now-dead child, to suckle a dying man.

The year 1936 alone saw 90,000 Okies enter California. Many did so after a four- or five-day journey, arriving to join family or friends already residing there. Of the perhaps hundreds of thousands of people who arrived during the 1930s, it has been suggested that fewer than 16,000 experienced the Joad chronicle of home eviction, despairing driving, and broken hopes upon their arrival in California.

"I am scared it will not be a popular book," Steinbeck wrote in his journal. The novel's release in the spring of 1939 brought an immediate backlash from Oklahoma, where Steinbeck's portrayal was considered insulting. It also raised the ire of employers in California, who felt besmirched. Libraries in places such as St. Louis and in Steinbeck's hometown of Salinas, California, banned the book over its use of "dirty words," despite the publisher's New York editor having ventured to California to persuade Steinbeck to tone down the language. (The editor then offended the reluctant telegraph operator, when she sent the "dirty words" editorial changes back to New York via Western Union.)

More than 430,000 copies of *The Grapes of Wrath* were distributed in the next eight months, a hint of the eventual millions to be sold—despite Steinbeck's fears of low readership. However,

The thunder of it all. Unimaginable. Untold tons of dust. Rapid, fierce swirls of dirt and grit. A sky turned enemy—an enemy with a decade-long vengeance that became known as the Dirty Thirties.

he never underestimated the impact it could have, writing in his journal: "If only I could do this book properly it would be one of the really fine books and a truly American book."

In a novel of thirty chapters, it is the twelfth chapter—fewer than five pages—that poignantly casts Route 66 into the world's literary pond, spreading ripples of recognition upon publication.

Steinbeck kept a diary in which he foreshadowed that this would be his big book. From these notations we also know of his anxieties and insecurities, notwithstanding his usual outward display of confidence. "I know this . . . a man got to do what he got to do," he writes in the Joads' story. The mental and physical demands of his five-month marathon of writing the novel left him so exhausted that he did not write again for nearly a year.

Fame undermines many marriages. The resounding success of *The Grapes of Wrath* affected Steinbeck's, as well, possibly helping to end the first of his three marriages in 1941.

A pattern was emerging in our travels. Peter and I were easily tempted away from pavement and contemporary roads. Peter never does anything halfheartedly, and when he'd said at the trip's inception that we'd find all the old parts and dead ends, he meant it. Nothing would be overlooked. During the early days on the road, we'd become particularly fond of finding old fragments of Route 66 that the guidebooks referred to as worth avoiding or that locals told us were "worth looking at, but not worth taking." Even as we drove through the gravel grounds of the garrison at Fort Reno, we knew we would jettison the rest of the post-1933 Route 66 and detour north on flat land to Calumet and its grain elevators, where earlier travelers and residents were forced to drive in their pre-1933 treks. That road would take us to Geary, Oklahoma.

Peter had read the night before that there were alternative roads immediately after Geary. Choice one was the paved U.S. 281: Well traveled and safe—and never part of Route 66—it would take us back down to join post-1933 Route 66, where it headed (more logically) straight between El Reno and a place known as Hydro. The other choice was "less traveled," and we were warned by the literature that it was NOT TO BE TRAVELED in the rain. It had remained a dirt road from the first decades of the previous century, when Route 66 was created. It offered a detour, and our eventual arrival near a once-thriving, now-destitute place called Bridgeport—a ghost town—*then* to Hydro.

After our swing by the out-of-use-and-soon-to-be-tumbling-down log jailhouse in Geary, I looked up at the heavy sky. The paved road south was pleasing—so much so that we drove clear past the turnoff to the dirt road. Peter, ignoring the omen of rain, said, in a drawl adopted from Gene-two at breakfast, "Stop . . . back up . . . "

Backing up, the detour came into sight, and I must admit I didn't hesitate. We pulled forward, turning onto the bank of slippery dirt, and gazed longingly at the deserted path of pre-1933 Route 66. The abandoned trail glistened before us.

"It looks quite beautiful," I said.

Peter opened his guidebook to quote: "Travelers should *avoid* if raining."

"It's not raining," I said.

"It poured last night," Peter said. Looking at the map, he cautioned, "It's seven miles of dirt."

"Only seven?" I nudged the Mustang farther down the road. "We should at least take a look." I veered onto the roadside, enjoying the sound of a soft shoulder. Then I moved the car into the center of the road, still not sensing any firmness beneath the vehicle. At that point, one of us should have provided adult supervision. Instead, all I heard was Peter laugh a little.

The car slid around wheel ruts that had been left by a heavy truck the day before. The truck's wider tires had made wide grooves for us to use—our narrower wheelbase could straddle the path, and all seemed well. I gave an easy push to the gas pedal, and we moved effortlessly.

"I wouldn't normally do something like this," said Peter.

Slowing, the Mustang slipped and almost stalled. Giving it gas, I found momentum, moving again into the grooves and gaining ground. Mud splashed over Peter's door and onto his jacket, and he rolled up his window.

There is a scene in many B-movie thrillers where the beautiful blond woman walks into a darkened room and everyone in the audience groans because the danger is blatantly obvious. Viewers say to themselves, "This is so stupid." After driving 400 yards on this road, I was feeling that obviousness.

"This is so stupid," said Peter.

"Really nuts," I agreed as the steering wheel bounced out of my hands and swirled unintentionally at the whim of the rut. "But fun."

We surfed red mud for a mile, then two. The road was bordered by shrubs, and trees had grown close to it. That narrowed our view. Where the trees broke, all we saw were fields, mostly level. No homes. Nobody.

The day darkened. A threat?

Each time we were gripped by the mud, the car hesitated and threatened to stop. So we had to keep going—not fast, just steadily. Grime splattered onto the windshield, and I kept pumping the wipers. The grade was a gentle decline, which helped our forward motion. I manually moved through second and third gears with the alternate shifter system, avoiding the automatic transmission's decision-making. Half an hour later we had all of three miles behind us and an uncertain four miles ahead. This, mixed with the emptiness of the land and a total absence of anyone in sight, morphed into tension.

Peter: "There's a split in the road. Pull over."

Rick: "Right, I'll drive up through the trees."

Peter: "In the center. There's grass."

Rick: "That's mud with weeds, Peter."

Not a hillock, not a triangle, but a spread of earth that farm trucks on dry days avoided as they either turned right or kept going straight.

"Where are the other vehicles?" Peter asked.

"Back on the paved road, methinks."

We crested where Peter had suggested and the car came to rest, not sinking. It was time to reconnoiter. Peter refolded the map, took out a guidebook and sought an indication of where we were. "Okay, we have two good options," he announced with feigned confidence.

"I'll guess that neither option is turning back."

Peter ignored me.

"That's where the 1921 Key Suspension Bridge used to be," he said, pointing at a downward slope, up which there'd be no return for days, possibly not until spring. "Little of the pilings left, though. We can go there." He made it sound oh-so *National Geographic*.

"*Or* . . . ?" I drummed my fingers on the Mustang's dashboard.

"*Or* we can try to keep going on this road another four miles," he said.

We stared ahead. I turned on the windshield washer and wipers so that we could see better. The sight was disconcerting, yet invigorating. Ruts. Red mud. Long puddles in the ruts. Ridges.

"I think it'll be OK," I said.

"Sure, then . . . " Peter replied, shaking his head.

The road became less passable every 100 yards. I could not get up enough speed to shift out of second gear.

"Slow down," advised Peter.

The wheels spun.

"Faster," he said.

My heart pounded. I was thankful the Mustang had a V8 engine.

The road got rougher. Then Route 66 from the 1920s started to incline before us. The slope, slippery and demanding, tugged at our wheels. There was no way to make the grade except with speed. I pressed the gas pedal.

"Got a favorite prayer?" I asked Peter.

"Please God, deliver me from Rick," he said.

Speed failed us as our treads filled with solid mud. They were packed so smooth they might as well have been bald. We whimpered along. The earth grabbed at our undercarriage, clinging, pulling us down.

Just in time, old Route 66 leveled, sloped downward, and became a mud run. We cheered prematurely and suddenly heaved forward and splashed through a five-yard-long puddle. Red mud flew everywhere. We smelled steam before we could see it. The aroma of baking mud rose from the engine. After navigating the puddle, we were relieved to see that the land remained flat. Slowly, patiently, we put another mile behind us. We became gleeful and unabashedly confident.

Then we turned a corner.

We gasped at the unwelcoming landscape ahead of us: a long pond had swallowed the entire road. Both shoulders of the road had tight-to-the-road bushes, meaning there was nowhere to turn. Emerging from the other side of the pond were half-foot-deep ruts carved by a heavy rig that had traveled this road recently. They led to an incline. If we slowed even a moment to reconsider our situation, we'd never get going again.

"We could be stranded here for days," I said, gripping the steering wheel. The Mustang crept forward.

Peter stared at the rivulets of mud and patted the dashboard. "Okay, Mustang, you can do it . . ."

"It looks pretty soft outside of the ruts," I said. We kept inching farther. Then I gunned the engine, the wheels spun, and we picked up traction from some rocks on the ground and shot forward. We swerved, and then headed straight toward the pond that more and more seemed to be a lake.

"How deep do you suppose it is?" Peter asked as we splashed into it.

"The car could use a wash," I said, ignoring his point and clenching my teeth.

Surprisingly, we shot through the water as if on ice. We had enough momentum to crest the near rise, veer right, and enter a long sleeve of sloping road half a mile straight and with widening shoulders. At first it was a slide—safe passage and gaining speed. Then the car suddenly stuttered ahead of a center patch of glossy mud. We hit a bump. And from there we plunged into deepening ruts, grinding, clinging, and crawling, struggling for control. It felt like we were hoeing a row of our own between the truck tracks.

"Pray," I said.

"Please God, deliver me . . . " he began.

"Not that one . . . "

The engine hissed after our pond dive. Mud attacked the Mustang's grill and pawed at the doors. We fought against the ground with low gear as the engine threatened to stall. I tried to climb out of the ruts to see if the ridge would save us, but the wheels were forced to track.

The car sighed, shuddered, and stopped.

The game of Mustang vs. mud was over. Mud, it seemed, had won.

Feeling only a little chagrined, I looked over at Peter and asked, "Where were you thinking we might spend the night?"

"I wasn't. I was thinking of dinner—a grilled sirloin steak, a side order of chicken enchiladas, and a bottle of Silver Oak Cabernet."

"Would you share the red wine?"

"I'm not in the mood to share anything with you right now."

I thought I caught a sly sideways glance of friendship, but could not be sure.

Nervously, we opened our car doors. Their bottoms scraped against clumps of mud. We stepped out and immediately sank into it, as had the Mustang.

We stared at one another across the hood. We were standing in mud up over our ankles.

Peter is particularly good at assessing lousy situations. It is how he has been successful in business and in life. He's astute, innovative, calm in a crisis, and known for his infectious optimism under gloomy circumstances. He can see a way out of the toughest dilemmas. So I asked, "What do you think?"

As is his wont, Peter thoughtfully took in everything—the miles of solitude, the endless mud, the immovable earth, our sunken car, the road's flooding, and the air's dampness. He took a long, pensive look at where our full-fledged travel-partner sat like a trapped plough.

I waited patiently, confident that he'd see an answer, a way out, that I did not. He always did.

Then he turned to me. "I think we're in deep shit," he said.

There are two travel gods: one for the innocent and another for fools. We'd been praying to the wrong one: She was busy looking after the innocents.

Steam enveloped the front of the car as we stood watching, wondering. I splashed back through the mud to the driver's side, reached in, and popped the hood loose. Back at the front of the car, I struggled to find the release hook that held the hood to the radiator frame. It felt mucky. As I raised the hood, I heard Peter swallow. "My Gawd."

We stared through the steam at an engine completely covered in red mud, caked as though it had been sprayed with chocolate icing and baked solid. It might have looked rich, even artistic, in a different setting.

"Tell me again about the red wine you're thinking of with that steak," I asked. He ignored me. I leaned over to have a look under the car. We had been ploughing the road, grading the mud. There was not a sliver of air between it and the undercarriage.

"Did you pack the shovel I asked you to bring?" I asked.

"You are such an ass," he said.

We looked up the road. We looked down the road. We were what is termed "alone." Very alone.

Peter said, "Well, here we are, stuck in the mud on Route 66."

I said, "Seriously, you have to love travel moments like this."

He repeated the bit about the donkey.

The travel-god-for-fools intervened. Behind us, over the crest of the hill, came first a mud-caked bumper and then the whole beauty of a white 4 x 4 pickup truck with a raised undercarriage. The cautious middle-aged driver crept nearer, seeming to take forever. I started walking up the road to meet him, thinking he might be upset to find his passage blocked.

He slowed, and rolled down his window. He did not stop. He kept moving through the mud hole as I walked backward to keep pace. He did not want to sink with us.

"Hi," I said. "We're stuck."

"*You're kidding.*"

I shrank a little, and he said, "I've been driving, thinking to myself, 'I don't want to be out here in my truck today; I hope no one else is,' and then I slide around that last corner and see a Mustang. *A Mustang!*"

"Yes, well . . . it seemed like a good idea at the time. Can you help us out?"

He pulled up, over and out of the ruts to stop beside the place where we were lodged on the mud median. His truck was scraped by the bushes, but this didn't seem to concern him.

He stepped down from the truck and into the mud. This man was nicely dressed, and our problem was not his problem; yet

I sensed *that* did not matter to him. He reached over to shake my hand. "Vince."

I tendered my muddy palm hesitantly. "It's okay," Vince said, giving me a firm, muddy grip.

Together Vince and I peered under the hood. Peter, anticipating a choice between getting muddy and staying clean, stepped out of our way in his self-appointed capacity as official photographer.

Standing there, we all realized that the median and shoulders, outside of the ruts, were actually harder-packed mud under a couple of inches of slop. It might be better to drive the rest of the way on them rather than in the ruts—*if* we could get out of where we were.

"I've got a tow-strap back at my ranch," said Vince. "I'd go get it if it was ten miles, but it's twenty. It'd take me hours to get there and back in this gumbo—if I could get through."

"Do you have a shovel?" I asked.

"It'd take you forever to dig out of this mess," he said.

"Any other ideas?" Peter asked.

Vince scrunched his hat with his left hand and thought a minute. Eventually he said, "I'll get the shovel."

He found it in the back of his pickup and gave it to me. "Sorry, it's a fence-post shovel," he said. Narrow and long, it made the job at hand nearly impossible. Our tires were so thoroughly covered with guck that they were without a sign of tread. I tried scraping them with the shovel, to no avail. The mud clung.

I knelt down in the mud and reached beneath the Mustang, scooping and carving at the muck where it was crushed tight against the car's undercarriage. Clumps of it stuck to my sleeves and pants.

"I might have a chain," Vince said suddenly. Our hearts soared, and we all walked over to where his tools and building materials were stacked in the pickup. He rummaged about, moved boxes, and concluded, "It's not here." He sounded genuinely sad.

Back I went, on my knees and elbows, digging us out of the predicament I'd created, when Vince blurted from his truck, "Here it is." He held high a short link of chain, sturdy enough to do the job, but barely long enough to wrap around the frame of the Mustang and connect to his truck's back bumper.

Now came the dirty part.

I'd already been in the bank of mud, scraping Route 66 off the tires with the shovel, but Vince was about to demonstrate how deep-in-guck we really were. He looked at me, talking to the three of us. "I can hand the chain down through the engine if you can dig out space below and crawl under the car to reach the end of the chain. Then you'll need to push the mud out of the way, wrap the chain around that lower metal bar and pass it back up through the engine to me. I'll hand it back, and you can loop it again and pull it out to the front of the Mustang."

"Right," I said. "You're the answer to our prayers, Vince." I paused. "You're not exactly what I prayed for, but apparently you're the answer."

There was no option. I lay face down in the mud, forcing my cheek into the grime for leverage. I stretched as best I could to create space under the car by pulling the mud toward me with the shovel. As I sprawled my legs and dug in my feet to keep in place, cold, muddy slime ran down the front of my pants, and soaked my underwear. I made decent progress by twisting the shovel and scraping more dirt away from the axle. I breathed in mud, which dried in my nostrils. Within ten minutes, there was enough room for me turn on my back in the slop under the engine, and then to reach up. Now covered from beard to boots in mud, I offered encouragement upward through the engine, where I could see the Oklahoman looking down: "Remind me to say 'Thank you, Vince,' when this is over."

Vince reached toward me, chain in hand, careful to avoid the still-hot engine. I took the dangling links, looped the chain as we'd planned, and pushed its end back up to him. Then he fed

Being "stuck in the mud on Route 66" may seem to most people a quaint occurrence from times past, but the danger is still there for unheeding travelers, one of whom was at the wheel of our Mustang when this mistake occurred and therefore was tasked with finding a way to get us out.

it down again to me. I wallowed in the mud under the engine, shifting to reach as far up as I could. Having wrapped it around the metal bar a second time, I crawled out from under the car with the end of the tow chain in my hands.

"You'll need a bath," said Peter, taking another in a series of pictures. Noticing his clean shirt and pants, I kicked mud onto his pressed slacks.

The three of us hooked the chain to the bumper of Vince's 4 x 4, which he had moved to the front of the parade while I was kicking mud at Peter.

I found my waterproof jacket in the trunk, tossed it inside down onto the seat of the Mustang and sat on it. Clumps of mud fell off

It was a common refrain to hear early motorists boast of an ability to drive their new jalopy anywhere, regardless of road conditions. Lackadaisical drivers believed they could conquer the new roadways even when harmful weather had caused the surface to become perilous muck. The author felt a kinship with them.

my boots onto the floor, and muddy dough flowed off my pullover and onto the inside of the car door. I wiped what mud I could off of my grimy hands and onto the crotch of my jeans. Finding my keys in a pocket, I started the engine. When I gripped the circle of the steering wheel, more mud flowed off my hands.

"Leave it in neutral," Vince shouted to me before boarding his truck. And he started to pull the Mustang out.

The chain held. At first the 4 x 4 spun its wheels, then the traction took. A minute later, we were on higher ground. Peter caught up and hopped in.

Unchained, we followed Vince for the remainder of the road. He sped up to make sure we could also race safely through pond patches or slip around the bend in silky-smooth sections without hitting him. One of the lessons learned from the pioneers who made their way across the continent in covered wagons was to keep moving when charging through difficult passages. No one yells "Whoa!" in the middle of a mud hole.

Eventually, and with great relief, we reached the pavement of the newer road. Vince turned left as we turned right, amid honks and appreciative waves.

"You get to do that once, buddy," said Peter.

"Right. Next time it's your turn."

"Not me," he said. "Not me."

Mindful of the mud clinging to the engine and undercarriage, we drove carefully. I was now shuddering from the cold and wet, so my enjoyment was mixed.

Map references indicated that the Canadian River lay ahead of us. Cartographers and historians have disputed the name's origin for nearly two centuries. Some say that early French hunters and traders who came down from Canada believed the river flowed that far north. Contrarians point to the Spanish language, via Mexico, where *cañada* means "a valley with gently sloping walls," an apt description of the landscape surrounding the river.

Whatever its provenance, the river did show up as promised. We crossed the river on a "pony bridge," built in 1932 across the South Canadian River. "It's almost a mile long. Well, no, not that much. Three-quarters, maybe." Peter was editing his commentary as he glanced ahead in the map book. "'Pony' is the arch. There are thirty-eight of them."

I began counting the ponies as we crossed, not from lack of trust in Peter's description, but because he made it sound like a challenge to my driving. He signaled the series of structures using his right hand to roll synchronized arches in the air. "The arch spans were the longest they were able to engineer eighty years ago," he said with some pride. Our wheels rolled over another patch of history and continued on what Jerry McClanahan's guidebook termed "one of the best drives on all of 66."

It was pretty here. The grassy hills seemed to heave, to sigh, and the setting stilled our conversation. My shivering eased and I felt warmth from the car's heater. I'd been chastised by both the mud of Route 66 and Peter, but the sting was fading. There was a rolling peace to the drive. This road once carried dreamers west with high hopes for a new life, with fewer hardships and more opportunities. I was not the first person to feel good simply being in this landscape.

This roadbed—"roadside," to be accurate—had been captured on film by the photo-essayist Dorothea Lange in August 1938. The sequence of photographs she took here, near Weatherford, shows a coquettish young mother hitchhiking in a provocative pose sure to catch attention, accompanied by one youngster in the arms of his dust-capped father, and a dressed-up little girl sitting on the family's suitcase.

Lange quoted one Route 66 farmer's opinion of the transients she had been following, traveling with, and photographing in her contracted role for the Farm Security Administration: "They're goin' every direction and they don't know where they're goin'."

When she came upon the hitchhiking foursome that summer, Lange persuaded them to let her photograph them in eight different poses. They were among the more fortunate of her subjects. A sawmill job was waiting for the husband in Arizona, so at least their travels had purpose, if not a guaranteed mode of transportation.

Social commentary was the thrust of Californian Lange's black-and-white portraits, whether the photos she took were of people left homeless, laborers working in drudgery, or families wandering west to escape the drought. For years she roamed

A family photographed by Dorothea Lange as they hitchhiked their way west from Joplin, Missouri, in 1938, here hoping for a ride along Route 66's concrete path in Oklahoma. If you look closely, you can see a car behind the mother's dress, heading west, having passed them by.

Route 66-connected states and roadways, Rolleiflex at the ready, in search of the disenfranchised.

Dorothea Lange, if less renowned than John Steinbeck, just as surely brought the heartaches of migrants into the American conversation in the 1930s. In fact, it is said that Steinbeck was inspired in his writing by Lange's photographs, many of them taken in government camps such as the ones Steinbeck visited. In her camera lens she caught powerful images of human suffering and brought them to public attention in newspapers, magazines, and, later with one-woman exhibitions.

Lange's lifelong profession—fifty years as a photographer—was a career choice she made at nineteen because she thought it would allow her to travel the world and live independently. Before Lange saw the world, that profession took her from her New Jersey home to San Francisco. Her studio work became well known, and California's wealthier residents retained her to take their portraits.

On the streets of San Francisco, however, Lange walked among the homeless and saw faces filled with disappointment. None of these people could afford to pay her to take their photographs, but all of them fascinated her. "There was a good deal of social ferment," she said of those days. She left the confines of her studio with the awareness that "there was a very large world out there that I had not entered too well, and I decided I'd better."

In January 1935, Lange teamed up with labor economist Paul Schuster Taylor, a University of California professor, on a field trip assignment: his words, her pictures. Their common topics included sharecroppers, out-of-work, down-on-their-luck individuals, and strife-driven families. Taylor documented the facts; Lange captured their insights on film. In Albuquerque, in December 1935, after each of them had obtained a divorce from the previous spouse, Taylor and Lange were married.

Lange explored those migrant lives, finding in her portraits of the characters and their settings a chance "to show the American people to themselves." One migrant woman she photographed told her that they had been "living on frozen vegetables from the surrounding field, and birds the children killed." And, said Lange, "she had just sold the tires from her car to buy food."

This was another, often impenetrable, America. The ability to create photographic stories required Lange to quickly earn the trust of people she had never met. She felt that by allowing themselves to be photographed, they were helped—somehow. She thought of herself as "a cipher." Photographs conveyed a reality and shared impressions with readers that writers could not portray as well. Lange was suspicious of storytellers, observing that people are "apt to prune the truth." She would not.

Lange called the social shift and economic dislocation of the Dust Bowl years "the landslide that cut this continent." She crisscrossed half a dozen states, intersecting Route 66 or using it to travel elsewhere in her tens of thousands of miles of road travel. She said that those tumultuous times in America had resulted in the "shaking off of people from their own roots."

Lange and Taylor's documentary book, *An American Exodus*, appeared in 1940, further entrenching the images of plight and flight

Dorothea Lange has been called "the greatest documentary photographer of her era." And her times delivered the harshest of circumstances—the Great Depression, creating an exodus of migrant workers moving west, searching for a fresh start at the American Dream.

that so often seemed connected with Route 66. One can blame aggressive planting by sharecroppers, or overgrazing by cattle ranchers, or greed that left no fallow fields—all are factors—coupled with drought. Taylor wrote about the magnetic draw of "the ever-receding western frontier" in North America and observed that "this tradition still draws distressed, dislodged, determined Americans to our last West, hard against the waters of the Pacific." The trauma that Lange revealed on film and Taylor evoked in his writing is captured in the subtitle of their book: *A Record of Human Erosion.*

In 1964, the year before she died at the age of seventy, Lange was asked by Robert Doud (for the Archives on American Art at the Smithsonian Institution) to share the most significant thing she had learned about fellow citizens. She replied, "I many times encountered courage, real courage. Undeniable courage. I've heard it said that [courage] is the highest quality of the human animal." Thinking about those days, those people, and her nation's current affairs, she added, "I am not sure that that quality is not dissipating in us as a people."

Social historian Peter Dedek writes about Lange's legacy from the 1930s as helping "to memorialize the tragedy. Lange's photographs depicted the Dust Bowl migrants in the arid western landscapes of Route 66 and helped to place their plight in the American consciousness."

"We've got to go to Bridgeport," Peter announced as we turned away from the peaceful hills. I turned off the good road and on to a bad road, and soon we saw a town that was once full of promise. Now, all of that was gone. There was not one open business, not a beating heart, not even a barking dog.

Bridgeport had lost its role to a new settlement on the river, and the ensuing decline in population never reversed. Most of its residents never boarded up their homes; they just left them. When Route 66 moved on, so did prosperity.

But being here in Bridgeport satisfied Peter's penchant for finding rejected parts of America, those left behind by rerouted 66. What began as his interest in finding dead-end roads had evolved into curiosity about the people whose lives dead-ended in the same way. Peter asked me to stop in front of a house whose drainpipe had fallen onto its porch, taking some roof shingles with it. The porch's hand railing had collapsed. Peter asked, "How would you feel if you had to leave the family home you'd built, because a road had moved and a bridge moved and your job broke away from you and floated downstream?" He didn't want an answer. His face looked lost in response to his rhetorical question and sad in the moment, the first time I'd seen this on the trip.

Peter has few bouts of melancholy, and recovers quickly—as he did while I was U-turning away from Bridgeport. There will be less there for the next visitors to see—should any others happen by.

To shift the mood, or perhaps to make me forget about my mud-caked jeans and soaked shirt, Peter offered a comment about the man who had helped us out of the mud: "Vince was the quintessential American—willing to forgive you for getting us stuck in the middle of his road."

I remembered, but did not voice, a Will Rogers quote, thinking this was perhaps the point Peter was offering: "Americans are generous and will forgive almost any weakness, with the exception of stupidity."

Weatherford, on the other hand, was a welcome sight! A car dealership greeted us at the entrance to town. We talked of getting a thorough check-up done for the Mustang, but our overconfidence returned and we devised a plan to pry off the mud ourselves, hand-wash the car, and give it a visual check-up. We spotted a self-serve carwash, one with hoses that hung from overhead, water wands, and soaped brushes, and that suited us fine.

Lifting the hood made the muddy mess clear. Heat from the engine had baked the mud wherever it landed—and it had landed everywhere. Black braces and silver couplings alike were covered with caked brown guck. Every crevice was plugged with it. We fed all the quarters we could find into the slots, buying a few minutes of water at a time, and began removing the mud from the motor. Clusters of dirt began to weep, then break apart. Eventually, the muddy clumps lost their grip on the motor and slid off. But there was more. Peter continued to prod the stubborn lumps with the nozzle and sheared the solid mud free by pointing the water's intense spray directly at it. Soon we were out of quarters and the wand went dry. We tried various denominations of dollar bills at the change machine, but it was broken. Peter spotted a McDonald's across the way and said, "I'll be back in a minute."

Over half an hour later, he returned with two cold coffees and an armful of bags containing chocolate chip cookies.

"I'm standing here up to my armpits in mud, I'm wet, I'm cold—and just this side of cranky, and where have you been? Getting cookies? Forty minutes?"

"The cashier wouldn't give me enough quarters," said Peter. "The manager wouldn't give me quarters. Seems he's having a fight with the guy who owns this carwash. And he wouldn't give me any quarters without a purchase. I had to buy food, beg for all my change in quarters, then go back and stand at the end of the line, each time, and do the same thing. I've bought seven bags of cookies. Seven!" Now *he* was indignant.

He also had nine dollars in quarters. And he had walked to a service station at the corner and returned loaded up on window cleaner, soft towels, scrub brushes, and interior wipes.

Peter suggested that since I was already dirty, I should power-wash under the car by lying on the ground. Foolishly, I followed his suggestion. As I lay there, thick, muddy water flowed to the drains around me. We even had to power-wash the floor drain's screen repeatedly to unplug it. There was too much dirt on the car to use the brush without scraping the paint, so we sprayed round after round of bought "time." Then we spent fifteen minutes on the engine and radiator, taking turns with a special soap nozzle and being careful not to spray too close. And we ran out of quarters, again.

Peter said, "I'll go see my friend, the manager at McDonald's." He was back in ten minutes with four more bags of chocolate chip cookies and a pocket full of quarters.

"Nice to see your relationship is developing," I said.

"Next time we see a bank, I'm buying twenty dollars' worth of quarters, in case you get stuck again."

Another nine dollars later, we were down to our last quarters once again; the Mustang sparkled on the outside; the engine glowed. Peter looked at my jeans and shirt, which were still covered in mud. My boots could not be seen for muck. Dirt covered my beard and caked my hair. Peter aimed the hose at me and said, "You get the last dollar. Stand over there."

And so it was that I received a personal wand-wash, up and down my trousers and jacket, leaving nearly as much mud on the concrete as the Mustang had. Completely soaked, I took my cleanest used clothes out of the trunk. I went over to the washroom at McDonald's, toweled down and changed while Peter vacuumed the car and wiped down the dirty interior. When I returned from the McDonald's, I brought Peter a bag of chocolate chip cookies as a treat.

Leaving Weatherford, we were in completely different terrain. Farms flowed into ranches, and the old roadway was topped with portland cement. Lovely examples of the original portland cement pavement remain in use today on Route 66, particularly in the western half of Oklahoma. Some of it is nicely curbed and all of it is drivable, regardless of the weather.

Portland cement, Route 66's original long-lasting surface of choice, had been in use for a century when the route was born. It had originated in Britain in 1824, where it replaced a commonly used material known as Roman cement, and where it took its name from the limestone cliffs on the Isle of Portland. For more than a decade before Route 66 was paved, the roads that prefigured it, particularly in city centers, frequently consisted of slabs of portland cement.

Early road surface protection came in the form of macadam (named after a nineteenth-century Scottish road builder, John Loudon "Mac" McAdam, who invented a road surface consisting of ground rocks rolled into a crushed pack and later covered with "tar" to keep dust down—thus, "tar-mac"). Initially the pavement on Route 66 was "concrete," an easy-flowing material that resulted from inexact mixtures of portland cement clinker (ground to a powder) and calcium sulfate. The other necessary ingredients, such as coal ash, sand, gravel, and clay, were easily available to Route 66's pavers and were interchangeable—so long as the foundation of sulfate and cement was in balance, to ensure cohesion. Just add water. The resulting portland "concrete" paved the way.

Pavement—whether gray, black, or mixed red with the earth—was always the color of progress. The pavement phases on the highway were defined by location, mix ingredients, and year of completion. Despite its eventual stature, Route 66 was not paved along its entirety until 1938.

Ghostly Texola, our goodbye to Oklahoma, is so near the Texas state line that it has changed its home state as often as its name—three times. Peter, now at the wheel, swung around in his excitement at the town's sagging storefronts and barely readable signs. He jammed on the brakes, pulled his Minolta from his pocket, and shoved it my way. "Get that picture. There. Take two of the store." He backed up, slipped toward a split between buildings and treated my work with his camera as if it were a video instead of a series of stills. "Look up at that, take it." Swinging the Mustang around Texola, he barked photo angles. "Back there. One more."

A sign smacked on the side of a building captured much of what we saw all along Route 66: "There's no other place like this place anywhere near this place so this must be the place."

A blink of the eye later, and we were in Texas. It would be easy to stay on pavement here and to cruise old Route 66 with only one piece of Highway 40 intruding.

But first, we doubled back in the old town of McLean to fully experience the street of used ideas. Its buildings wept with peeling paint, its worm-eaten wood held together by rusty nails and faded hope. It was not particularly enjoyable to be stopping—starting—stopping, but Peter was constantly getting out of the car to photograph sights such as the first Phillips 66 station in Texas.

We chose not to take the Route 66 pavement running west from McLean—that would have been sensible. Instead, we headed south under a Highway 40 overpass and continued, for a mile or so, to a gravel road that promised to turn to dirt soon enough. Our map posted the turnoff for us, and I can't say we weren't warned: "A place that sucked up cars in its mud." But the sun shone and the road was dry.

The Mustang pulled onto this mostly ignored stretch of Route 66, and we headed for the lonesome, oft-renamed town of Alanreed (variously: Eldridge, Spring Tank, Springtown, Gouge Eye, and Prairie Dog Town) eight miles hence, where this 1926–32 dirt road joined a post-1932 paved Route 66 alignment, taking us again within sight of Highway 40. The road rose, sank, climbed slow hills, and, often as not, had foot-high weeds as a center stripe—which our car pushed over and under, sucking part of the stalks into the motor. The smell of their cooked, shredded parts wafted up through the engine. We jostled, bumped, and slowly overcame obstacles on the surface that might one day become ditch-deep—we literally scraped by, savoring the total absence of other vehicles.

At the end of it, we explored Alanreed's dead ends, dead motels, and dead 66. At one time, people would swap hard goods for farm groceries at the now-closed store, or pass the time with neighbors on the street corners while chewing tobacco or wiping dried cow dung from their boots. Now, no one swaps, passes the time, chews, or wipes anywhere near here. The party has moved on. A song playing on the Mustang's stereo—"Used to Be" by the Red Dirt Rangers—seemed to capture the scene. I reset the disc so we could listen again. A voice tinged with regret sang, "There used to be a place to go dance in this town."

The road through Alanreed led us west, and miles later we were forced to choose: Highway 40 or the dusty, dippy Jericho Gap. Peter asked my opinion as he bounced onto a packed-earth section of Route 66 known for never, ever having been paved. This piece of road is rough, four-wheel-drive rough. We were roustabouts, but we weren't road-stupid. At least, Peter wasn't. Stopping to look at the road ahead, he said, "I'm thinking my luck may be about to run out, and given that *your* luck *has* run out . . . "

We drove only as far as the first serious rise in the dirt, where our muffler scraped the road and seemed likely to break free. Our left wheel sank into an unavoidable hole. The Mustang tilted enough that we could see this was the beginning of a worsening road, and understood its car-swallowing reputation. We could have blundered forward, but in a strategic retreat, we turned back to Route 66's late-1930s alignment and slipped onto Highway 40. The Mustang liked it more than we did, and as soon as we could return to the "old" route we did, finding Groom. We backtracked east a mile or more out of Groom on the dirt road of the Jericho Gap, thinking we might make it farther heading in from this side. But the road was inhospitable. Peter never does anything by half measures, and scouted ahead of the car to see if the short break in the road led to a better surface ahead. Dejected, he returned, slumped back into the Mustang, and finally acknowledged defeat.

Route 66 is mostly paved comfort westbound from Groom to Conway. It's a pretty stretch, out of sight of I-40 for most of its twenty-plus miles, giving a sense of distance from the cares and concerns of the current century. But night was falling. A sprinkle of rain turned into a drizzle and then into a full-force downpour. I'll credit Peter's penchant for finding more of the old road, even at that hour and in the unhappy weather, as the reason why we pulled off the pavement after Conway and dirt-roaded our way toward Washburn. But good sense pulled us from the narrow road back to pavement and then up to where Route 66 abuts the airport lands. Having selected this course, full of pride at our accomplishment, we stopped, unsure of where we were. Rain pelted the Mustang's hood and the wind howled, its gusts forming ripples visible in the canvas ceiling above us.

"This'll be the back way to Amarillo," I said, trying to justify our being lost as a temporary situation.

"What?" yelled Peter his voice competing against the thundering rain. "I can't hear you."

I repeated my observation, yelling back at him.

"It's real Route 66!" said Peter, clearly excited by the predicament. No time seems more immediate to a traveler than when being lost. For someone always in control, always setting goals, always heading somewhere specific with purpose, the specter of dislocation is disorienting. That specter looked both strange and good on my travel companion. Something was happening to Peter in response to the decaying towns, dismantled lives, and dead-end roads; he was captivated by what's left of Route 66 and the road's reluctance to be anything other than itself.

The rainfall hardened against the windows. It fought with the road, bouncing off the pavement. It hid street signs from view, pummeling the car, road, and ridge into one hazy vista. We seemed to be swimming in the dark. Both of us were certain we had intuitively taken a proper turn, but soon Peter pulled over in a puddle, splashing water up the side window of the car. We turned on the reading light: It was 9 PM.

"Give me the guidebook you don't use," he said.

I shuffled in the glove compartment and pulled out two. "I don't use either of these. Leave me with my map."

"Your map has left us on the roadside, in the dark, miles from dry weather," he said.

"Don't blame the weather on my map."

"Your map is harmless. You are not."

"Here, this is where we are." I said this before he could fiddle open the guidebooks. "We're on the right road. Put your lights on high beam."

As he did, I huffed. A Route 66 sign was posted not twenty feet ahead.

"If we'd stayed on the interstate, we'd be in Amarillo by now," I said.

"That comment is unworthy of our trip."

I accepted the reprimand. He was right. Weather is an agent of freedom—a challenger of entitlement. We would get where we needed to get, however circuitously.

Amarillo was less accepting of us than we'd been hoping, perhaps a demonstration of its own discontent with the evening's downpour. We circled back on our map, persuaded that we had missed a friendly entry road in our hunt for the real 66. Wire fences protected buildings that elsewhere might have been left to fall down on unwitting passersby. These closed motor courts and gas stations from the 1950s are said to have been "sixty-sixed." As have been the disowned restaurants that hadn't offered a good meal in decades, not since the near-death of downtown America.

We hunkered down in the Mustang, leaning forward as the torrent of rain crashed onto the convertible's roof, inches above our hunched shoulders. "There'll be a place to stay . . . "

This inconvenience was, I recalled, our only hardship on a road where others had frequently traveled in grief and danger. Our warmth, vehicle, maps, and a credit card quelled our anxiety. Only rain dampened our confidence. The windshield wipers, although they were in overdrive, failed to provide much of a view.

It had become our habit to drive past the first one or two motels we saw every evening. Encouraging this behavior was our unyielding assumption that there'd be a "character enterprise," a survivor, a roadside motor court from the "real" Route 66 days waiting for us, if only we were patient. But on this night, a mile into being patient and with no ending of the downpour, we decided to do a U-turn, stop at a gas station and inquire about our options. Rain swirled around me as I gassed up the car. Peter went into the store.

He returned with a six-pack of Bud Light, fulfilling his promise that we would never again endure a dry evening like the one in Baxter Springs.

"Bud Light?" I complained.

"What's wrong with Bud? It's my favorite—since that's all the store has," said Peter.

"It's for people who don't want to get drunk but still like to pee a lot."

Peter's trip inside the store had confirmed that our accommodation choices for that night were few, unless we cared to drive farther—in which case we'd have to forgo the dinner special at the nearby Mexican restaurant. It made the sighted motel our best bet, and that's where we headed; it was near, open, and dry.

On a trip where every diner and dead end seemed one of a kind, I could always count on the routine of our arrivals at motels. Peter's nightly need was to barter, as though anything less would leave him unable to sleep. This evening I simply said to the desk clerk, "He'll negotiate our rate. Here's my card. I'll square up with you in the morning." With that, I went to finish unloading the car in the rain and scout the building in the adjacent lot to ensure that the restaurant, Ruby Tequila's, was not closed.

Our rooms were clean and on different floors, and I accepted this as a good omen. Mine was designed by a trapped decorator, holed up with left-over carpet, hand-me-down furniture, mismatched curtains, and a toilet that took two flushes to down a Kleenex. I tried not to think of who had slept here last.

We headed out for Ruby's and cornered four Corona Gold. Peter asked the waitress to order up two plates of chicken, tortillas, white and yellow grated cheeses, and red and green chilies—variously grilled, baked, or fried.

"No onions," I said.

"I love onions," Peter countered.

"Onions are non-negotiable," I said.

Thoroughly warmed, we pulled up a couple of chairs under the hanging television to catch championship baseball.

"Do you really watch baseball?" Peter asked.

"Of course. It's like life. It's about anticipation. Nothing happens. Then everything happens."

Peter sipped his Corona. He was having distant thoughts; I could sense that this was the day Route 66 was settling in on him, with all its uncertainties and inevitabilities. He eventually spoke into the quiet. "Lord, I hope they got where they were going."

"All the children of the mother road," I added, finishing the song's next line and giving its title. We'd been listening to CDs constantly, and the Alan Rhody song had come up a dozen times, the guitar stroking our ears and the drum keeping a car piston's beat. Rhody sang about growing up in a small town and watching the faces in the cars on Route 66 as they drove by: "The restless and the desperate, the young ones and the old, all together like a river flows."

It was late when our waiter and one of the cooks swept the floor around our chairs. Our delicious meal had been consumed long ago. We weren't bothered; we were enjoying a baseball game in which team names didn't matter—the autumn ritual was all-important. It was later still when the waiter stopped serving Corona and asked us to leave.

Lying in bed that night, a comforter pulled tight to protect against the winds and rains lashing the window of our motor court, I read a biography of Will Rogers. I was coming to understand his observation: "No wonder American people are filling roads, trains, and air. There is so much to see. What we lack in reading, we make up in looking."

7

The Dust Bowl Highway

"The past decade's been a tough time to be an American. I meet people from all over the world traveling here. They don't understand us. Many don't want to understand us."

—Chris, traveler

America conspires with its promoters to distort reality. The conspiracy is called kitsch, and it has its place. Of interest to anyone who reads about Route 66 is the Cadillac Ranch, that head-butt of art. Here, latter-day versions of Monsieur Antoine Laumet de la Mothe, Sieur de Cadillac's namesake, are buried waist-deep in the earth. When the French officer founded the fort of d'Etroit around 1700, he could not have envisioned the horseless carriage, let alone Detroit's Cadillac Automobile Company—to say nothing of this ranch.

It is not that the land on which this attraction is located lacks other purposes. It sits beside a viable farm. This, in the name of public art, is a confirmation that Route 66 is a highway without any fashion sense. It has gained such prominence that its photograph graces many articles and books about Route 66—and it is not *on* Route 66!

Saps that we are for making fun of such temptations, Peter and I left Amarillo on Highway I-40. Exit 60 brought us a row of fence posts dotted with dozens of unmatched running shoes and leftover gym boots (part of the public art). The brightness of the morning lit the ten vehicles in their careful positioning, stuck in the mud up to their rubbers. They sat in a well-crafted nosedive posture. Trunks and back seats were angled out of the ground to coincide with the angles of the Egyptian pyramids, it is said. Ten tilted Cadillac cars mooned the sky—it is as though Salvador Dali had collaborated with Monty Python.

Cadillac's first fling with fins occurred in 1948. That year's model is represented among the tail-light display, which also includes Cadillac coupes and sedans up to 1964, when consumers' weariness of the gimmick and public taste dictated the fins' demise.

Graffiti blazes over the cars. The above-ground portion of these vehicles is periodically repainted with a base color, and the graffiti competition begins anew. To the credit of the organizers, they keep a tight rein on continuity in this installation. Each car is painted in keeping with a loose thematic approach; the current rendition included strong swirls of reds and greens, and splashes of yellow with blue highlights. Variety is what this display is all about. An earlier version had pink as the base color; another had blue waves. This exhibition is not evolving toward anything.

It would have been silly for Peter and me to have missed this. And the absence of other visitors meant that we had the display to ourselves, perhaps because the previous night's rains had left the ground inhospitably slippery. We sloshed through a courtesy corral gate, down a hundred yards from the road toward the pagan idols, and walked freely about this latter-day Stonehenge.

One may ponder the star-linked, bumper-to-sky symbolism or consider the religious significance of the spacing between the vehicles, but the truth is stranger. It all began with "Stanley Marsh Three," as the project's commissioner prefers Stanley Marsh III to be voiced. He and his cohorts from the offbeat collective known as Ant Farm fiddled with a whimsical artistic interpreta-

Synonymous with Route 66 and travel oddities, Cadillac Ranch isn't actually on the route (though it's near). It is as much a tribute to America's fascination with the automobile as it is a celebration of hard-wrought, unexpected road art.

tion of the American Dream, or at least the American Fantasy. In an interview with Michael Wallis, Stanley Marsh III said that owning a Cadillac was "all part of a boy's coming of age and reaching manhood. The idea was to get a good-looking blonde, get a Cadillac, and then go west on Route 66 to the California beaches." The display was moved to this location from its 1974 birth lot, a few miles east, in 1997. It has been mythologized, anthologized, and patronized as a visual Route 66 whack job.

The Spanish surrealist Salvador Dali, who never learned to drive, enthusiastically participated in America's love affair with the automobile. The 1941 Cadillac touring sedans were featured in his painting "Dressed Automobile." When he drove Route 66 to Los Angeles in the 1940s with his wife, Gala, at the wheel of their 1941 Cadillac, Cadillac Ranch did not exist—though surely Marsh would have loved to have coffee with Dali if he'd stopped by. Dali traveled Route 66 all the way to L.A., where he eventually worked on film projects with Harpo Marx, Alfred Hitchcock, and Walt Disney. He became so inspired by the Cadillac that he wrote the company to recommend designs and to propose that they use Gala's name as an insignia.

Of all the vehicles that have cruised America's main streets, none has been as weirdly commemorated as the Cadillac. As Dali said, "The one thing the world will never have enough of is the outrageous."

Soon we were once again alone on the road, traveling a long-ignored section of the route. A stencilled Route 66 badge had been spray-painted on the path, but was now faded. The road itself seemed lonely. The cracks in the pavement looked like lines in a grumpy man's face; this part of the route had seen its share of unhappy travelers.

Many Texas towns tumbled in the rust decade that followed the interstate's arrival. Trees grew in empty buildings, rock columns crumbled, planks fell from barns, and birds nested where neon once glowed. The only sign that has never left Route 66 is "Vacancy." As highway crews erected barriers on the road, its pavement split and weeds overwhelmed it. It is easy to get lost hereabouts, and there is no traffic to console you—it has gone the way of Cadillac fins.

Route 66 crosses Texas only in the Texas Panhandle ("panhandle" being an American term—strips of land on the map that look like the handle of a frying pan—and used to designate parts of the states of West Virginia, Idaho, Oklahoma, and Alaska, as well as Texas). The Panhandle here is not an inconsequential patch of ground; it is one-tenth the area of the state. A 1915 citizens' movement in the Texas Panhandle culminated in a bill being introduced in the state legislature aimed at using the provisions in the Act of Admission to enable the Panhandle to separate from Texas.*

Had it come to a successful vote, Route 66 would now pass through the state of Jefferson.

Texas has a different approach to road designation: "Old Route 66" replaces the "Historic Route 66" signs of other states. It matters not; the route is the route, and we found long stretches that surprised us with their lack of traffic. Driving a dozen or more miles without encountering even one vehicle adds to the sense of open road and makes accomplishing this part of the drive very gratifying.

Soon we paralleled Interstate 40 for many miles, separated by 100 feet of sloping berms of dirt, weeds, and barbed-wire fence (known as Devil's Rope). Now trucks and cars whizzed by us on that nearby highway. We were happy when our road moved away, immediately putting decades between us and the hurrying drivers.

There's a scene in the movie *Cars* where the enthralled Corvette-inspired character, Lightning McQueen, is converted from his speed-fiend obsessions to a state of being considerate

* Many Texans believe that when Texas joined the Union in 1845 it reserved the right to secede. That belief is erroneous. But when President James Polk signed the "Joint Resolution for Annexing Texas" (also called the "Act of Admission"), it did provide that the state of Texas could one day devolve into as many as five equally viable states of the American union. The U.S. Constitution is clear on the matter of Texas's ability to devolve into five states: "New States may be admitted by the Congress into this Union; but no new States shall be formed or erected within the Jurisdiction of any other State; nor any State be formed by the Junction of two or more States, or parts of States, without the Consent of the Legislatures of the States concerned as well as of the Congress."

of slow, intentional travel. McQueen muses to his friend Sally, the animated Porsche, as they look down from a mountain pull-out of Route 66 onto the modern interstate's rush of traffic, saying that everyone drives right by without slowing to see the towns. It was the same as what Peter had said to me the day before: "People don't even know what they're missing."

The Porsche character gets pensive, remembering that it wasn't always that way, and talks about the days before the frenetic freeway cut across the land.

Lightning McQueen learns that car travel forty years ago didn't slice the country like the interstate does. Sally, a Porsche 911, describes how old Route 66 swerved with the land, rising, falling, moving where the earth naturally went, not where it was forced to go. I recalled my book club night in Chicago at the start of the trip and one of the women talking about the film, saying, "Cars didn't used to drive Route 66 to make good time; they drove it to have a great time. I think I'm paraphrasing the movie," she said. "Anyway, I hope that's what you find." We had.

On April 14, 1935, these lands were subjected to nature's wrath. It was "Black Sunday," a day that Woody Guthrie sang about as witnessing "the worst of dust storms that ever filled the sky." The storm appeared first as a rain cloud without moisture; no rain fell. There was no dampness in the earth, nothing left to evaporate. The wind swept and re-swept the land like a nervous janitor. The land became drier by the day; and when the dirt was drier than dust, it got still drier. People who live by the ocean might think of it as the tide going out—and staying out. No replenishment.

This disaster did not start in 1935, but it peaked then, with darkness overhead, around, and within people's lives. The massive shift of airborne earth to dust foreshadowed a parallel shift in society. The magnitude of neither was anticipated; both shifts were beyond "managing" in any sense of analyzing,

"The blackest and worst of the many duststorms of recent weeks swept down on the vicinity out of the rolling black cloud pictured above. 'It was no darker in the cyclone cellars after the storm arrived than it was outside,' one farmer said."

shaping, coping, or responding in a timely manner, either by individuals or by governments. Only some large corporations could see commercial opportunity within the human heartache, and that mostly came from owning the foreclosed lands which their patient money could afford to hold until better times—if those times ever came.

Unexpected weather conditions had seared these parts of America in the spring of 1930. The heat had come in waves, each wave compounding the one before. Rain was elusive—it was not here, not there, not anywhere. And that was merely the first year. It was only months before the media announced "The Great Drought," and the alarmist tone was prescient.

There is a term foreign to those from non-farm states, but familiar to those who know of arid lands and parched breezes: "blackout," that swirl of discarded dust, dry topsoil, and swift winds that blocks the sun without easing the heat.

The High Plains, that giant lay of land across Missouri, Kansas, Oklahoma, and the Texas Panhandle, suffered intolerably. The earth and its people could barely breathe. The economy choked. There was nothing to hold on to—not earth for roots, not land for farmers, not jobs for workers. Pride evaporated. Hunger spread. Farms failed, ranches fell, and people fled.

In 1932 the new president, Franklin D. Roosevelt, took office as life in the Midwest worsened. He launched his radical New Deal when matters looked salvageable, but they worsened: 1933 made 1930–1932 seem like only the first act in a tragic play that would climax in 1935 with Black Sunday.

Across the nation, newspapers, radio programs, and political speeches ramped up the tension; the crisis deepened by the week. The newly coined term "Dust Bowl" came to mean a land, a people, a situation. The resulting migration was not "to" anything, but "away from" everything.

The hard times of the Dirty Thirties, far from eroding Route 66's appeal, enriched its mystique in song and story.

A lean man with an even smile, wearing a workman's open-collar, long-sleeved shirt over an undershirt, figuratively hitchhiked across America's musical landscape as he literally hitchhiked along Route 66. He was twenty-ish, had sallow cheeks, a straight nose ridge, and a crop of curly, untended black hair. Thin of bicep, he also had thin fingers that were most at home on a guitar. He played the harmonica backwards, cupping his hands with the bass notes to the right. He could play the washboard and was given to say, "This country's a-getting to where it cain't hear its own voice." He let that sentiment reverberate for generations, doing whatever he could to hear that voice, replicating and repeating its truths.

Route 66 shaped the gravel-voiced Woody Guthrie into the "dustiest of the dust bowlers." In turn, he made road travel, hard work, and misfortune the heart of the more than 1,400 songs that he either fine-tuned or originated, mostly between 1936 and 1954. Many of his songs were crafted from phrases uttered by migrants in roadside camps on their way west along 66 or in conversations colored by despair.

Born in 1912 into a troublesome Democratic family in Oklahoma, he was named Woodrow Wilson Guthrie after the then hopeful candidate and later U.S. president. Throughout his life, Guthrie awaited the arrival of socialism in the United States, the need for which he saw whenever he rode the rails or walked into migrants' tent cities.

As a fifteen-year-old balladeer full of songs, Woody Guthrie left Okemah, Oklahoma, "one of the singingest, square dancingest, drinkingest" of towns, for Pampa, Texas. In 1934 the newly married twenty-two-year-old singer in the Corn Cob Trio watched as devastation took root in his world of Pampa. As others left, he wrote the ballad "So Long, It's Been Good to Know Yuh" in commendation of the land, not the people. He prepared to head out.

Guthrie said he'd "traveled Route 66 enough to run it up to 6666." He would sing of his fellow Okies that they "come with the dust, and go with the wind." He would have first hitched on to Route 66, the Dust Bowl Highway, coming south from Pampa in 1937, his paintbrushes in his hind pocket. Fortunately he had the fallback skill of sign-painting when his guitar playing did not pay enough.

Both good times and tough times came to Woody over the years, through his finding and leaving of wives and his career ups and downs. Invariably he left stability behind and took to the road, using Route 66 to crisscross his country, seek his people, and learn their songs. The highway became his soapbox.

The socialist in Guthrie found a voice in his songs about migrants and unions. "I sing songs that people made up to help them do more work, to get somewhere in this old world, to fall in love, and to get married and have kids." He fashioned himself as one of the downtrodden, a bindlestiff, writing that he'd go "out and sing for a bunch of working people . . . and they'd holler and roar and yell and raise so much ruckus that you just know damn well this country was gonna come out right in the long run."

Woody Guthrie shared the workings of his guitar and his mind with "song circles," gatherings of like-tuned players and like-minded participants. At the time, he was "eating twice a week whether I was hungry or not." He reassured those who cared about his well-being that he was "never spending money foolishly unless I'm alone or with somebody else."

Guthrie's ballads would tell of hardship; his audiences heard him talk of "dust pneumonia." And he reinforced his image of being "just a lonesome traveler; the great historical bum." Route 66 was his road, and it legitimized his songs. It is where he talked at roadsides, strummed for audiences large and small, and listened beside campfires. He felt at home on the road, as only a rootless man could. It was from these travels that he formed much of his first song collection, *The Dust Bowl Ballads*.

Woody would capture moments in a westbound transient's life: "Out of your dust bowl and westward we roll/And your desert was hot and your mountains were cold."

In New York, Guthrie fell in with others who were playing "people's songs," notably Burl Ives, Leadbelly, and Pete Seeger. They formed the Almanac Singers, taking their name from the homespun wisdom of *The Old Farmer's Almanac*, commonly found on farms and ranches across America.

Joe Klein, in his book *Woody Guthrie: A Life*, writes of Woody eventually distancing himself from this group while staying with them. "He remained aloof, and the others stumbled into an uncomfortable and debilitating parody of Okie-ism, which seemed to mean that you didn't admit to reading books, didn't talk philosophy in public, didn't wear bourgeois clothes like suits or ties, and, in extreme cases, didn't bathe." Once, longing for the road, Guthrie asked a New York friend, "How do you get from here to the United States?"

In the early 1950s, illness slowed Woody's creative work. Its specific source and nature eluded him, as he avoided hospital care. Little was then known of Huntington's disease, except that it robbed the victim of the ability to think, to control motor skills, and to make good judgment calls. Guthrie had watched his mother's body shrivel, her mind becoming frightened at its loss of control; he now found himself experiencing the same decline. He died at the age of fifty-five in the autumn of 1967, soon after the "summer of love." Artists as varied as Bob Dylan, the Kingston Trio, and the Almanac Singers' successors, the Weavers, built

In words that leap across the century, Guthrie wrote about bankers and mortgage lenders and funny men: "Some will rob you with a six-gun/And some with a fountain pen."

upon the themes celebrated in Woody Guthrie's road repertoire. Guthrie never knew of their tributes.

Juxtaposing the word "ugly" with anything American is a dangerous thing, yet an establishment in Adrian, Texas, has made a reputation from it. Few Route 66 entertainments get the repeated recommendations that the Midpoint Café's ugly crust pies do. Without them, you'd blink and skip the small town of Adrian. With them, you dawdle at the Midpoint, order more food than you can reasonably eat, sample things your mother warned you away from, and spend good money without qualms.

Tommy latched on to Peter and me the minute the screen door slammed behind us. "We've been waiting for you all day," he grinned. "Have a seat and some ugly crust pie." His banter has lost none of its humor in the repeating.

"I'd order a hamburger if I was you," said Tommy. "We don't know how to cook much else." He walked away from us and over to where a lady poured gobs of sweet icing over doughnut twisters filled with raisins and cinnamon. They're labeled "Tommy's Twisters," and there's a story. Tommy Loveless told us his dad had named a nearby restaurant and gas station after him, and the twisters started there. "He ran those operations until his age and the shifting highway business got the better of him. Now I work here for Fran. She'd like me to buy the place, but it's tough to keep up with the downturns."

The café, operated by family and friends, dates back to proprietor Zella Crim's opening in the late 1930s, when it competed with several other roadside diners in Adrian for the attention of passersby on the busy Route 66. The original building is still, in part, couched within the new.

"This place could give a lesson to Lou Mitchell's," I told Peter, remembering the first breakfast spot we'd visited on our trip. Here, a gift shop off to the side was filled with Route 66 souvenirs. The diner oozed highway collectibles. Anything rumored about Route 66 was given prominent notice on the walls by way of calendar pictures, photographs, and homemade hangings. The booths had the 1950s aura of slippery vinyl seats and chrome adornments. A father and daughter, she perhaps in her mid-twenties, ate at a Formica table close to our booth. He forked into "upside-down cake" and she into carrot cake. Neither of them paused to talk to the other until he placed a map on their table after they had finished eating.

"Fran's 'never-fail meringue' pie," Peter affirmed as Tommy told us it was time to order "or you won't get any more coffee." And Tommy promised me there was one piece left of this morning's baked peanut-butter-and-chocolate ugly crust pie, "since I haven't had time to eat the last of it yet today." I took the piece before he could, but not before his advisory: "Fran makes it with half a cup peanut butter and one cup of powdered sugar, you should know."

Peter asked Tommy how many people came through Adrian each year.

"Lots on motorcycles. They get organized by tour operators out of L.A. Most go west, though, so they ship the bikes to Chicago to start there. Hundreds ride them hogs."

"What about in cars?"

"Buses, cars. Thousands. Most stop here. We're midpoint on the route. You're halfway to L.A., if you care about that. Take a look in the guest book. You'll see names from all over. Don't forget to sign it."

The café's guest book was spiral bound, with thirty lines to a page. I looked back a dozen double-sided pages, seeing names from the U.K. and Asia and an expected quotient from Canada, but it was the dominance of Europe – Spain, The Netherlands, Germany, and France – that was surprising. That and the absence of travelers' homes noted as "U.S.A."

Here you are in the heart of America, a once-thriving-still-existing business with a good road to and from it in either direction. Here Route 66 looks once more to be relevant.

"It won't ever again be what we dream. Still, we dream," said Tommy responding to Peter's now inevitable question. "Business is good for us this year. Because of the Euro dollar. They want to see what once was." Heritage tourism, with its preference for preservation and replication, may yet provide a way to prevent Route 66 from becoming a road of ruins.

Tommy was serving pie that, to be charitable, was downright ugly. Fran came over and told us she had worked at maintaining the "ugly" recognition since she had bought this spot two decades ago. "My grandmother made the most wonderful pies. Somehow I can't make that happen," she told us while signing a copy of her cookbook, *Ugly Crust Pies Favorite Recipes*, with the admonition "Life's too short . . . eat more pie!"

The pie tasted mellow and sweet. Fran had let hot bubbles in the pastry shell form lumps on the rim and had made the crust too large, so that it overlapped the pie plate in an inelegant wave. Those deformities ensure that no one will ever call her pies "pretty."

Chris, the father at the table near us, left his daughter there and came over to see Peter and me when he saw us spread out our map. He was dressed in a way that displayed every state they'd traveled through: a slick belt from Illinois, a plaid shirt that shouted Missouri, denim slacks that claimed Oklahoma, and a beige hat from Texas. He told us of their trip west for a wedding, and glowed with envy when he heard of the time we had set aside to seek out the original Route 66. "That's another trip for us," he said. "You have to know how lucky you are to have that experience. You can drive Route 66 and say you've seen America."

Then he surprised us by offering an unsolicited comment. "The past decade's been a tough time to be an American. I meet people from all over the world traveling here. They don't understand us. Many don't want to understand us. We'll recover. I want to be proud again to be American—the way I once was."

As I walked to our car, Chris was driving out of the parking lot. Not seeing me, he was singing, and through his open window, the truth came out clear and loud: "If you ever plan to motor west, Travel my way—the highway that's the best . . . get your kicks . . . " and as he drove on his voice faded, but not from any lack of his pride in America's heartland.

With the end of the Second World War, Route 66's role as conduit for military supplies and personnel quickly ended. The war years had filled Route 66 with transport trucks and armed forces vehicles that required services from the towns along the road. All that changed quickly, and with it the economic circumstances. Rubber tires and petroleum products were no longer being rationed. Returning troops and discharged personnel were getting a formal education, marrying in unheard-of numbers, purchasing new homes, having lots of children, and buying flashy cars. The late 1940s ushered in workplace changes, expectations of prosperity, and the concept of vacation time. The time and money available for visiting family and friends, wherever in the nation they lived, meant travel. And that travel needed both better highways and more motor courts.

Not far behind those necessities—building on the railroads' example—there emerged on the highways a variety of stores and stations selling whatever young families wanted to buy. Or could be lured into buying. That included trinkets parodying Native cultures and distorting history. Every aspect of travel was commercialized in the boom of late 1940s–1950s road tourism that saw vacationers drive around the country in a swirl of dollar bills.

The road itself was still being paved then, and its curves were being made less dangerous. It is now clever to say, "It's the journey, not the destination," but back in the 1920s, "getting there" was often a chore. Those were the pre-nostalgia days, and travelers were intent on arriving at their destination efficiently rather than coping with unwanted thrills of getting there.

As hundreds of thousands of new cars took to the road year-round, Route 66 struggled under the weight of its reputation as a travel experience. Its quality varied from state to state, even within a hundred miles, and yet variety became Route 66's greatest appeal. Though accommodation expectations

From the first conversation before our trip began, our goal was to find the discarded parts of the road, the left-behind portions. Once, its name meant the very definition of traveling in America. Today, Route 66 teases more than ever: "Find me if you can."

had changed since the 1920s, when travelers slept in whatever tent or shelter they carried with them in their flivver, it remained chancy. Tourists found service on the route to be unpredictable and inconsistent in the independents, although the variety of names—Arrow Courts, U Drop Inn, Munger Moss Motel, Rest Haven Court, Texas Longhorn Motel—was an entertainment. There was no pattern to the food on offer; instead, families stopped where the name or the reputation appealed, at places such as the Hinton Junction Cafe, the Golden Spread Grill, Hank's Hamburgers, or Miz Zip's Cafe, and at service centers such as the Blue Dome Station and the Magnolia Station.

It is a paradox of travel that a special and pleasant travel experience or destination becomes popular and therefore no longer "one of a kind." And it soon gets worn, congested, and overused. In the 1950s, Route 66 became dangerously popular. It could not sustain itself as a novelty, nor could it cope with the volumes of travelers it attracted. Friction arose between those who preferred the leisurely approach and those in a hurry. Speed won out. Faster roads were wanted and, admittedly, needed.

The guidebook Peter was reading hinted that our nearing Glenrio would mean that the trip "drops down off the high plains," as he quoted. The last eighteen miles to Glenrio, located on the Texas-New Mexico state line, are on I-40. We exited at Glenrio, a ghost town, and Peter pulled out his photo revolver, shooting as we crossed the Santa Rosa River on a narrow bridge and hurled ourselves onto one of three versions of Route 66 connecting Endee (an abbreviation of "N D Ranch") with San Jon. Our chosen road was an unpaved but passable road built before the 1950s. Reliable information warned us to "avoid if muddy," but the day was good and the road was dry. We drove eighteen miles without incident!

At San Jon we stayed on the old road and drove past shuttered shacks, stations, and motels, avoiding the still-visible Highway 40 to Tucumcari. Then we ducked through an underpass tunnel flooded with three inches of water and turned left onto a decent road with I-40 bustling not far away. We were humming along at a good speed, and this open stretch of Route 66 seemed to promise freedom. At a slight turn, with a beautiful stretch in front of us, we saw the road shimmer ahead. I had a premonition—a flash from the movie *Cars*, where Mater, the animated tow-truck character, tells vehicles like ours they'll be kissing the pavement goodbye and finding mud clinging to their car in places they'd never imagined.

Peter had the good sense to ease up as we neared a reflecting pool ahead. The road was badly flooded. Wide tire tracks in the mud showed where the 100-yard washout had been forded on the left by a big rig. Similar tread marks showed a successful attempt on the right side of the lake. None of these tracks matched the narrowness of our Mustang's tires.

"Easy, now," said Peter, patting the dash with his right hand and keeping his left on the steering wheel.

It was not possible to gauge how deep this water might be. It might be two or three feet deep, and look not half that. Out of respect, Peter simply nosed the Mustang into the water and stopped.

"We might try to crawl over the left rim," I suggested, pointing to where the tracks had sunk only a little into the mud, and where at least one set of tracks showed successful passage. "And we could let the right-side wheels ride in the water."

"Or not," said Peter.

"There's got to be pavement down there. It should be shallow," I encouraged. "And I could walk in the ruts behind you, in case the car fills with water and you drown."

Peter backed up, then headed to test the right side's bank of dirt.

"It looks more solid," he said.

"It looks like quicksand."

Travel's trials reveal more about travelers than do its happy experiences. Peter had his jaw set at an angle, and nothing would dissuade him. He dared the mud to suck us in. This approach was soon seen to be obviously dumb. We did well entering the soft dirt shoulder. Less than two feet after that—water to the left of us, mud to the right—we slipped.

"Whoa!" yelped Peter.

You may have read this before: We looked up the road. We looked down the road. We were what is called "alone."

I respectfully repeated to Peter his own line from the day before: "Well, here we are, stuck in the mud on Route 66."

To his credit, he sighed and reminded me: "You have to love travel moments like this . . . "

Our attempts at rocking and pushing the car only splattered the wet earth all over my pants. Red mud flowed around three of the Mustang's tires. In such situations, it is important to get your first full attempt at self-rescue right and be patient in preparing to do so. To that end, we were fortunate that railway tracks crossed a strip of land abutting the road. We walked to the rail bed and scooped up its gravel. We could put it under our tires for traction. We cupped handful after handful of pebbles and rocks to use as stuffing around the sides, behind, and in front of the tires sitting in the shallow water and mud. This would give us steering ability once the traction took hold—we hoped.

Nearly half an hour later, we were still picking up small branches, pieces of brush, and gravel as landfill. We wedged the debris wherever tires and mud met, placing it up to a foot behind and in front of the tires, providing some traction both ways. When we felt all set, Peter tossed me the keys. "Have a go." He pushed from the front right, his feet slipping in the mud, as I nursed the car into reverse. The wheels spit rocks, but gained no traction.

We didn't want to risk going far forward, but we tried, with Peter pushing from behind to see if we'd rise out of the mud. No luck.

"Well, look at this," said Peter, pointing behind us. Two 4 x 4s were pulling up. "Here comes the cavalry to the rescue."

A young woman in a brown sweatshirt and dark denim pants jumped out of the first truck to arrive. "Hi, I'm Kate. I was driving over there"—she pointed south—"and saw you were having problems. I called my friends, and we've come to help you."

Both doors popped on the pickup behind her and two men her age jumped out, eager for action. "Chancy," said a blond, muscle-bound man.

"I'm Jonathan," the taller one said. "You stuck?"

"Think so," said Peter.

They pushed down on the Mustang's trunk to jostle the rear end. Then tried to lift the car and found it too heavy. Finally Jonathan said, "Yup. You're stuck."

Why they looked at me, I'm unsure. Maybe because they suspected I was wearing my last semi-clean threads. Whatever the reason, Chancy made the suggestion: "If you could crawl under the back and hook up my chain, I think we can pull you out."

I looked at Peter, thinking it was his turn to get dirty. Looking away from me and at them, he said, "Great idea. Thanks, guys."

As Chancy and I worked the chain's fierce claw over a piece of immovable steel underneath the Mustang, Jonathan repositioned his truck right behind us. He faced the car's trunk. Jonathan's Ford had a double metal bumper and a winch at the front. When we were tied securely, I walked through the water on the driver's side and got into the car. Jonathan shouted to me from the cab of his truck, "Put it in reverse." He backed away slowly, picking up the chain's slack. When the chain was taut between the Ford and the Mustang, he revved his engine to take on the Mustang's weight and kept driving slowly in reverse. And out we came.

We were all pretty proud of the accomplishment. Everyone reached out to everyone else and shook hands. Chancy hugged Kate.

I looked longingly at the pond, feeling both success and defeat.

"They dammed this roadway months ago, not leaving a drain. Stupid-dumb," said Chancy, gazing over the impediment. "That's quite the lake they made, right in the middle of the road."

"Do you think we could drive through it?" I asked.

"Hmm," said Jonathan, pursing his lips in thought.

"Let Chancy and Jonathan drive through it first, in their truck," Kate suggested. "You'll see how deep it is. If they don't get stuck, then maybe . . . "

Jonathan smiled at the challenge and leaped for his rig. He drove cautiously into the water, but kept up a proper speed, splashing thick brown water everywhere. His truck climbed steadily to the other side, showing us that the little lake was over a foot deep.

Peter shook his head and smiled. I nodded, looked over at the water, and cocked my head toward where Jonathan and Chancy now stood on a solid Route 66, 100 yards away.

"I can see how much you want to do this," said Peter, moving to the passenger's door. "Go for it."

We got back in the Mustang and I maneuvered it to the center of the road, facing the flood head on. Steady and sure, we entered the water, keeping the Mustang in second gear. Muddy water sprayed everywhere, coating the car and, to my satisfaction, splashing on Peter as he hung over the windowsill to get the perfect video shot.

He smiled at me and said, "You know, I'm not comfortable with some of the stuff you get us into."

Hesitation would have stranded us in the middle as surely as it would have wreaked havoc on the car's motor, so I kept on—momentum was what counted. We emerged on the other side, dripping water and soaked in accomplishment. Jonathan and Chancy hooted and hollered. Kate followed in her raised truck, reminding us how deep the water actually was, and jumped out when she caught up with us. Hands were shaken again, and thanks given.

Chancy said, "Probably not a good idea for you guys to drive through water or mud in a Mustang, unless you've got a 4 x 4 lifeguard on either side!"

It is usual for travelers on this part of the trip to accept the overlapping of Interstate 40 and old Route 66 and to cruise the shared designation, shared pavement, and shared scenery. That would make sense, and it would be safest.

We took the Cuervo Cutoff instead. It is an oft-forgotten bite of 66, out of use since the interstate's intrusion. It begins as gravel, then becomes tired asphalt, then dirt, leading eventually to Santa Rosa in a circuitous 1950s path. The railway tracks provided our guide to the north, out of sight of 40.

Then the Cuervo Cutoff itself offered a cutoff.

Seven days into our journey, we had not sated our lust for back roads. Nor had we shed our disposition to ignore signs that were explicit in advising caution. The sign for this pre-1950 piece of Route 66 stated: "Unmaintained Road—Travel at Own Risk." The guidebook advised: "Very bad shape" and "Not recommended." This seemed reasonable to us, and we barely slowed. Peter wanted me to capture a photograph of the warning sign before he drove on. It read: "Road Closed Ahead."

The going was bumpy, but good. Chunks of some parts of the dirt road had disappeared, while other sections suffered from serious erosion. A Mustang is a Mustang, and I could almost hear it snort denial at the rugged road's challenge. We jostled as we made our way for a mile, then two, then four. Peter, driving, patted the dash once too often, saying, "Good work," when I said, "That may be bad luck, talking to an inanimate object and all . . . you'll need counseling when we get home."

Our car top was down. The sun shone. In the center of this decaying road was a sporadic line of grass, and then it too disappeared. In spots, weeds scratched our car's belly, its undercarriage barely clearing the potholes.

The alchemy of travel is one part being in the moment and one part anticipating regrets. Peter said, "I've been thinking we should take this car home with us."

"How so?"

"We could buy her—split it fifty-fifty, you and me."

Suddenly, the pitted road's gentle bend was complete and we pitched forward, slanting downward, while approaching a narrow river. Peter temporarily eased our descent. The closer we got, the faster the river seemed to flow. The road went through it; would we? Should we? We had a poor track record when it came to such things. And while I trusted my driving and Peter trusted his, neither of us trusted the other's. Such things are conveyed by sideways glances, grunts, and by how one grabs a door handle in case of the need to exit quickly. These subtle signs were coming from both of us, which was worrisome, especially since Peter displayed his behavior as the driver.

Suspense has its purpose at such times, and it is particularly effective if the person demonstrating it actually has the potential to do something really stupid. Peter had sped up and kept going as though intending to ramrod straight through the swift-running river. From our vantage point of ever-increasing closeness, we could see that the river turned to rapids right where we'd needed to pass through it, and that the expanse was thirty feet across. There was no indication of the water's depth. On the other side, the dirt road inclined upward.

Peter adjusted our speed to slow, methodical, and intentional. He aimed the car down the center of the narrow road. The one assured fact here was that the dry road would turn to mud two feet after we were into the water. Our score card so far was MUD: 2; RICK/PETER: 0; and why, I wondered, would Peter offer MUD a hat trick? He hit the brakes suddenly as the Mustang's front wheels entered the swirling water.

I jumped out, for no other reason than that I could, splashed into ankle-deep water and slipped on the mud, regaining my balance by leaning on the Mustang's haunch.

Peter yanked on the emergency brake, let the car idle, and climbed out over the driver's door, jumping to the back of the Mustang and out of the water. He put his camera on video and caught my contemplative walk around the car's trunk, gauging the situation, and when I looked up at him, he recorded my advice: "I say we put on our bathing suits and go for it."

Peter is nothing if not practical. He hopped back in the Mustang and engineered the car's withdrawal from the river, saying, "I've got a better idea."

Detours had become Peter's obsession. If he had the slightest idea where he might be going, he would drive miles just to turn back, if it meant seeing seldom-traveled roadbeds that were once part of the cross-country road. His early promise that he'd seek out-of-the-way stretches had become an obligation. And his pursuit of yet another one had become inevitable. I climbed over the passenger door, my boots dripping water on my seat, and inserted myself into the Mustang.

We backtracked four miles, shedding mud as we bumped over the curb on reentering I-40 near Cuervo, where I-40 equals Route 66. We drove west to Exit 277, which linked us with New Mexico's paved 156, heading *east*. We then drove ten

The more obscure and rugged an alignment we found of old Route 66, the more likely that something would be in our way, like these rapids in a river running across what was once "The Dust Bowl Highway."

miles. There we found the southern connection with what the guidebook defined as "Rough!!!" road. Dust filled the air behind us on this very dry day. I felt tanned and alert in the moment, fit in the traveler's sense of the term. We were now traveling on what would have been the latter part of our uncompleted dirt road drive—had it not been broken by the river. We were dead-ending, again. Eventually, driving through fields of high, useless grass and over knolls of scrub, we came to a hill and looked directly down on the river and rapids we'd wisely refused to cross from the other side.

This was a bad land for silly drivers. Wrecked vehicles were frequent in the area, overgrown with brush, decades of rust camouflaging them with the land, their abandonment complete. There was a lesson there for anyone who noticed. Peter did not. He swung partway down the hill, backed up, and angled forward on the slope. Then he put the car in reverse and backed down, giving no indication that he had something smart on his mind.

"I'd like to get out, please," I said, fearing the worst, and he stopped, tossing me his camera.

I climbed the incline, thinking I may have to walk out the way we'd driven in—alone. When I turned around, I saw Peter gun the Mustang backwards toward the rapids. Then he slowed, letting the rear wheels of the car enter the water. Across the way, he'd avoided driving through the rushing waters. Now it appeared as though he'd be willing to reverse his way across the river. He was becoming unpredictable. Then he stopped midstream, just before the rapids.

"Get this," he shouted. So I took a video clip of him driving out of the river, ostensibly completing the crossing. Once we were home, when this faux image of him gallantly exiting the roiling river was spliced onto one of the car entering on the other side, the hoax would convince many a skeptic that, at last, Peter had bested water and mud.

Sometimes authentic adventure needs to be contrived.

A short stretch of two-lane roadway took us through the lovely architecture of Santa Rosa. Then we drove the I-40/Route 66 shared surface toward our goal of Santa Fe.

The biggest shift in Route 66's history of changed alignments occurred when Santa Fe was eschewed in favor of a straighter route across New Mexico. In 1927, politics rerouted Route 66's path away from New Mexico's capital city, the oldest established community in the nation. The new route took people directly east from Santa Rosa to Albuquerque, eliminating the Santa Fe bulge, which required motorists to take a ninety-eight-mile hump north to Santa Fe, then south to Albuquerque.

Today the road north to Santa Fe is a delight to travel, as smooth as any in the country. When Route 66 was being built in 1926, the fourteen-year-old state of New Mexico had roads that were as steep, twisty, and treacherous as its political landscape. The state was said to be controlled by a nefarious coalition of self-serving politicians (no news there, but hold on) based in Santa Fe and supported by both elected and appointed officials in collusion with the business community. That alliance, known as the Santa Fe Ring, had the Republican Party as its calling card, controlling public office until the surprise election of Democratic governor Arthur Thomas Hannett, in November 1924, for the 1925–1927 term.

Running for re-election, Hannett was vigorously attacked by his opponents. He accused them of inappropriate actions, dirty tricks, and compromising supporters in his own party. When Hannett soon met his inevitable defeat, he used the two months prior to the January 1, 1927, handover of the governor's office to exact revenge against the "Ring." He targeted Santa Fe, the center of their corrupt influence. Hannett's remaining days in office focused on building a new sixty-nine-mile road directly between Santa Rosa and Albuquerque. The new road was many miles shorter than the existing route from Santa Rosa *up* to Santa Fe and *down* again to Albuquerque. It diverted traffic from the capital, damaged its businesses, and forever altered the flow of travel, political decision-making, and commerce.

Even using today's road-building technology, sixty days is inadequate to push a new road through mostly unmapped, unfamiliar territory, even if the necessary equipment and workers were at the ready. They were not anywhere near ready in those final two months of 1926. The first month was taken up with acquiring materials, securing workers, and moving the road-building rigs into position.

In many instances, the state lacked ownership of the land the road would traverse, an awkward detail that former State Highway commission member Hannett told his highway engineer E. B. Bail to ignore—these kinks could be ironed out by the new administration! It was a race against an unforgiving calendar and harsh weather to complete the new road before Richard Dillon took the oath of office on January 1, 1927. Every day of Governor Hannett's last thirty-one days in office was a long day's work for the road builders, who were not given a day off even for Christmas.

Although Hannett focused on hurting Santa Fe, many communities were affected by the diversion of traffic to the new route. Unguarded road-making machinery was vandalized, survey markers were destroyed, and bitter confrontations ensued, all against the backdrop of fierce storms and unbearably cold winter temperatures.

On January 1, 1927, as the alternative road was only two days from becoming a through road, the new Governor Dillon attempted to halt the road's construction. But the weather that had plagued Hannett's strategy now became its ally. As Dillon's representative waited for a break in the weather so that he could deliver his stop-work order to work crews, progress on the new road continued. It was completed on January 3, the day the cease-to-work order arrived.

Initially known as New Mexico's Highway 6, the shorter route was designated the official Route 66 in 1937, the year those sixty-nine miles were finally paved. As a testament to the route's utility, this course was later followed by the new interstate.

Staying true to the original route required Peter and me to head north, to Santa Fe. Before doing that, we drove beside Highway 40 for a ways, taking an exit before Santa Rosa so that we could go as far as possible on the area's oldest dirt route, knowing that it too was a dead end. Crossing a cattle guard, we saw a terminating sign and a metal gate across the road. From here, what was left of 66 dwindled to barely visible tracks on private grounds, then to nothing: Grazing rights trumped car-access rights here. The ruts before us signified the route before 1937. This road is not maintained for "outsiders," though it is passable with a four-wheel drive. This was once the northwest route to Dilia, and from there it once ran to Santa Fe. It has been circumvented by a handsome new road, Highway 84. There is no alternative.

We retraced our way, connecting again on Highway 40 while looking for 84, joining the flow of traffic as America clicked along. Technically, this is a widened version of Route 66, and we motored west on the interstate. Then we took Highway 84 up toward Santa Fe. The rising elevation saw the foliage change from flowery shrubs to scrub brush. The hills gave way to mountains.

The temperature plunged with the onset of dusk. I was enjoying this part of the drive—top-down days in a convertible Mustang are to be treasured, and we didn't want to put the roof up. Instead, as the day cooled, we turned on the heater, flipped the fan to full blast, and leaned toward the dashboard to keep warm. Our windows were up against the wind, but the chilly evening air came right over the windshield and blew down the backs of our shirts. Peter kept his hands near the top of the steering wheel so that the heater vents directed hot air at his knuckles. I placed my palms an inch away from the vents. We shivered in contentment, turned the music up loud, and sped along to the sounds of the wind and the road.

We took what Jerry McClanahan's guide calls "Dirt 66" down into Romeroville, regretting that we didn't get to test the book's warning to "avoid if muddy." We descended the side road as evening habits settled in around us, chickens crossed the path, and children scurried for home. We could smell America in the woodsmoke and meal preparations on this early autumn night. We passed a man smoking a pipe, and the aroma calmed our uncertainty about the neighborhood where we traveled.

Then, under early moonlight, we took the Old Pecos Trail exit off 25 and headed northwest into the heart of history—downtown Santa Fe and its adobe buildings. This city has the classiest suburbs in America, its council having had the temerity to require developers to adopt a pueblo revival style in their construction: They refused to allow a mishmash of building heights and uncontrolled density. The community, as a result, melds together. Every building is a part of the neighborhood rather than being a stand-alone structure.

Peter got out at the hotel we'd settled on, and I drove off to park the car for the night. I caught up to him at the check-in desk, a long branch of dense wood hiding computers. La Fonda, built in 1922, became a Harvey House in 1926, a stature it held for the next forty years. The cavernous lobby ached for activity. Business was slow, so Peter once again morphed into negotiator, angling for the best room rate.

Front-desk clerk David L., new to this property, but not new to the business, angled back. "It's the best rate we have, sir."

Peter, nonplussed, took that as an opening and suggested the rate was fair for one room. But given that we'd take two rooms, notching the rate down twenty dollars apiece could ensure us a place at their hotel rather than see us walk down the road to spend our money someplace else.

"Ignore him," I said, nodding toward Peter as I arrived.

"Be thankful. I'm saving you money," Peter barked my way.

"Keep stretching . . . " I said. "I'll tell you when you're getting funny."

"You two together, then?" asked David L.

"Separate, but together," stressed Peter.

"Can I have a room at the opposite end of the hotel from his?" I asked.

"That's the old wing," I was told by the other clerk, David K., who was wearing a bolo tie. Younger than, and unrelated to, David L., he had longer service at this establishment.

"That's okay. As long as the mattress isn't old," I said, about to invoke the Five-Second Pause Button.

Peter snickered. "You've taken to using a mattress?"

"Ever since you started sleeping indoors . . . "

David L.'s head swayed left and right, from Peter's face to mine. "You two must have been married in an earlier life."

"And for that sin," Peter asked, "two rooms for a reduced rate?"

"Only Lisa can give you that. She's the manager." It was David K. He nodded toward a woman who was occupied on the phone at the other end of the front desk.

Peter went silent and waited a full minute while Lisa finished her phone conversation. When she hung up, he pitched his price. She hummed to herself, keeping her head down and looking away from him. (Never lock eyes with a predator.) When she'd finished thinking, she accepted Peter's offer.

Behaving as though he was providing her with an incentive, Peter expanded his position. "We'll pay that, on condition that each room has a king-size bed."

"I'll do the rate," Lisa said, still not looking up from the register. "But your friend has a smaller bed in his room."

"Deal," Peter agreed.

Lisa looked at Peter's chest and nodded.

"And you'll throw in free parking, right?" said Peter. I caught his wink, meant for me, not for her.

Age, abruptness, and the art of assumption were on Peter's side. Lisa didn't dare glance up. She murmured a shy confirmation. "And I'll throw in free parking." She didn't mention that parking was always free.

Retreating to my room, I tossed my canvas case and shoulder pack on the bed. I leaned against the worn stand that hid the television behind wood doors and was thankful that it was out of sight, as the rest of the room was ragged and alluring. It felt like fifty years in the making; modern without trying to be, dated without being old. A photograph on the wall hearkened back a century. I breathed in the history, then I jumped into the shower. My goal was to be the first one down to the lounge, to catch the stage band before dinner—and to have time to myself.

On my way to the bar, I went to the restaurant's concierge and bumped back the dinner reservation Peter had made by half an hour.

The bartender pulled a pint of Santa Fe Pale Ale. I swallowed it whole, watching a two-stepping couple swoosh around the floor to the accompaniment of Bill Hearne's Roadhouse Revue. The dance floor swelled with a dozen people out of sync with one another in various stages of a step-dip, step-dip motion. After the set, Hearne encouraged the dancers to buy one of the Revue's music discs. I was picking up *Heartaches & Honky-Tonks* for the next day's drive when Peter entered the bar.

He wore a fresh shirt and said that mine smelled, as it probably did. I caught the attention of the bartender and ordered Peter a particular beer that I wanted to see, but not to drink: "A State Pen Porter, please."

When it arrived he hoisted his glass in a toast, but I beat him to it. "Here's mud in your eye," I said, clinking our mugs. We pushed the dinner reservation back further and ordered two more pints. Then Peter began to speculate: "Americans are the best friends to have when you get into trouble." He sounded reflective about his own stuck-in-the-mud drama.

"Are you planning more trouble?"

"I thought *you* might be," he said.

"Want another beer?"

When it was served, Peter reached for his wallet.

"It's done," I said as the waiter passed me the receipt to sign.

"Only on condition . . . " began Peter.

"Stop it!" I said. "I'm buying you a few beers. That's non-negotiable."

Peter nodded agreement, and as an aside he caught the bartender's eye, signaled two fingers and thereby doubled our last beer order on my tab.

I accepted this. I'd come to understand his love of dickering. If Peter faced a firing squad, he'd negotiate his preferred time of execution.

He switched to a new insight. "Do you notice that if you get us into town before dark or, say, even before ten o'clock, we have time for a nice meal?"

"You should write for TripAdvisor."

Over dinner we proceeded to get what Woody Guthrie called "drunker'n old billy hell." The maitre'd at La Plazuela Restaurant suggested a glass of Pinot Grigio for each of us as he decanted Peter's long-sought bottle of Silver Oak Cabernet.

Juan, our waiter, was Mexican. He fell into the philosophy of our trip across his adopted country. He knew about the route, of course.

"I hear people over dinner, I listen. Kids. Adults. Lots of times they mention Route 66. Is important. They do sample parts. Yes. I talked with a few people doing everything. Whole Chicago-to-L.A. thing. All of it."

That roused Peter's comment. "That is our quest."

"Quest, maybe," said Juan. "More I think is pilgrimage."

8

The Great Diagonal Highway

"They've paved over memory lane."

—My son Sean

I was at a convenience store in La Fonda the next morning, looking for deodorant. I chose a brand I'd never seen before. A woman behind me said, "Yes, take that one. It'll make you smell like flowers. Women like a man who smells like flowers."

Peter, overhearing this, said, "I am *not* getting into a car with a man that smells like flowers."

That sold me on it.

Peter was a little groggy, and admitted that the effects of last evening's overindulgence lingered. "If I'd known I was going to be so thirsty this morning," he moaned, "I'd have had more to drink last night."

We walked around downtown Santa Fe, a town made for strolling. Coffee and cranberry muffins were offered in a restaurant with wooden benches to slide in on. It looked welcoming, and we accepted. Replenished, we found ourselves keen to hit the road.

As we were stuffing our bags in the trunk, passersby stopped to gawk. The Mustang's sides were still covered in mud, hiding much of its silver paint, and the wheels were dirt-brown. The car looked like a road warrior, fresh from battle. Peter, his head throbbing, curled into the passenger's seat, tapped the dash, and sighed, "I might nap."

As I eased forward on to San Francisco Street, seeing Peter slouched over with a pounding headache, I couldn't resist. I dialed up the volume *before* turning on the car's stereo. Then I pressed "On." Nelson Riddle's arrangement of "Route 66" thumped loudly from the speakers. Peter bolted upright.

Bystanders swung around to the music and looked straight at us. It was a pitch-perfect scene, music and all. As the top-down Mustang pulled out into the sun-lit street, two nearby couples broke into applause.

"Fifty-nine miles from Santa Fe to Albuquerque," I said.

"Not with you driving."

"Maps are honest," I said, having heard that in the United States, distances between cities are measured from local sheriff's office to sheriff's office. (In Canada, they are from post office to post office.)

We were gassing up before leaving Santa Fe when a kid on a skateboard slid by the pumps. He cackled at the splattered mud on our vehicle and asked, "You been bogging in that car? In a Mustang?"

"We should wash her," Peter said, checking the oil and clearly offended by the suggestion we'd mistreat a car. "Clean the grill and hose off the radiator." Not seeing a place to do that, he closed the hood and we motored on, aiming for a fifty-mile drive south to a place where we'd rejoin the alternative Route 66, constructed in 1927.

But . . . right away there were dirt roads to be found off an old alignment, and we started down one, toward a formidable

Route 66 is pockmarked with signs of past neglect. Often they are long stretches of roads that never found their way into sufficient use to give them a chance at lasting.

mountain climb up, up, and over La Bajada Hill on a 1926–32 continuation of Route 66. It was a marvelous switchback reputed to take away the breath of driver, horse, and carburetor (in that order). It really is intended for daylight travel only, and owing to the dozen or more steep switchbacks, is a 4-x-4 road unless you're nuts and don't care about your car's undercarriage. When this was the main route, a sign was posted at the crest. It read, in part, THIS ROAD IS NOT FOOL PROOF BUT SAFE FOR A SANE DRIVER.

Clearly it was not for us—this time. Faced with the absence of raised four-wheel drive capabilities, we turned around after we'd feasted our eyes on what might have been.

Back on the crowded highway heading south, Peter said, "A splinter road is coming up. We can get on it. Old Route 66. Next exit. Take it." He had become staccato when translating his guidebook directives, keeping color commentary to a minimum.

"Puts us off this four-lane monster and smack-dab onto 66 to Albuquerque," he said. He flipped the pages back and forth. "Know what? There's also a dead end we can take."

"Another dead end? How good is that!" I feigned.

"Look," he said, holding up the book to present his case and win the argument. But I was cruising at sixty miles an hour and was determined to keep my eyes on the road, so he lectured me instead. "A commitment is a commitment. We said '*all* the old parts of Route 66,' so take the exit, turn back over the highway on the overpass and head north again toward Santa Fe—on the old pavement. Go as far as you can, maybe five miles. What's left of Route 66 pavement then turns to ditch."

"That is *so* special."

The resulting drive was nondescript, disappointing, and even lacked the lustre of a rusting sign or an abandoned motel. We were back on rugged Route 66 history, returning northward until encountering the ditch—where the road ended and the new highway smacked the former by running on top of it all the way back to Santa Fe. I pointed to where we could no longer proceed. "They've paved over memory lane," I said, quoting my son.

"Keep going," Peter said as I made a move to turn around a hundred yards before the ditch, where I saw a DEAD END sign up ahead.

"I can actually see the ditch from here, thanks," I said. "You're pretty exciting to travel with."

"What . . . is . . . that . . . ?" said Peter.

Beside us loomed three giant boulders, weighing several tons apiece. Two of them were being reduced to dust and rocks as workers chipped away at them. Wire fencing, bent where a truck had careened into it, separated the Route 66 roadway from a platform supporting the three boulders. Soon it became clear that the rocks were not merely being pulverized. Two men, oblivious to our arrival, were skillfully wielding power tools to sculpt stone. A hand-painted sign, the size of a billboard, announced

"Tres Artistas" and backdropped the artists' working stage, the bed of a transport truck.

Nearest to us, set gracefully in stone, was what looked to be an oversized woman. Its sculptor shut off his sanding machine as we got out of the car and approached his work. He removed the protective mask from his face and extended a dust-covered hand. "I'm Jon. Jon DeCelles."

"Who are you doing this for?" Peter asked.

"Myself. Same for the other two artists. For ourselves. Maybe we sell. Maybe we don't. I cannot stop carving stone. It is my life."

"Are you carving a woman?"

"It is a shawl dancer," said Jon. "I am Plains Indian. It is from my people. This," he held the electric sander shoulder high, "smoothes the drapery—the shawl—I'm putting on her." He explained that his piece was being sculpted from Kansas limestone.

Next to it was a stone-carved 1951 Chevrolet pickup with a sculpted family in the cab. "That's Marco's. It's Texas limestone. Weighs ten tons, or at least started out as that much. Marco's cut away as many tons as he has left."

"Who's Marco?" I asked.

"Our ringleader. Another sculptor. Marco found Martin, who owns this place. That started it all. But he's not here. Come and meet Kevin." Kevin finally noticed us and put down his diamond-toothed chainsaw. "That's three tons of Indiana limestone," Jon told us. He's sculpting 'Mermaid with Two Dolphins'—I think." Kevin approached, and Jon confirmed: "You doing two dolphins or three?"

"Two."

Kevin's jeans were barely blue through the covering of white rock dust. He doffed his hat, ran a muscular right arm across his forehead, and gripped our hands in turn.

A truck yard stretched behind the area where they carved. It was strewn with automotive parts and trailers.

"The revitalization of Route 66, a symbol of America, represents a revitalization of ourselves," observes Kaisa Barthuli of the National Parks Service. Native American stone carvers create a new reason for today's passersby to stop and linger along an unwanted section of Route 66.

"Why here?" I asked.

"A trucker who hauls rock from Belen quarry heard what we were going to do. Said he's got space. Man, has he got space—and it's free! He hauled our rocks here."

A pickup truck swung into the yard and braked when the driver saw us. He climbed out of his rig. This was the site's owner, the trucker. "Martin Quintana," he said. Right away he noticed our rental car and our being at the dead end of a famous road that ran nowhere, and piped, "This is the *new* Route 66. This is it. The artists want to carve three more each. More after that. Perfect place. People will come. They'll stop."

"That's right," said Kevin. "We can do these six months a year. We're fighting time to beat the cold and get these ones done before winter."

"Sculpting brings people together," said Jon. "We give a week-long course in the mountains. It draws artists from everywhere. All students carve large stones. You could do it," he said, looking at Peter. "Non-artists make the most beautiful things. We help you chip and chisel. We teach." He had a tensor wrap on his right biceps, a hint of the grueling work and awkward angles he was forced into while holding heavy grinders.

By the time we left, I could see that Peter had a stone carving in his future—not one he would buy, but one he would create. Jon's final words seemed to stay in his mind: "Come carve with us."

Crossing Highway 25, we drove for an hour on a lazy, winding road through once-bustling service stops like Algodones and Bernalillo. All this pleasing pavement was Route 66 from pre-1927, when many westbound travelers took this approach to Albuquerque, south from Santa Fe. Until 1938, when it lost official standing as Route 66, this road was the smoother alternative. We slowed down to absorb the El Camino Motor Hotel and its reminder of more active days, when its OPEN sign stated a fact.

Peter simultaneously kept an eye on the map and flipped through the carvers' brochure that Jon had given us. I could tell that the builder in him was enthralled by it. He'd become keen on the rock carvers we'd encountered and was thinking out loud: "I'm going to make me a carving. One so large, my mistakes won't show. I'll go to their seminar in the woods within the next few years. I'm going to become a carver."

I encouraged him. "They'll send you home with a chunk of granite so large your family will complain about the lost parking spot. Not to mention the shipping fees."

"I'm serious. I want to do this. It is so strange, and so undoable. I don't know anyone who has even mentioned it. That novelty alone . . . " He pushed their information papers into the pouch on the side door, his mind made up. "I think we'll make Gallup for dinner," he said, his mind moving to more urgent matters. "There's no rush, so let's lunch in Albuquerque."

American cities often convey carelessness about their entrances in many ways: in an abrupt end to a freeway, with an off-ramp disgorging too many cars into too-narrow roadways or, as we saw here, erratic displays of commerce in strip malls and half-occupied buildings—those dismaying harbingers of big-box stores and remainder outlets. The one hopeful sight was a Laundromat, but when I pointed it out to Peter, he dismissed it: "You can wash your clothes at the hotel, if you can get us there before midnight."

Albuquerque's downtown, however, is more welcoming. It benefits from having kept its stone and wooden buildings in use. Too many inner towns elsewhere, even those with interesting buildings, have withered and suffered from civic ambivalence, the departure of shoppers, and the inevitable result: neglected premises. Not so here.

Smack-dab in the middle of town is a tall sign with a westbound arrow, LOS ANGELES—790 MILES, and an arrow pointing back from where we came: CHICAGO—1,345 MILES. Peter handed me his camera and rested against the sign.

"Let's find the other parts of Albuquerque's 66," Peter suggested, holding open his guidebook after lunch. "There were once three ways to get into and out of town. Go around the corner here, hit 2nd Street, and we'll see what's left."

As we'd experienced elsewhere, taking the time to see more than one of a city's Route 66 options meant gaining more than one perspective—architecturally, and in terms of what the town had done with its heritage. Some of Albuquerque has been left to deteriorate, as occurs in many parts of vanishing America. Other sections of 4th Street had been commandeered by newer buildings, breaking the old visual line and portending that eventually the rest of the city's historical reference points will fall to the wrecker's ball.

At Central Avenue and 4th Street, Route 66 scissors and crosses over itself, a testament to shifting routes and shifting politicians, illogically leaving only one block separating 4th Street from 8th Street.

Cynthia Troup liked this town's name. Long after her husband Bobby's song had become a classic, she said, "What I really can't believe is that he doesn't have Albuquerque in the song." Bobby Troup said he considered it when writing the lyrics, but felt it was too cumbersome to fit in.

The Route 66 alignment from pre-1937 headed south across the Rio Grande to Los Lunas. From there we'd be able to drive more directly west, lured by the promise that the original Route 66 resumed "rough and partly unpaved . . . " Peter several times mentioned the likelihood of an early-evening arrival in Gallup, his anticipation of a leg-stretching walk, and a choice of good restaurants.

Heading out of Los Lunas we traveled west and a bit north, finding what the *EZ66 Guide* describes as "bits of old 66 along the way." Eventually we met, and shunned, Highway 40 at Mesita so that we could keep meandering toward Cubero.

Our happiest stint on the entire trip may well have been here. We drove sixty miles of old Route 66 without encountering another vehicle. It was a lost heaven. This part of Route 66 has been in use since the booster Cyrus Avery and others began promoting "the Great Diagonal Highway" in 1926. Slab-topped mesas emerged from the horizon and came into full view. Sunlight bit the lip of land a mile away and gave a layered depth to the bald hills. We were never more alone, yet enchanted. Where we stopped—on a remote dirt road—I danced a jig in a roadside field. It was spontaneous; minutes of freedom in the middle of open lands, unfettered by plans or worry. Peter videotaped my antics. I didn't care; the expanse was humbling but exhilarating.

Another hour into the drive, a lasso flew in the air in a corral beside the road, and we heard yelps. We were driving at speed, entering Villa de Cubero. Another loop of rope whipped high, and another yelp was let loose. Wooden fence slats blocked the view, then a horse trailer was in the way, and a black pickup parked beside us made it hard to see what was happening.

Route 66 has long been the ultimate road trip, yet today it is the lost and found of highways. A hidden-away America. It offers a different kind of alone.

A man yelled instructions and a woman shouted back at him—that much we could hear. I slowed down and pulled over.

Here's what was interesting. Three men and a woman were practicing roping, taking turns with two of them teamed against one calf. Cattle charged across the corral, one at a time, and seldom won. When they did, it was on rider error. And the calf never celebrated.

An attractive cowgirl on horseback approached us as Peter crossed his arms over a fence railing, watching, and I leaned on their fence post. She was waiting her turn to head down the corral, forcing a calf to run between her and the long fence. "What do you think?" she asked.

"Looks complicated," said Peter.

"My husband there is a champion," she said. "If he wants to win at the rodeo, he needs these practice nights. My name's Randy. His is Kerry. He's a dentist. This is his sport."

At that, a calf ran from the holding chamber toward the other end of the field, fifty yards away. Motivated by food released through a chute when the run was completed, and no doubt propelled by its fear of the nearby horses, the calf bolted. Two male riders gave chase. Kerry used his horse to keep the calf from heading mid-field while raising the wide oval of his lasso overhead. In fast synchronization, the other rider kept behind the calf, lasso at the ready, waiting for the leader to force the calf to turn into the open. In link-sync, the two riders let roll their respective ropes, the lead rope aiming to wrap over and around the calf's neck while the other rope had to capture both back hooves. Up and over went the calf.

"It's a five-second penalty against your time score if you get only one back hoof," said Randy.

"Do you go for the front or for the hooves?" I asked her.

"There's a 'header' and a 'heeler.' I'm riding header tonight. We change up, but you're better at one or the other."

Across the roadway was the reason Peter and I had planned to stop here, and we went over to visit. Villa de Cubero Trading Post is a dot on the map, its listing in the guidebook annotated with a note that it still has a service bell that rings when cars pass near the 1950s-era gas pumps. We walked down the store's short aisles, loaded as much with goods needed by locals as with those sought by snoopy travelers. I found a stack of Cracker Jacks, shook the rectangular box and, from the solid sound of the popcorn contents, determined they were stale. I bought a box for Peter.

As we crossed toward the car and corral, Peter munched on the Cracker Jacks, read aloud the paper joke, and showed me the ditzy prize, a whistle. Kerry had dismounted and was standing near the fence where we'd parked the Mustang.

"How's your dental practice?" asked Peter.

"Busy. Lots of people eating Cracker Jacks," Kerry said.

He pointed out the motel rooms that half-ringed the area behind the Trading Post. "The actress Ethel Merman used to visit here. Ernest Hemingway wrote part of *The Old Man and the Sea* while staying here. That room right over there." He pointed to a corner room along the tired façade of the motor court. "It used to be bigger, and he liked the privacy."

I looked over Kerry's shoulder, at Randy and the two cowboys, and asked, "Do the four of you rope often?"

"A few nights a week."

"What do you practice for?"

"Used to be we had the rodeo here, but it's grown. Good to grow, but it meant that we had to move it. Now it happens down the road in Albuquerque. We call it the 'Route 66 Shootout.'"

"Where's your home? Your original home," Peter asked.

"Here," said Kerry. "Born not far down the road. This is my family's place on Route 66. That's what's left of the Gunn Café beside us. My aunt Mary and her husband Wally Gunn owned it." He waited to let this settle in. More humbly, he said, "This land is my land."

Kerry's parting words hung in the air as we drove away from the Villa de Cubero Trading Post; it made me hum.

For many, Woody Guthrie's name brings up the lines of one song: "This land is your land, this land is my land . . . " Heard always as a testament of praise and national confidence, that is not how Guthrie wrote it. Stripped of two controversial stanzas, the song was recorded throughout the United States, being erroneously thought of as the heartfelt statement of a balladeer's unquestioning faith in his country. That mistaken notion grew with the song's popularity, while the truth behind its writing lay undisclosed.

Woody Guthrie wrote: "All you can write is what you see." His honesty did not resonate well with those who determined what the public should hear. He was censored: Many of his original words in "This Land Is Your Land" were kept from the public, as was his original message. Legitimacy gave way to political pretending. (Currently, however, all the verses appear in the sheet music and choral editions of the song, and all verses have been recorded by other artists.)

Woody would write on any surface that stayed still long enough—scraps of paper, cardboard, the corners of newspapers. And he'd write at any venue—on stairways in flophouses, by the side of the road. In February 1940 (a month before he and Pete Seeger met at an "Aid for Workers" fundraiser and became lifelong compatriots), an angry Woody Guthrie found himself in the rundown Hanover Hotel in New York City. He laid out his frustrations about his country in a notebook, intending to balance a celebratory Irving Berlin song made popular at that time by singer Kate Smith: "God Bless America." Guthrie's satirical scrawl titled his own song "God *Blessed* America," which he began with the words: "This land is your land."

Guthrie's years of Route 66 travel, nights of sleeping in migrant tents, and days of witnessing the plights of many disenfranchised citizens gave him a view contrary to that held by most Americans. "This Land Is Your Land" is implied by some to have begun as a Marxist tract, a leftist retort to Berlin's bewitching portrayal of an America at odds with the one Guthrie had encountered firsthand. It is, perhaps, more of a parody.

In a stanza excised from "God *Blessed* America," prior to its being retitled "This Land Is Your Land," Guthrie wrote about what he'd experienced as a common divide in society: "Was a big high wall there that tried to stop me/A sign was painted said: Private Property/But on the back side, it didn't say nothing/God *blessed* America for me."

An early edit by Guthrie, in which he dropped the last line above, replaced it in that stanza with "That side was made for you and me."

Guthrie's original sarcasm gave way to his own edits, his retitling of the song, and his replacement of each stanza's last line with "This land was made for you and me." That was after his original writing of the soon-to-be-deleted closing verse: "One bright sunny morning in the shadow of the steeple/By the Relief office I saw my people/As they stood hungry/I stood there wondering if/God *blessed* America for me."

He first recorded the song in 1944, and then still included verses four and six (as above) in that unreleased version. The sanitized version would become America's most popular folk song and was proposed by some as a replacement for the "The Star-Spangled Banner."

Pete Seeger did not admire "This Land Is Your Land" when first he heard it, saying: "That's the most ordinary tune." Seeger would have recognized the melody from a 1930s song made popular by the Carter family in "Little Darling, Pal of Mine," whose tune was borrowed from a church hymn "(Oh My Loving Brother) When the World's on Fire." Back then, Seeger felt it to be "one of Woody's lesser efforts."

It is now speculated that no singer has sung this song more often than Pete Seeger. Indeed, at President Barack Obama's Inaugural concert, "We Are One," in front of 18,000 fans at the Lincoln Memorial on January 19, 2009, Seeger and Bruce Springsteen sang "This Land Is Your Land" with the original verses intact. Springsteen had once introduced the song by saying, "With countries, just like people, it's easy to let the best of yourself slip away."

Guthrie's only recording of the complete song was done in a New York session with Moses Asch in April 1944. On shore leave at the time, merchant mariner Guthrie recorded many songs with Asch, who later founded Folkways Records. They began with two songs on April 16, and Guthrie recorded another sixty-three(!) songs in an extended session a few days later, coming back for bouts of recording two or three

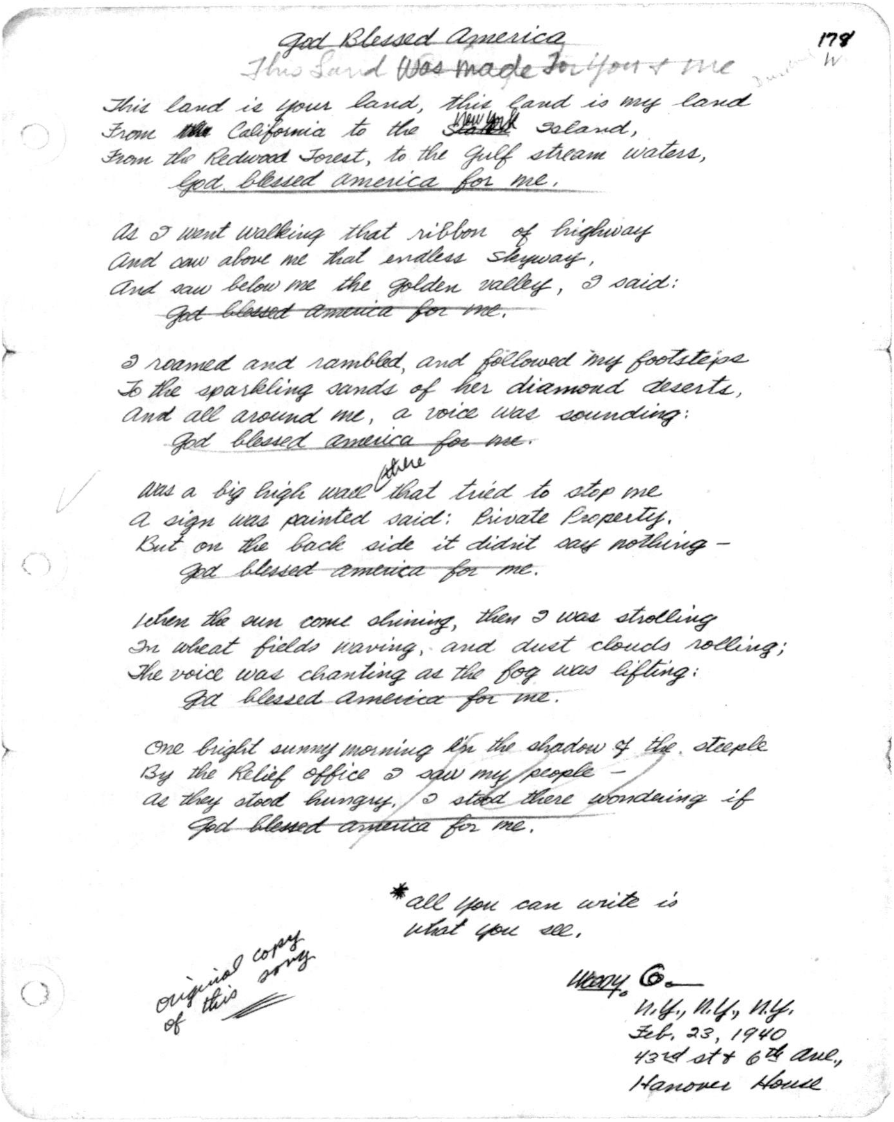

~~God Blessed America~~ 178

This Land Was made for You & Me

This land is your land, this land is my land
From ~~the~~ California to the ~~Staten~~ New York Island,
From the Redwood Forest, to the Gulf stream waters,
God blessed america for me.

As I went walking that ribbon of highway
And saw above me that endless skyway,
And saw below me the golden valley, I said:
~~God blessed america for me.~~

I roamed and rambled, and followed my footsteps
To the sparkling sands of her diamond deserts,
And all around me, a voice was sounding:
~~God blessed america for me.~~

Was a big high wall there that tried to stop me
A sign was painted said: Private Property,
But on the back side it didn't say nothing –
~~God blessed america for me.~~

When the sun come shining, then I was strolling
In wheat fields waving, and dust clouds rolling;
The voice was chanting as the fog was lifting:
~~God blessed america for me.~~

One bright sunny morning in the shadow of the steeple
By the Relief office I saw my people –
As they stood hungry, I stood there wondering if
~~God blessed america for me.~~

*all you can write is what you see.

original copy of this song

Woody G.
N.Y., N.Y., N.Y.
Feb. 23, 1940
43rd st + 6th Ave,
Hanover House

Woody Guthrie wrote this, his original draft of "God Blessed America," having seen a different truth about his country than the boosterism being portrayed by businessmen and politicians.
(This Land Is Your Land by Woody Guthrie. Courtesy of the Woody Guthrie Archives. © Copyright 1956 (renewed), 1970 and 1972 by Woody Guthrie Publications, Inc. & TRO-Ludlow Music, Inc. (BMI).)

dozen of his written songs at each session. In one of these get-togethers, Woody recorded a version of "God Blessed America" in which he and Asch changed the last line and gave it the title "This Land Is My Land." Guthrie himself recorded a modified version without the protest verses in 1947, and when Folkways did release the bowdlerized song in 1951, it was that further revised version. In 1997, as an archivist at the Smithsonian Institution was transferring various recordings to digital format, he listened to a number of songs by Guthrie and "discovered" the Asch-recorded version of Woody singing his original words in 1944.

Woody Guthrie's daughter Nora, now executive director of the Woody Guthrie Foundation in New York, remembers the frequent, rapid flow of her father's lyrics from his typewriter as the kids played nearby. She recalls her father giving scraps of song-filled papers to his children to use as coloring paper. Even his most famous song was thought by the Guthrie kids at that time to be simply a family ditty.

When the family moved to New York City, and Nora and one of her brothers arrived for their first day in a new school, their surname meant little to most of their teachers or fellow students. At the start of that day's assembly, they stood up with the rest of the kids and placed their hands over their hearts, preparing to sing "The Star-Spangled Banner." Surprise overwhelmed them when the entire class broke into the morning's first song, bellowing, "This land is your land, this land is my land . . . "

We had left the Mustang's roof down. The road was open, its black pavement leading into dark hills that thinned into a starlit sky. Stars were everywhere. New Mexico was on its best behavior.

We fancied the diversion of a dirt road near the Continental Divide and soon found ourselves at an altitude of 7,300 feet, one of the highest points on Route 66. There was no one else in sight. We slowed to admire the cliffs—mountains, really—in their darkening, red beauty.

Doing thirty miles an hour, I turned off the headlights.

"Wha . . . ?" said Peter.

"Shh . . . listen . . . "

The road sang, accompanied by the voices of wind and rubber on pavement.

Peter broke the silence. "I've read about El Rancho, in Gallup. That's where we should sleep tonight. It promises to be *real*, and the food write-up says it's terrific, and they offer beds, sheets, hot water—all the things I care about and you don't."

Gallup greeted us with a splendid mix of dark and color along a strip with aging neon signs that glittered, one boasting LARIAT LODGE with FREE COFFEE. Among other benefits, we almost changed our plans because the Blue Spruce Motel's sign promised steam heating and bragged "TVs in every room." And, at the posted $26, it was affordable.

The railway owns the land all along one side of the highway, and that side is backdropped by mountains, modest in height, but striking in their dominance. Because the railway lands are track and side yards, there is little to spoil the view.

Darkness always has a role in welcoming travelers to a strange town at night, and here it made the neon-lit El Rancho stand out as the haven of movie stars. This motel was home to moviemakers and actors from the 1930s to the 1950s. Here they could film in the "real West," on location, rather than in the pretend-Western locales less than a mile from Hollywood studios. The likes of Errol Flynn and Ronald Reagan ventured here for weeks of filmmaking. Their stay of choice in Gallup was the El Rancho, which had been built in 1937. It was lit up then, and it's lit up now—adorned with neon at its most stylish and wrought with care.

I had not wanted to alternate our evening ritual, but I was beginning to think the pattern of "Peter—rooms, Rick—bags" should change. This time as I entered the foyer, Peter bantered with Phillip.

Peter: "We aim to pay less each night for our accommodation as we progress west along Route 66."

Phillip: "Good for you. I'm sure there's an affordable place in town to meet your expectations."

Peter: "We like it here with you—the large lobby, the reputation, and the smell of good food."

Phillip: "Then, as I say, it's $62."

Peter: "What if my friend here sleeps in the car?"

Phillip: "Then his parking spot is $62."

The lobby had a woody charisma, and the lower level had log walls that featured paintings, dried animal parts, and leather stretched over hefty chairs. Upstairs, the rooms were small (I looked in two open doors as I walked to my room), the nub of them being a bed and a basin, but each was a treasure house of movie memorabilia. The hallway featured a gallery of both known and little-known Hollywood guests. Walls in the open loft were covered with photographs of actors and actresses such as Jane Wyman, Katharine Hepburn, Kirk Douglas, Jackie Cooper, and Humphrey Bogart. Hundreds of thin-wood-framed, autographed black-and-white pictures rimmed the balcony. As I walked up a wide, wooden balustrade to view them, the stairway creaked beneath my step. I found myself humming in time with it, "Dun-da-da-dun-da . . . Bonanza."

9

The Long Concrete Path

"Road used to be busier. You're first car today. How come you're not on the good road?"

—Eugene

Having passed the state line into Arizona at Lupton, we parked the Mustang beside the Rio Puerco River and double-checked the map's caution: "Apache County Road, Pre-1931 Route 66," dirt all the way. The guidebook advised: "Not recommended."

What more could we want?

Peter pressed the gas pedal with the Mustang in neutral just to hear the purr in anticipation of forbidden pleasure. Sun had caked the road recently, and the last vehicles' ruts, created a few days earlier, had hardened. We flipped down the visors and clipped back the roof anchors. Peter depressed the switch that lifted the Mustang's canvas roof into an arc and packed it away neatly between the back seat and the trunk. A sturdy sign, with a misspelled warning, stared at us: CAUTION/16 MILES UNPAVED ROAD AHEAD/MAY BE INPASSABLE [sic]/DURING INCLEMENT WEATHER.

Ready. Our wheels spun and we drove on to the territory of the Navajo Nation.

The scratch grass and bushes near the road had attempted to become forests, but the land could not sustain that. The vegetation remained stunted in this ground. A few homes appeared, but distant from the road, as though their locations had been selected to ensure their remoteness.

First impressions: When this road carried migrants and early travelers it must have seemed to do so reluctantly, offering only sparse services and every indication that visitors had best keep going. There were no hopes of homesteading or raising a family here, let alone of raising crops. Those who already lived here would have been hospitable enough to provide food and gas for travelers, but the area was so barren that they'd obviously not done enough of that to create a community or town. That role, the map promised, was fulfilled by a modern post office and an oft-rebuilt diner ten miles away, at the end of the dirt road. Our short-term priority became breakfast at a diner in the settlement of Sanders.

"Hitchhiker ahead." I pointed to the left side of the road, a horizon away.

"We're in the middle of nowhere," Peter cautioned.

"Let's pick him up," I suggested.

"It might be dangerous."

"You insured?" I said. "Am I among the beneficiaries?"

Peter slowed somewhat to avoid covering the hitchhiker with dust. The man waved us down, and we stopped well short of him. He started to limp toward us.

"Ya-Ta-Hey," he said. "That's Navajo for hello."

"Good morning," Peter replied, wary.

"I need a ride." The man smiled, the skin of his face darkened by inheritance and sun. "I've got friends to meet at the post office. You going that way?"

There was no other "way." The presumptuous hitchhiker had already walked around back of the car and arrived at my door.

He walked like a comma. His back was curved from overuse, and his posture had bunched his shirt. His single upper tooth made his smile seem sincere.

"Eugene's my name. It's my birthday."

"Happy birthday, Eugene."

"See." He opened his wallet and pulled out an identification card, confirming his date of birth.

"Hop in," I offered. "Not much room, but climb in where you can in the back."

He clambered into the uncomfortable back seat and, folding his legs into a wedge, began to talk freely.

"Road used to be busier. You're first car today. How come you're not on the good road? See that hump?" Eugene pointed at the middle of the road, where a remnant of concrete was barely visible beneath the surface. "That was part of a trading post. This road's built over it now. This was the original—the first—Route 66, you know. Lots of trading posts here. Well, a few. We traded blankets. Well, my parents did. Navajos make good blankets."

I turned to see him better, and saw a face wrinkled with a thousand legends.

Eugene told us he was a "bull rider," when we asked what he'd done for a living. With a laugh, he said, "Caught my knee between a horse and a fence, tore something. I'm sixty-two."

I wished Peter had worn the T-shirt I'd bought him that morning at El Rancho's gift shop, so that I could have got Eugene's response. On the shirt was a photograph of four Native Americans under the banner of "Homeland Security." The text beneath the image announced: "Fighting terrorism since 1492." And when I thought Eugene might tell us that the indigenous peoples had lost all of America because they had a poor immigration policy, he pointed to a gravesite marked with a U.S. flag that was draped over a whitened marker. "My uncle's buried there. He fought in Vietnam. Died there for America. He was a good boy. Twenty-eight. Miss him, but it was good he fought for us. You should buy a Navajo blanket."

It was all interwoven. Eugene said that he had recently painted the grave marker. "Can't forget."

Vietnam marked the return of the Navajo warriors to the Pacific theater of war.

During the Second World War, Navajo servicemen had provided the United States with the most sophisticated secret code of the war. It proved to be an unbreakable code and was pivotal to many U.S. victories, including Okinawa and Iwo Jima. Without the Navajo code talkers, who served as fully trained members of the U.S. Marine Corps, the number of lives lost in Pacific conflicts would have been much larger, and victory more elusive.

The Navajo language does not have an alphabet. It is unwritten and tonal. It consists of syllabaries, wherein symbols imply syllables, and the syllables are translatable. Barely half of the 300 native languages spoken when Columbus arrived in the New World were still spoken when the Second World War began, and most of those languages were spoken only among the elders. Fortunately, Navajo was among those in use.

At the outset of the U.S. war against the Japanese empire, fewer than thirty non-Navajo understood the hard-to-comprehend language—and none of those thirty were Japanese or German. The natives conversant in the language lived on lands that are home to what has been called "the largest and most influential Indian tribe in North America, the Navajo Nation." They were all Americans.

The first Navajo recruits were gathered at Camp Pendleton, California, in the spring of 1942. Their assignment: to prepare a verbally dispatched/verbally received code that could withstand the genius of Japanese code breakers.

The resulting Navajo Code was, to the untrained ear and mind, a nasal jabber of mixed and halting words. Each message could be understood only by a Navajo, who would translate the word into its English counterpart, the first letter of which was the relevant component of the message. To further confuse enemy decoders, every letter in the Roman alphabet could be conveyed by one of three different Navajo words. For example, "E" could be transmitted as *AH-JAH* (for Ear), *AH-NAH* (for Eye) or *DZEH* (for Elk).

One option to convey the word "route" would be: *AH-LOSZ* (Rice), *NE-AHS-JAH* (Owl), *SHI-DA* (Uncle), *THAN-ZIE* (Turkey), and *DZEH* (Elk). There were many permutations of the code.

The code developed at Pendleton included specifics for military terms not common in Navajo, such as "Platoon" (*HAS-CLISH-NIH*), meaning, literally, "mud." "America" was *NE-HE-MAH*, meaning "our mother." Given the frequent need for the word "route," it could also be *GAH-BIH-TKEEN*, or "rabbit trail."

The first deployment of Navajo marines on the front lines during the Second World War occurred in the battles against the Japanese for control of the southwest Pacific Ocean island of Guadalcanal. Their secret task was to transmit orders for supply movements, troop maneuvers, and intelligence about the enemy's actions. Despite being impenetrable to non-Navajos, the code was efficient, fast, and accurate, conveying in minutes what might take hours with the more conventional, and riskier, Morse Code.

A Marine team of six Navajo Code talkers working with memorized codes is credited with the error-free communication of over 800 strategic transmissions during the bloody first days of the battle at Iwo Jima. According to Major Howard Connor, 5th Marine Division signal officer, "Were it not for the Navajos, the marines would never have taken Iwo Jima."

The patriots remained unsuspected and unacknowledged until the relevant documents were declassified by the military in 1968. Only then was their heroism revealed to an appreciative public. Their clandestine work was finally formally recognized in 1992 at a Pentagon ceremony attended by thirty-five U.S. Marine Corps veterans, all Navajo Code talkers.

Eugene, Peter, and I had driven five miles on the Navajo Nation section of Route 66 when I asked Eugene if he was cramped in the back seat. He smiled, his thick lower lip playing with his tooth, and said, "No rush. Lots of time." He held up two strapless wrists indicating no watch. "Time doesn't matter."

This reminded me that we were in a new state, and I asked him if we had entered a new time zone.

"Arizona doesn't do Daylight Savings Time," he said. "But the Navajo Nation does. We span three states, and so we decided we would." We laughed when he observed, "Only a white man would think you could cut a foot off the bottom of a blanket and sew it on the top, and get a longer blanket."

"How much farther is it still Navajo land?" Peter asked.

"We're Diné now," said Eugene, ignoring the question, and opting to educate us. "Navajo is from the Spanish, and it means 'The Thieves,' which we're not!" It was the only time he raised his voice. "Diné means 'The People,' so call us that now."

We parked at the post office so that Eugene could get out, and he pointed us to a diner that he called "authentic," which seemed anachronistic coming from a native.

He climbed awkwardly out of the backseat. Leaning on me for support, he whispered, "Would you have anything to help?"

I palmed him five dollars and wished him a happy birthday.

On departing, he spoke what he'd written out for me in Navajo earlier on the drive: *"Ha-go-A-Na."* Goodbye. He wandered off, singing a salute for us, repeating it as a chant. "On the road again . . . "

The Route 66 Diner, not the first to claim the name, certainly deserves the moniker: reclaimed siding, ungraciously painted pink, sets this place apart—though the diner doesn't need that distinction, as it sits alone on a large gravel lot, backing into the bush. Its roof tries to be blue, and two posts near the door fight with white paint.

We popped the screen door and walked through an alcove that served as a "mud room" when the weather was sloppy—meant not as a space to remove your boots, but as a place to stomp them and shed their muck before going in for a meal. The rest of the mud would be shed on the linoleum floor. A U.S. Navy poster took up most of one wall: "Life, Liberty, and the Pursuit of All Who Threaten It." We were in the epicenter of America, where dirt and pavement dueled, and no one questioned America's Main Street philosophy.

Debbie—short, clean-smocked, and grinning—shuffled two clean mugs down the counter, not offering the tables in the back room. We obediently took to our stools, in front of which the mugs slowed to a halt. She hailed that cooperation with, "What'll it be?"

Modest keepsakes cluttered the shelves. For the only time on this trip, I saw salt and pepper shakers styled as Route 66 gas pumps from the 1940s. A picture, curled at both top corners and wanting to fall to the floor, portrayed the Chevrolets of the 1950s. Debbie's polished, aligned teeth contrasted nicely with Eugene's. A printed sign above her head announced: "Prices subject to change, according to customer's attitude." A Route 66 shield adorned the menu that Debbie slapped down in front of Peter.

Peter asked her what she thought of Route 66. She considered that question at some length and eventually said, "It's like a once-grand hotel, neglected and in need of new carpets, steam-cleaning, and a can of paint."

I looked at her, expecting more, but Peter had moved on, digesting his menu. “What’s a 66er?” he asked, flipping the two-sided menu over for other options.

“A three-quarter pounder,” she said, “with three slices of cheese.”

“And a Double 66er must be . . . ” speculated Peter.

“Yup. With five slices of cheese.” Debbie topped up our coffee and sprinkled plastic milk thimbles beside our mugs.

“Okay, now, what’s in the Ultimate 66—Blaksley Special?”

“Mushrooms, green chili, Swiss-white-cheddar cheeses—swarmed all over a Double 66er, plus whatever we have out back.”

“Blaksley?” I asked. “What’s in the name?”

“Dunno. Ask Ena. She’s the owner.”

It seemed curious that the origin of the most expensive and oddest-named item on the menu was unknown to the waitress. Ena walked in, as if on cue. She was prim, older, better-coiffed, in an “I’m the owner” way. She had overheard the conversation and offered up some history. “Mr. Blaksley was a school teacher nearby. Loved by the kids. Used to eat here once a week and kept adding ingredients to the Double 66er. It became a meal that would swamp most folks. He finished it all, every time, and then he would have a banana split. He moved on years ago.”

In what seemed increasingly like a private movie set created for our personal education, Peter and I ordered huevos rancheros at Debbie’s recommendation. Ten minutes later, she returned from the kitchen wearing oven mitts, grasping two pans that sizzled and spat. It should have been a warning. The cook’s creation flowed all over each pan. At the bottom of the pan was a flour tortilla supporting a sea of food. It was filled with pieces of green chili, and brown beans spread deep and steamy. The hash browns—crispy ones, the kind seen in restaurant photographs that never match the actual food served—were real, and were pressed to the side in a half-pan serving, where cheese bubbled and swirled. All this was covered by two fried eggs, sunny side up, their thin whites curled and crispy.

It was the best breakfast of the trip. Maybe my best breakfast ever.

Feeling plump, we walked over to a 1923 bridge, part of the road that became Route 66. It was blocked to traffic by piles of dirt at both ends. Debbie had pointed it out, across the way from her diner: "We call it the Golden Gate Bridge." The name was inspired by the bridge's once-yellow paint, now leaching rust. It was typical of Route 66 relics—unused but still there. As we approached, we saw that only a few girders remained to support it. The wood that had at one time added bracing had mostly disappeared.

Back in the Mustang, we crossed over the highway, straightened onto a road, turned left, and meandered to where I thought the guidebook was leading us. Then I overguessed: we made a wrong turn. But we kept going, on my assurance that we were righting a wrong and that the road would naturally wind up where we needed to be: "It's shorter this way. Trust me." I always should be at the wheel rather than at the book.

Peter did not share my confidence.

Half an hour later, having zipped up and down many hills with nary a Route 66 comfort sign in sight, we came upon three erratically parked trucks, about a dozen native people, and a welcoming wave. Pulling onto the gravel bed by the roadside, Peter slowed down to avoid creating a dust cloud. It seemed we had run into a family reunion centering around a burly grandpapa, four young girls and as many boys, and a middle-aged man and what looked to be his wife—perhaps the mother of the kids. They seemed happy. The oldest man, who was holding a post-breakfast beer in a loose grip, almost tossed it at us when he motioned me closer.

"You're lost?" he asked.

"Naw, wandered a bit out of the way," I said.

"Lost," Peter said over my shoulder.

"Don't ask me the question," the man said.

"What question?" I asked.

"Don't ask me the question," he repeated.

I didn't have a clue what he was getting at, so I changed the topic. "Where's this road go?"

"*That's* the question," he grinned, having sprung the trap.

I was out of my league or in a different ballpark than he was. I asked again, "Where's this road go?"

"Road stays. You go!" He howled as though he'd just invented comedy.

One of the little girls came up to us with a plastic bag that she emptied into her hand. *"Piñon,"* said the oldest man. "Like the sunflower seeds. Not salted. Chew. Spit."

The little girl looked on with pride and said in a voice we could barely hear, "I roasted them this morning." She held the seeds out to us, and we took some.

Peter got back in the driver's seat, spitting his chewed gift-seeds on the ground, which I thought poor diplomacy. The oldest man, still chuckling over his joke, said to me, "I know what you're looking for—the long concrete highway. Stay on this road. It goes where you want to go." He sang us on our way with "You'll get kicked on Route 66 . . . "

Robert Wesley Troup, the son of a Philadelphia music store owner and a self-taught piano player, was a jazz musician who did not want to go into the family business: Bobby Troup wanted to be a songwriter. While studying business at the University of Pennsylvania in 1940, he'd written "Daddy," a song that became surprisingly popular on campus. It caught the attention of Sammy Kaye, whose orchestra recorded it. "It was the best-selling song of 1941," according to Troup. Elated, he put his first royalty cheque toward buying an olive-green drop-top, a brand-new 1941 Buick.

Cynthia Hare, a singer one year his senior, married Bobby in 1942 before he joined the navy. After extended tours of duty overseas, Marine Captain Troup returned from war and was discharged while still in his twenties, dark-haired, clean-cut, and with a smooth, youthful face. He later reflected: "I decided to give myself one year in Hollywood to see if I could really make it as a songwriter." Cynthia, beguiled by Bobby's stories of shore leave at bases on the California coast, agreed. "We've got to go to California."

Troup persuaded his mother to look after their two little girls while he and Cynthia motored west, planning to settle in the Los Angeles area. The grandmother and two girls could come out by train later, on the all-Pullman Super Chief.

Twenty-six-year-old Bobby and Cynthia packed up their convertible in Philadelphia that February and headed along Highway 40 to St. Louis, in search of a Louis Armstrong performance at Club Plantation on Route 66. Near Pittsburgh, they stopped for lunch at a Howard Johnson restaurant. Cynthia, "quite hesitantly, really," as Troup recalled, then suggested that he write a song about Route 40—a road tune, a traveling song. He shrugged off the idea, considering it silly, since they'd soon leave that road behind them and be traveling on U.S. Highway 66, joining its swoop down from Chicago to St. Louis.

Three days later, along Highway 66, Cynthia kept playing with combinations of "six, nix, picks, kicks," making rhymes and laughing at them. Finally she vamped in Bobby's ear, "Get your kicks on Route Sixty-Six."

"I almost drove the car off the road," Troup recalled. He told her, "That's a darling title. Goddamn! That's a great title."

Troup started to compose the lyrics around the title as they drove west. The first half of the song came together in a few days, despite his sense that "it was possibly the worst road I've ever taken in my life." They would use seventy-five quarts of oil during the rugged trip, the tires becoming "badly worn" and the canvas roof a bit tattered. They also endured a snowstorm. En route, in motor courts, they'd spread out their maps, eventually determining that Route 66 was "more than two thousand miles all the way."

Within days of arriving in Los Angeles, Troup's new agent, Bullet Durgstrom, arranged for the songwriter to briefly meet his idol, Nat King Cole, whose trio was playing that night at the Trocadero Club on Sunset Boulevard. Following the dinner show, Troup was introduced to Cole as the writer of the hit song "Daddy," and Cole asked whether Bobby had written any other songs. Troup was well aware of the late hour, of the waiters and staff cleaning up around them, and that Nat King Cole had been performing all night. He felt unprepared to audition, but Cole's piano was right there, so he sat down.

"I was so nervous, I got on the riser and . . . the bench slipped off the riser and I went backwards," he remembered. Regaining his composure, Troup got back on the bench and played a song he'd written and was confident about: "Baby, Baby, All the

Bobby Troup's 1946 road trip across the United States with his wife Cynthia included Highway 66 and swerved into a serendipitous song that captivated America and the world, and set in place forever the rhythm of the road.

Time." "Nat just loved it," Troup recalled. Impressed, Cole asked for anything else the young songwriter might have in the works.

Troup admitted, "Nat, I wrote a song—actually, half a song—coming out to California, and because I don't own a piano, I've never played it. I think you might like it."

Troup had only the first six lines fixed in his mind. He had hummed the half-composed tune, run it around in his head while on Route 66, and now it was about to become live music for the first time. The self-taught pianist tinkled the keys on Cole's piano. A tired but curious Cole watched. Uncertain how the tune would sound in real life, Bobby Troup began playing and singing: "If you/ever plan to motor west/Travel my way/the highway that's the best/Get your kicks/on Route Sixty-Six." He finished by singing the only other part of the song he'd written: "It winds/from Chicago to L.A.,/More than two/thousand miles/all the way/Get your kicks/on Route Sixty-Six."

Cole "liked it so much, he started playing piano with me," Bobby reminisced in an NPR interview. Cole told Troup to finish the song by the following month, and committed on the spot to recording both of Troup's songs for his new album, which was right then heading into final production. Cole had driven Route 66 himself, and the synergy of Troup's song and Cole's personal memories proved compelling.

Bobby and Cynthia got out their AAA maps to help frame the next verse, concentrating on overnight stops, considering the song's momentum, and at first trying for realistic distances of 250 miles between place names. Destinations and poetry combined into a practical rhythm. "I wasn't aware of what a great lyric I'd written," Troup admitted in the afterglow of subsequent success.

The trip's lyrical salutation was soon completed in words and music: "Now it/Goes through Saint Louis/And Joplin, Missouri/And Oklahoma City is mighty pretty/You'll see/Amarillo/Gallup, New Mexico/Flagstaff, Arizona/Don't forget Winona/Kingman, Barstow, San Bernardino."

And, "Won't you/get hip to this timely tip/When you make/ that California trip/Get your kicks/On Route Sixty-Six."

Ten destinations joined with Chicago and L.A. and leapt to fame, thanks to the vagaries of a jazzy rhyme (would Win*ona* be there without Ariz*ona* begging for a rhyming partner?). Many a traveler has since driven Route 66 guided by Troup's musical itinerary.

Keeping his word, Nat King Cole put aside other planned songs from his March 16, 1946, recording session to make room for the two tunes written by Troup. He accepted Troup's eastern pronunciation of *root* instead of the more Americanized *rowt*. It has stuck with the song for over sixty years, through riff changes and clever intonations in recordings by more than one hundred celebrities, from Bing Crosby to the Cheetah Girls. The song's popularity has never waned. Mick Jagger and the Rolling Stones recorded it for their first album, *England's Newest Hitmakers*. Jack Kerouac's own road trip, resulting in his book *On the Road*, is said to have been inspired partially by Troup's song and Cole's recording of it. And everyday reference to the road's name changed from U.S. Highway 66 to "Route 66."

There is a controversy about Bobby Troup's Route 66 song lyrics that merits disclosure, and is resolved here after decades of dispute. In 1959, the crooner Perry Como released a version of "Get Your Kicks on Route 66" that startled knowledgeable people by including different lyrics—indeed, a complete verse with additional place names that were unfamiliar to anyone who had heard the song before. And it included a playful intro and closing to the song with even more new words. There were subsequent claims that this rendition by Como actually included all of Bobby Troup's original lyrics for the first time—words claimed to be the songwriter's intended version.

Were the additional words really part of a longer work initially composed by Bobby Troup before either he or Nat King Cole shortened the original for the popularized release in 1946? If not, where did the new words come from, and when? The Como version, with its extended storyline about Route 66 and expanded list of destinations, soon slipped into listener obscurity except for people playing the song from RCA's long-out-of-circulation album *Como Swings*.

This is how the fuller song goes (with the surprising lines shown in italics, courtesy of an article by Johnnie Meier published in *Route 66 Magazine*):

Mister . . . you may . . . have traveled near or far;
But you haven't seen the country,
'Till you've seen the country by car!

Mister . . . may I . . . recommend a royal route?
It starts in Illinois, let me tell you boy!
If you ever plan to motor west,
Travel my way, take the highway, that's the best!
Get your kicks . . . on Route 66!

It winds from Chicago to L.A.,
More than two thousand miles all the way!
Get your kicks . . . on Route 66!
Now you go through St. Louis, Joplin, Missouri,
And Okalahoma City is might purdy!
You'll see Amarillo, Gallup, New Mexico
Flagstaff, Arizona, don't forget Winona,
Kingman, Barstow, San Bernardino!

Won't you get hip to this timely tip,
When you make that California trip?
Get your kicks . . . on Route 66!

Springfield, Illinois . . . Springfield, Missouri too!
Seven states, count 'em, seven,
Spread out in front of you!

You'll like the aroma, of Tulsa, Oklahoma,
Albuquerque and Tucumcari, make
New Mexico extraordinary!
You'll wanna own a piece of Arizona,
Needles, Essex, Amboy, Azusa,
No one in sunny Cal is a loser . . .

So . . . get hip to this timely tip
When you want that California trip!
If any Joe . . . tells you to go . . . some other way,
Say nix!
Get your kicks . . . on Route 66!

The ubiquitous source of information, Wikipedia, stated that these additional words are part of the valid original composition written by Bobby Troup, and rationalized that the unfamiliar lines have simply been "seldom heard." The Scottish comedian Billy Connolly, in his book about a celebrity traveling on a celebrity road, asserted that such research is true—writing about the "shortened version of the song that omits a couple of verses and doesn't mention a string of towns that appeared in Nat's original . . . "

However, in *Route 66: Iconography of the American Highway*, Arthur Krim writes that when Bobby Troup received his first royalty check soon after the release of Nat King Cole's album, the Troup family moved into a new home. There, Cynthia made a collage of their trip snapshots, placed on a base of the actual AAA maps that she and Bobby referenced when finishing the song's lyrics for Cole's recording. She did this in May 1946. Krim's reproduction of those artifacts in his book shows that

Cynthia included only those song lyrics commonly heard, lyrics she attributed on the document as "written by Bobby Troup and Cynthia."

And, there is a lovely 1946 recording of Perry Como and the Nat King Cole Trio, *Live at the Supper Club* (which was an NBC radio show that the always-sweater-wearing Como hosted, sponsored by the Chesterfield cigarette company). In the segment that culminates with Cole singing his newly popular song, Como nicely plays straight man to King's joking around during the introductory sequence as they banter about Cole's recent achievements, and then Como introduces "the tune you recently recorded, dedicated to that famous highway to California, Route 66." The lyrics then sung by Nat King Cole are only those very well known ones, clearly and confidently portrayed as the complete song. The Como/Cole verbal duet is absent any hint of alternative words, let alone a longer version of the song.

In the process of researching this book and seeking (paying for) "permissions" for reproduction of appropriate quotes and song lyrics, the Library of Congress provided to the author a copy of Bobby Troup's February 27, 1946, application to register the copyright of "Get Your Kicks on Route 66." That complete copyright submission, signed by Bobby Troup, is reproduced here with permission from the Library of Congress, and it makes it unequivocally clear what Troup had written in his original. Bobby Troup wrote the words so well known today. And that's all he wrote.

(following page) The original copyright deposit for "(Get Your Kicks on) Route 66," registered in the name of Robert William Troup, Jr., February 27, 1946.

(***Route 66***. *By Bobby Troup. Copyright © 1946, Renewed 1973, Assigned 1974 to Londontown Music. All Rights outside the U.S.A. controlled by E.H. Morris & Company. International Copyright Secured. All Rights Reserved. Reprinted by Permission of Hal Leonard Corporation. Image reproduced by permission of the Library of Congress.*)

"ROUTE 66"

Words and music by Bob Troup

Carl Fischer, Inc., New York.
No. 4-12 lines.
Printed in U.S.A.

(OVER)

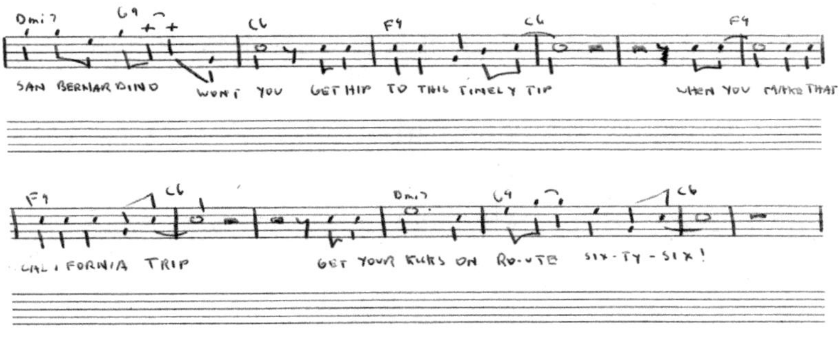

Of course, the jaunty travel song lends itself to easy extensions (as has been done for fun by many performers over the years, though with more modest riffs than the extended wording purported to have come from Bobby Troup and/or Nat King Cole, and as later released by Perry Como). More likely, Perry Como and his crew made up the controversial variation in a musical jest—jamming for their own enjoyment and not feeling obliged to let the history books know the true story behind the fabrication of their 1959 recording.

The original "Get Your Kicks . . . "—short, not long—is complete as written by Bobby Troup in 1946, and is the wording offered in recordings by Nat King Cole.

Cynthia Troup, after she and Bobby had divorced, remembered their drive on Route 66 as arduous. "It took ten days!" she recalled. "I'd never do that again." Their journey has taken on elements of serendipity and folklore, but Cynthia saw it otherwise: "It seemed to me it was just a long road with cheap motels and restaurants. I wonder how we ever knew where to go."

"If you ever plan to motor west" began a "little ditty," yet it is admired now as a definitive cultural statement. Bobby Troup said, "I just thought I was writing about a road—not a legend." For Nat King Cole, the bebop song became the one he was most requested to perform. It set in place the lure of Route 66 travel more than any tourism promotion could have, and it became both a musical road map and a travelers' anthem.

When Bobby Troup died of a heart attack at the age of eighty in 1999, eulogists had many of his achievements to comment on—his acting in movies (*M*A*S*H*) and in television (*Emergency*, with his second wife, Julie London), and eight record albums. There were various mentions of his hit songs "Girl Talk" and "Baby, Baby, All the Time," but not one of the obituaries overlooked the admonition: "Get your kicks on Route 66."

In Arizona, Peter and I backtracked on a few occasions—taking time, finding short sections of Route 66 that ended with unfriendly concrete walls or a fenced barrier. Each time we turned around, we were satisfied—it seemed inevitable that we would be denied passage at some points. These spurts of history attracted us; we'd exit a good road to find a bad one.

However, Peter's intensity about dead ends, born of a personal pledge to find them, had eased somewhat. His manner had become more nonchalant, a simple expectation that we'd learn of more dead ends as we traveled, and, of course, find them. It no longer seemed a preoccupation, but rather an acceptance that the road broke off, and where it did, we'd turn around or head elsewhere. All in good time.

We took a promising loop through the Painted Desert, an austere, blisteringly attractive land. The desert was immense, and the loop twice crossed an inaccessible dirt-road piece of 66. As we curved between lookouts, where a man-made ridge helped visitors know where to stop, we also drove perilously close to the edges of several cliffs that lacked any protective barrier. But I felt no need to reenact *Thelma and Louise*.

A rolling flatness took us into Winslow, Arizona, where the highway offered little to warrant attention, let alone affection, until we noticed that the guidebook stressed two Route 66 access points there. It advised us to get off the westbound one-way through town and to retrace the trip on the eastbound route. Here, a 1937 realignment of the original route resulted in Route 66 crossing over itself.

At the corner of 2nd and Kingsley stood a hollowed-out, barren piece of property that ended with a two-story brick wall braced by strong supports. It was the one wall left standing after a fire. Its symbolism became clear once we saw the other side, which faced the street corner. Painted into the wall's large window was a picture of a pretty girl in a flat-deck Ford slowing down to take a look at me. Standing on the corner next to the wall was a brass sculpture of a male singer, his right hand atop the neck of a guitar. The depiction captured the Eagles song that made Winslow and this winsome street corner famous.

Peter said—but did not sing—"You're standing on a corner in Winslow, Arizona, and you're such a sad sight to see." Then he added, "You need a shave."

We strolled the neighborhood, looking for a barber. It wasn't long before we found a red-and-white pole that had once signaled a drugstore. It led us into a side alley, and from there to the Antler Barbershop. Antlers, on display as souvenirs of the owner's various kills, covered the wall. The hunter was now a barber.

"Would you do a straight-razor shave on a beard?" I asked. John Lewis looked at the eight days of growth that covered my face with charcoal-colored splotches.

He nodded at me, and pointed at Peter. "Him, too?"

For men who are not into manicures and pedicures, a straight-razor shave is as close to self-indulgence as it gets. And it is hard to find a barber who will do it; indeed, some jurisdictions restrict the practice for insurance purposes. It's a dangerous treat. Looking around the Antler's decor, I thought twice before lying prone, face-up, under a warm cloth that was covering both my eyes, while a hunter-turned-barber took a strap-sharpened blade to my throat.

After I had been scraped clean, I waited while Peter settled into the chair, was tilted backward for a pre-shave scrub and had his eyes covered by hot towel. Then his face was lathered-up by the barber. Through the warm foam, he said, "I've never done this before." At that, I made sure that both he and John Lewis knew the story of Sweeney Todd's escapades as an English barber. As Lewis slapped his razor on the leather belt tied to Peter's chair, I told them of the nineteenth-century London barber's habit of drawing down his shop's shades while out-of-town clients rested their eyes under a damp cloth. "Then he used his razor to slit the traveler's throat," I told them. "Scot-

People we met along the way were beguiling and enlightening about this country's quirks and quandaries, as well as about their own hopes and fears. Route 66 is America writ large, as well as America in small type. Let it be. Let it decay and renew. Let it be real.

land Yard was eventually tipped off when fingernails started showing up in the tasty meat pies in the store next door. That was run by Todd's wife."

Peter peeled back one eye's worth of hot cloth and kept his eye on Lewis. The former hunter and taxidermist leaned Peter farther back in the chair and replaced the hot towel over his eye. He slapped his razor on the leather strap once again, undiscouraged.

Mounted on the wall next to the barber's chair is a wild turkey's foot modeled by Lewis-the-taxidermist so that it curls upright, with the middle toe making an "up yours" thrust. "That was the last thing the turkey did before I shot him," John told us.

A man who was sitting on the barbershop's couch worked for the local newspaper, whose premises were next door. He was hanging out between booking advertisements for the weekly edition. I mentioned to him that we'd found the Roadworks store two blocks away and that I'd bought *Their Greatest Hits* by The Eagles. He hinted, as only a local can on such topics, that the Eagles didn't originate the song "Take It Easy," with its famous line about standing on a corner in Winslow, Arizona.

"They didn't ever write it. It was Savoy Brown who wrote it," the newspaperman said.

"Savoy Brown, the British blues band?" I asked.

"Well . . . not blues. And . . . not a band."

"Or maybe you mean Jackson Browne. The American songwriter."

"That's the guy. He wrote it."

Indeed, Jackson Browne did write the song, in collaboration with Glenn Frey, the lead vocalist for the Eagles. It was on their first album, and was their first "single."

Routes 66 and I-40 are one and the same after Winslow's westbound main street merges through an on-ramp with forty-two hectic miles of freeway. Our exit off that road and back on to a relaxing 66 at Winona offered a pleasant alternate routing into Flagstaff. Curiously, Bobby Troup's lyric "Flagstaff Arizona; don't forget Winona" makes this the only town that is sung out of geographic sequence.

The road rose gently, approaching Flagstaff through Ponderosa pine forests. The temperature dropped, due as much to altitude as to the end of the day. Route 66 here has benefited from consistency: It runs, proudly signed and with good blacktop, right into a thriving downtown. In many other cities, developers' greed and poor planning means that those cities have lost their "sight lines," and tall buildings spike the sky, blocking longer views. Flagstaff avoids that trend.

But it did not always do so. The guardians of civic atmosphere were too busy celebrating on New Year's Day, 1927, when the builders of the Monte Vista Hotel opened their new property with a giant sign on its roof. The sign can still be seen miles away. Given its age and type font, the sign now seems comfortably "in place" rather than an affront to the skyline of five-story buildings.

I dropped Peter off at the hotel's ornate front door so that he could negotiate the room rate while I explored the town's one-way streets and sussed out the evening's options. And I made a mental note of the Laundromat two doors in on a side street; my clothes were going to rot if I didn't clean them soon.

Only a block away from the Monte Vista was the historic Weatherford Hotel. This is the home of the Zane Grey Bar—named for the writer of "dime books," the creator of stories by the dozen, a writer of prodigious output who penned (or tapped, on his Underwood typewriter) more than ninety books, five dozen of them Westerns. In this one-time rooming house, he'd written *The Call of the Canyon*. In return, the hotel's current owners have designated their loveliest room, a second-floor bar and balcony, as the Zane Grey Room.

Eventually, I gave up touring in hopes that Peter would reappear at the front entrance of the Monte Vista. It was not to be. I parked at the hotel, entering the lobby to find him in the final throes of negotiating the application of his AAA membership discount to both our room rates for the night. More importantly to me, we were able to stay in the town's most prominent hotel. I'd heard it was haunted; I wanted to find out more.

We hauled our bags up a stairway. When I opened my door, I felt at home in a room fit to serve as a movie set in a hundred "duster" films. The small, tidy bed was covered with a quilt, and had a brass headboard. The closet was a wooden wardrobe, styled in the 1800s, its narrow doors adorned with brass handles. A porcelain sink jutted from the wall. The floral wallpaper covered the walls in deep blue and white swirls. I was embedded in the 1890s.

Arriving downstairs before Peter, I asked the desk clerk to tell me one of the hotel's ghost stories.

She threw her head back, not to laugh, but to clear her hair from her eyes. She looked right at me, all serious. Her eyes were a penetrating green. "Well . . . " she began.

My left elbow found the countertop, and I leaned on it. She and I were alone.

"About forty years ago, a trio of bank robbers pulled a job not far from here. They got away from the bank, but not 'cuz they were what you'd call clever. They stopped at the Monte Vista for a drink before heading out of town. One had been shot in the getaway, don't ya know. Good robbers? Yup. Smart? Not so much."

"He died?" I asked.

"Bled to death, right here in the lounge."

"And?"

"And . . . people say he still haunts the lounge. He shows up now and then, looking for a bandage and a drink. A spirit among the spirits." She laughed.

The Monte Vista boasts a long list of paranormal phenomena, including voices in hallways, a ghostly couple dancing in the bar, cries from the basement, and someone who cannot be seen, but mysteriously moves objects.

The American Ghost Society has many chapters. One of them is a group known as the Ghost Hunters of Northern Arizona.

Starting in spring 2004 and throughout the summer, the Ghost Hunters undertook a study of the paranormal goings-on at the Monte Vista, using advanced motion detectors, voice surveillance recorders, and video monitoring. Deploying heat scanners and equipment to monitor the electromagnetic field, these "certified ghost hunters" went looking for evidence of the apparition of a bellboy (which the movie star John Wayne swore he once saw) and the lounge ghost.

They found photographic evidence of orbs ("ghost lights"), both circulating and stationary. Their report also claims that "cold spots" have been found by thermoscanners, a near-sure sign of spooky activity to those who believe in such things. The researchers charted "high levels of electromagnetic energy fields" on occasion, and their "ghost-cam" caught movements on film. A phantom was reported to frequent certain rooms on the third floor—where Peter was staying.

The night clerk stared at me, her green eyes now slightly more penetrating. She told me that her predecessor had heard heavy bags being shuffled across the lobby's floor at midnight—more than once—but "every time he looked up, no one was there."

I said, "What would you do if you heard that, and were alone?"

She shrugged, then dramatically suggested, "Who ya gonna call?"

Whoever designed the lobby of the Weatherford Hotel did so knowing that a winding staircase would make it seem larger and provide space for a check-in counter at the hotel—while providing visitors with period decor. Up the stairway was the writer's lair. The long bar, bordered with thick, dark rims, was crowded when we entered. The Zane Grey Bar was hosting a political rally next door, and the attendees mingled with the regulars and tourists. The bartender proposed American Blonde Ale from the Flagstaff Brewing Company and drew two pints at my behest. I nudged through the crowd toward Peter, who was talking with a man and woman. He pointed to me.

"Meet my driver."

I handed Peter's beer to the man, and mine to the woman. Peter did penance by making it his business to get us the next couple of beers. Before he turned to force his way through the crowd he noted, "Cliff and Jenny are here from Australia. Retired. On a house exchange."

By the time Peter had wound his way back with the beer, the three of us had commandeered a table in the corner, pulled up extra chairs, and found a waiter. Peter put our two beers on the table. That, and a pot of popcorn, primed us for the essential American political setting, resplendent with people wearing U.S.-flag-embossed jerseys, flag-emblazoned T-shirts, and flag-themed chef's hats. In political gatherings in this country, much of the attire is consistent; the candidates' names may change or a party symbol may accent the wardrobe, but the American flag as trademark is ever-present. As a promotional logo, it is more popular than Nike's swoosh or Disney's Mickey Mouse. It no longer seems to be only a nation's flag—it's a product brand.

We fell into easy talk, and Jenny spoke of their affection for Americans. When Cliff asked, "Where's the nation going to be in ten years?" the waiter plunked down more beers and unintentionally answered the question with each landing: "Here! Here!"

10

The Road of Flight

"Driving'z life. Life iz a highway."
—Motormouth Mike

I woke early and walked down a staircase and out the Monte Vista's side door. The sun was barely up. Silence. The day seemed speechless. I walked alone, eventually trying the Late for the Train coffee shop in an effort to find some local cooking or baking. The shop was closed, and I had to admit there was such a thing as getting up too early. I headed back to the hotel's Rendezvous Coffee House. Peter would soon be up, sorting himself out, and it seemed our best choice for breakfast.

In the Rendezvous a woman, looking utterly bereft, sat on a stool. Her clothes were disheveled. One of her buttons had been stretched into an unmatching buttonhole, while another buttonhole remained empty. The gap showed the swell of her braless breast. Finding some consolation by staring into her coffee, she then turned her weary eyes to me. "You're not from here," she said.

I told her where I was headed and, since Peter wasn't here, asked his inevitable question about the road.

"Route 66? It brings men." She tried to smile, fought a smirk, then admitted, "And it takes men away."

I didn't know what to say, and didn't reply.

She asked, "Is that why they call it the road of flight?"

Still waiting for Peter, I retrieved my gear from the room and brought it downstairs. New staff had begun their shift at the hotel, and as I approached the front desk I noticed the lobby was empty. Behind the desk, an innocent-looking teenage girl fidgeted with strands of her blond hair as she punched something into the register.

"I think I saw a ghost in my room last night," I said.

"Might have." She smiled. "It happens."

"Tall, blond, attractive woman," I said.

"I think you're making that up," she countered. "If it was *one of our ghosts*, it'd have been a bellboy or a dancing couple."

One of the three alignments for Route 66 when it leaves Flagstaff is covered by the I-40. We chose to leave that one alone as we swung through Bellemont, heading for pine forests and the gravel road that had been Route 66 before 1941. Through the pines, we could see its predecessor, the 1921 National Old Trails Road, now potholed, gradually yielding to nature's encroachments.

Peter read aloud the posted sign announcing the route we sought. Bullet holes punctuated its warning: PRIMITIVE ROAD—CAUTION—USE AT YOUR OWN RISK. He turned to me. "Sounds like your kinda road, being primitive and all."

I let his comment pass, happily reading the rest of the sign to myself: "This surface is not regularly maintained."

The mid-morning air cooled as we climbed Forest Road.

"Fortynine Hill," said Peter as we crested it, claiming, "This used to be one of the highest points on Route 66."

We pulled up, got out of the car, and leaned against a wooden-rail fence. Ahead of us, blocked off from vehicle access, was the National Old Trail roadbed.

"I'll be back in a while," I said. I wanted a few minutes to walk with history, to think of the jalopies and the families they had carried, the flappers and loners, the hopeful travelers who must also have stopped at places like this to wonder about what was ahead in their journey, to ponder what had passed.

Both Peter and I were looking forward to the town of Williams because this is said to be the place where Route 66 got its final comeuppance.

October 13, 1984, was the day of reckoning for Route 66. On that Saturday, it became a no-through-road. In the eyes of many, the new four-lane freeway reinforced the image of interstates as parasites. Here, the efficient six-mile freeway rerouted travelers from a six-mile stretch of Route 66, eliminating the last stoplight that travelers on Highway 40 "needed" to observe and ending any necessity to travel on Route 66 to get from Chicago to L.A. "The day the noise died," is how Bobby Troup saw it at the ribbon-cutting ceremony. Then he sang his song.

That event temporarily broke the spirit of Route 66. Local historian Teri Cleeland reported that there were "no official temperature readings" that day in Williams. It was said that "the high was 66; the low was 40."

The *San Francisco Examiner* headlined its article about the opening of this bypass with "No more kicks on Route 66." A reporter reprised the history of interstates that, piece by piece, had now replaced Route 66 from Chicago to L.A. and lamented that "portions of Route 66 were either torn up as part of the interstate construction effort, reduced to frontage road, or bypassed and abandoned." The town of Williams was granted three off-ramps from the new I-40; those exits helped increase its draw as a gateway to the Grand Canyon. Today Williams thrives once again, with period street decor, relics, and an atmosphere of "all this happened before my time."

Distractions are tough to overcome; travel temptations all the more so. "Grand Canyon exit," said Peter, pointing to a posted turnoff from Route 66 . . . but we motored on. I could not tell if he was keen to go or was letting me make the decision for both of us. I saw his fingers tapping on the steering wheel and noticed the taps were a second apart. A proposed side trip off Route 66 to the Grand Canyon would not pass the Ten-Second Rule.

One of the two longest continuous old-road stretches of Route 66 is the 158 miles from Ash Fork to Seligman, Arizona, to the California state line and Topock.

Neglect—the result of being bypassed—is obvious in Seligman. It has been left a stretch of Route 66 that is too wide for the town's need and the limited traffic today. But one sure stop is the self-described "most famous diner" on Route 66: Delgadillo's Snow Cap.

"When was the last time you had ice cream with marshmallow topping?" I asked Peter when we were still a few miles from Seligman.

"Never," he said, keeping his eyes on the road.

"Well," I looked up from the guidebook. "You're in for a treat. If you're good."

It would be inaccurate to say that Delgadillo's is on the outskirts of town, as the whole drive through Seligman seems to be on the outskirts. There is no "there" there—not in the sense of a town center or a spot where you'd stand up and say, "I'm in Seligman." Instead, you seem always to be heading out of town. I don't mean to oversimplify this, but it is that simple.

All true, except for Delgadillo's Snow Cap. The location has the most gawdawful decorations imaginable—a cluster of directional signs, each made from different material and coming from different decades; red paint applied where white didn't work, and blue over both of those; and a conflicted backyard/

frontyard/sideyard that has collected an outhouse, a picnic table, and car bits from the last century. We pulled over and parked beside a rusted-out pickup truck, circa 1940.

Peter approached the diner's entrance door and grabbed the handle right below the sign that said PULL. He pulled gently, and when the door didn't move, he yanked harder. Nothing. We could see the cook laughing inside. Then Peter pushed the door with his left hand while his right hand still tried to pull it open. As soon as he pushed on the left side, where the hinges would logically be, the door opened "in."

"I smell a jokester," he said, not at all embarrassed.

Ahead of us in line to order was a curly-haired, paunchy father of about forty years old, an attractive mother ten years younger and twenty years slimmer, and three kids: We heard them talking about the milkshakes they'd ordered, and one of the kids hung from the lip of wood that was the serving counter. The paper-capped teenager who had taken their order handed out five glasses of various sizes, some half full, one empty, but all dirty. The kids smiled at the gag, while the parents gasped. The server laughed as though he'd never stop. "Gotcha!"

Then he retrieved the dirty glasses and provided his customers with clean plastic cups, filled to the brim with their milkshakes—four chocolate and one strawberry. Clutching a handful of used straws, broken, covered with dried slime, a half dozen of them in torn paper shells, he asked, "Straws?" Again the kids thought this was great and reached for them as the parents stepped back.

"Gotcha!" The teenage server nearly fell over himself with the funniness of it all.

"I'll wait outside," Peter said. I watched as he pushed and pulled the door in opposite directions to ensure his efficient exit. I walked to the order window; it was my turn.

"Chicken?" asked the teenager. "We've got really good dead chicken." And with this he tossed two rubber chickens at me.

Some days our trip was like an easy drive down a forgotten road—winding, stopping now and then to gawk at bygone times. Route 66 evokes the quintessential America travel experience: recognizable yet elusive.

Both were attached to elastics, and sprang back out of my reach and into the wicket through which he prepared to take my order.

"I know it's boring, but could I have two ice cream sundaes, please?"

"We're out of sundaes, but we have great Saturdays." He laughed.

"Right then," I said. "One with caramel and marshmallow toppings, please. The other . . . "

"Ah," he interrupted, "Ketchup. Makes for the best on ice cream."

"And the other—" I smiled "—with butterscotch and marshmallow."

Outside, I passed Peter his ice cream creation. We walked around the museum of surrendered items. A slender, middle-aged man wearing a loose-fitting black blazer over a black shirt and black tie smoothed a table and organized his display box. It was full of sports cards, mostly portraying baseball players I recognized from the 1950s and 1960s. He had a Honus Wagner "from a kid's cereal box series" that he'd labeled 1942, and one of Milwaukee Braves pitcher Warren Spahn, from 1958. And Andy Pafko, "probably from the time before they included bubble gum in the packets," the man said. He had others: Willie Mays, Duke Snider, Hank Aaron.

"How many people stop by here?" I asked.

"Oh, hundreds. More if you consider all year."

"Sell many baseball cards?"

"One last week. Two the week before."

I still have a shoebox of treasured baseball cards at home, mostly from the TOPPS Company, from the 1950s and early 1960s. "Got any Mickey Mantle?" I asked.

"He was such a star for so long, so many seasons, there are so many cards. His is the one card people keep—even if they don't like baseball. They don't sell Mickey. I've got one at home I could get, if you're serious about him."

He fussed with a second display case, forcing it tightly beside the first one to make room for another display that was still in the trunk of his car.

"Is this how you make your living?" I asked.

"No. It's a sideline. I keep the restaurant yard tidy for the owners, sweep up, and collect garbage after people eat and leave. They pay me and feed me."

With that, he went to his 1962 Chevrolet and took the final display out of the trunk. "I'm here all afternoon, if you want the Mickey Mantle."

Route 66 from Seligman to Kingman is one lovely stretch of driving. I was at the wheel and the top was down. Later this day, we'd be driving on my most anticipated part of the trip: the Oatman Highway, which has a fearsome reputation. As it climbs a mountainside, the road takes some steep and frightful turns and eventually crests at Sitgreaves Pass. We hoped to be there long before sunset and to drift through little Oatman and into California for our first night in the route's eighth and final state.

As we drove, we encountered a series of signs, less than a foot high and three feet wide, posted about a hundred yards apart. They appeared to be silkscreened. Peter began to sing, in short bursts broken by three-second pauses—a timing suited to a singer moving at thirty-five miles an hour and reading sequential signs.

HE PLAYED

A SAX

HAD NO B.O.

BUT HIS WHISKERS SCRATCHED

SO SHE LET HIM GO

BURMA-SHAVE

Route 66 was once home to these "jaunty little signs" along much of its length. They were planted beside many U.S. byways, particularly in the West. "Burma-Shave" became a common reference to a sequence of posted words as much as to a drugstore offering. That national awareness started in 1925 with an idea sprung by Alan Odell, the son of the owner of a little-known company with a lesser-known product.

Odell's father, Clinton, was son of an inventor who made a cream concoction that he claimed had originated with sailors from overseas. The application of that cream eased skin rashes and smelled medicinally mean. In deference to its oils, sourced from Southeast Asia, particularly the country of Burma, the liniment struggled with the unlikely name Burma-Vita, the latter word meaning "life" in Latin. "Life from Burma" was more descriptive in English, but was felt to be a less commanding product name than Burma-Vita. Thus began the Odell family's foray into marketing.

In the family folklore there is a chemist whom Clinton senior befriended and who, in return, helped Clinton reconstitute the British brushless shaving cream called Lloyd's Euxesis into the family's second product—and later into an American phenomenon. Their market advantage was that men using this new product would no longer need to fiddle with the mess associated with the morning ritual of lathering and shaving. Their early chemical formula failed, however, and not until they had tested nearly 300 hundred variations did they discover the magical ingredient: aging. And that they discovered by testing a three-month-old jar of experimental Formula One Forty-three! They named it Burma-Shave.

A 1925 drive to Joliet, Illinois, on what would the next year become known as Route 66, provided Alan Odell with the inspiration for the Burma-Shave promotion. He noted the logic of a series of signs along the route. The simple GAS/RESTROOMS/FOOD postings always concluded with a sign pointing to the service station. The idea sprang into Odell's mind fully formed. "Every time I see one of these setups, I read every one of the signs," he said. "So why can't you sell our product that way?"

The family business's promotional budget was thin, so Alan and his younger brother Leonard found discarded pieces of board, used brass stencils for the letters, and hand-painted the first Burma-Shave signs themselves.

Peter asked me to slow down so that he could photograph the next set of replica signs at the side of the road. As he did so, he shouted their words:

THE ONE WHO
DRIVES WHEN
HE'S BEEN DRINKING
DEPENDS ON YOU
TO DO HIS THINKING
BURMA-SHAVE

The signs disappeared in the mid-1960s, when the company's new owners, Philip Morris Inc. (American Safety Razor Products), deemed the 35,000 signs old-fashioned and removed those splinters of fun and banter from America's roadsides. The Smithsonian Institution claimed enough of the originals to complete a display, and Arizona highways thoughtfully erected half a dozen examples for the entertainment of today's drivers along old Route 66. This approach is still considered the best way to slow down speeding drivers, usually at their family's request.

It was good going that day—Route 66 all the way, rolling over the Sacramento Valley and rising as we neared the Black Mountains. I was caught up in awe. We put our hands to the wind and let them aeroplane as we drove at sixty miles an hour. The Mustang's engine paced beautifully, never emitting a chug or a whine. It was early in the evening, and that made for a carefree drive—the day still held ample time for us to take our chosen route through the mountain pass before dark and then to motor on at dusk to the Arizona-California boundary, a nice meal, and a good night's rest.

Kingman faded in our rear-view mirror, and, what was better, the I-40 disappeared south, taking a belly loop out of sight. We were in the Sacramento Wash, the great escape course for flood waters in the rainy season. Dips in the roller-coastering road had distributed flash-flood waters down broad gulches during their times, which thankfully were not occurring now. Up next was the Oatman Highway. Before us were, in Steinbeck's words, "The broken, sun-rotten mountains."

To early travelers on Route 66, the steep climb to the 3,523-foot summit of the Black Mountains was onerous enough: People driving wagons and harnessed animals found it hard going. For those who came later with cars and trucks, the winding incline and precipices challenged their hearts and camshafts. This is

Route 66 at its most unforgiving: the seemingly endless curves, the cliff-clinging, the road force-cut into the mountainside. We were told, "No one willingly drives this stretch of Route 66 in the dark." Improvements over the years have involved little more than repaving, and, where the road curves sharply, steel cables strung between wooden posts give drivers a sense of security. This road is best crawled up. Signs implore trailers or trucks longer than thirty feet to turn back.

The wind whipped over the windshield, its sound blending with the Eagles' ballads on the car stereo. We climbed the road's first miles relaxed and happy about our day. The skirt of the mountain was steady and steep: The flatlands, and dusk, were only two hours away, on the other side of the mountains. (California, here we come.) Our road was empty behind, empty ahead. We headed up the mountain toward Sitgreaves Pass.

I was singing along with the Eagles, lip-synching the part about "We may lose, and we may win, but we will never be here again . . . "

Peter chimed in with the chorus at "Take it e-a-s-y."

We shared a serene feeling of confidence.

"Why are you slowing down?" Peter said.

"I haven't seen *that* light flash before."

"*What* light?"

"Hold on," I said, stopping, shifting into reverse and backing into an open spot at the edge of the cliff.

"*What* light?"

"That one," I said, pointing to the red light glowing on the dashboard so that Peter could join in the alarm. "Temperature. Engine. Trouble." I pulled on the hood release, and got out to open the hood.

The engine hissed at us. It was not happy; the culprit was not the road—it was us.

"Mud on the radiator," Peter speculated.

"Engine couldn't cool," I confirmed.

Guthrie's "Talking Dust Bowl Blues" drifted my way from old listenings where he's driving "way up yonder on a mountain road" as were we, but more salient was his line "'A-bouncin' up and down, like popcorn poppin'." I mumbled just that one line, but did so twice. Peter looked at me and huffed, his chest sinking.

A pickup truck soon pulled alongside, and two local women looked at us through their rolled-down window. "Need any help?" they offered. Being men, we declined. They took our assurance that all would work out, and left saying, "Get off the road before dark."

"When was the last time you checked the water?" I asked.

"I didn't. I thought you did."

"And . . . I thought you did . . . "

"Sorry," Peter said to the Mustang, once again preferring awkward talk with the car to conversation with me. Then he remembered the gallon of water he'd stowed in the trunk and went to get it. "This," he announced, holding up the jug, "was brilliant on my part."

Of course it was, but I couldn't bring myself to acknowledge that. The driver of the day should check the tire pressure, top up the fuel and fluids. It was my day; my mistake.

Peter put the full jug on the ground in front of the car. We waited fifteen minutes for the engine to cool. We were certainly not the first drivers whose radiators had boiled over on this hill, but 1930s drivers encountered that problem due to the lack of a cooling system, not due to a lack of thinking.

Looking around, Peter said, "I need a rag to twist off the radiator cap. Where are your muddy jeans?"

They were scrunched up in a plastic bag in the trunk, still wet from their dousing after our mud hole escapade a few days ago. They had not been laundered and were now this side of moldy—so Peter didn't hesitate when placing them over the hissing motor. He twisted the cap loose. The radiator spat at him. He bunched my jeans around the radiator cap and pried further. As the radiator spewed green water over them, the mud-soaked jeans kept his hands from blistering. Everything, including the two of us, slowly cooled down. And when Peter tilted the refill water, the radiator gulped the gallon without a burp or a spill.

Fifteen minutes later, I turned the motor on. The red light stayed off and the warning gauge had reset itself to midway on the dial, where it should be. We decided to keep heading for the summit at Sitgreaves Pass, believing that it levelled off afterwards. Right now, it wasn't even in view. Once through it, though, we could head down the other side of the mountain, the rushing air cooling the motor as we continued westward. That would ensure a functioning engine, as well as power steering and power brakes—both assets on a mountain drive.

The needle on the temperature gauge stayed steady for half a mile and then again started to rise with the incline. I commented on the problem. Peter, leaning over from the passenger side to take it in, said, "This don't look good."

The road was narrow and ever winding. There was no shoulder, only carved-out mountain on the left, and a sheer drop-off on the right. "I need to pull over, *now*," I said.

Peter shouted, "*Don't you . . . dare.* It's straight . . . *down!*" He put his head out the window and looked hundreds of feet down. "*Don't . . .* "

"*Now!*" I repeated as the red light flashed. I stopped in the middle of the road.

"How bad?" he asked.

"It's the end of the world as we know it."

We sat there a minute. Finally I said, "Got another brilliant bottle of water?"

"Actually," said Peter, "I do." He retrieved a half-gallon bottle of drinking water. "Thirsty?"

It took nearly half an hour for the engine to cool enough for him to once more wrap my muddy jeans around the radiator cap.

Woody Guthrie returned to my mind with his singing talk of a mountain road and a heavy load and the inevitable hot motor, but I dared not even hum the tune, let alone pop a line about "poppin'."

A single headlight approached. A Harley-Davidson motorcycle pulled up and the rider got off, propping his motorcycle in the middle of the road. "Need help?" he asked, having already arrived beside us and now peering under the hood.

"How far to the summit?" I asked.

"A few miles."

"How far on the other side is Oatman?"

"Few miles."

"What's in Oatman?" asked Peter.

"A mine."

"Any place to stay?"

"Nope. It's a ghost town."

He stayed with us as Peter fed the half gallon of water to the radiator and he talked us through our debate about heading back to Kingman, or not. He thought the engine would cool itself while heading down into Oatman. "You just have to get to the summit," he reminded us.

He kicked his Harley on, and his headlamp shone on the nearby mountainside. "Get to the summit soon," he warned. "And get off the road before dark." And off he went, downhill.

Dusk claimed our side of the mountain, and the sky became momentarily lighter in the distance beyond the mountains. The summit was still out of sight. The stunning yellow peaks slowly faded to pewter and then turned the colors of early night.

I nursed the Mustang for another mile, the needle in a steady, disappointing rise as the car continued to climb. "Start looking for a place to pull over," I said.

"Last chance to turn for downhill-Kingman," said Peter.

"Find a spot," I said. "Red light's on."

"There's the summit!" declared Peter.

I saw a gap in the mountain, one that was within reach—for most vehicles.

"It's too far," I said, slinking onto a soft ledge.

"Don't!" he shouted. "The car's weight could topple the ledge."

We went another hundred feet and I had no choice. I stopped.

Hood up, we stood beside the Mustang and stared together at the engine. I said, "I don't suppose you . . . "

"Nope."

(previous page) Sitgreaves Pass was to be at the crest of our relaxed hill-climb over a once-treacherous mountain road that brought dreaded anticipation to travelers on Route 66 in the 1920s and 1930s. Our overconfidence proved us unequal to the task; we were unprepared for the unexpected.

Survival strategy gets pretty simple at times: stabilize the situation.

My idea: "We should turn back half a mile to that mountain-side hollow. We can park there and sleep in the car."

Peter's idea: "Or we could wait an hour for the engine to cool off, and then risk the summit." We both looked longingly at that gap, up, up, and away.

In the distance, a pair of headlights crested over the summit. We waited patiently until a pickup slowed and pulled up beside us.

"Need help?" said the driver.

"Got any water?" I asked.

"Sorry, no. How'd you overheat?"

"We've been driving a long way. We should have checked the water. He didn't," Peter said, pointing at me.

"It's a new car," the man said. "I never check my water. Never. You should have been fine."

"Well, we took on a bit of mud. Probably blocked the radiator," I offered.

"That'll do it," the man said. "You only have half a mile to the summit." And he left us, his taillights receding and finally trailing out of sight.

Half an hour later the sky was pitch-black, except for a billion stars. The silence was overwhelming—except for an engine hiss. Peter and I hadn't spoken to one another for most of that time. The Mustang's roof was still down, the hood was up, and Peter sat outside, leaning against the passenger door; I perched on the trunk.

It was impossibly black. Peter finally broke the silence. "There's something to be said for the dark."

"It brings out your inner owl," I said.

I knew Peter wouldn't endure much more of this. So I got back in the Mustang, tested our luck, and we won. Taking deep breaths, we approached the summit. And reached it. I knew now that we'd make our final destination, even if we had to rely on the rest of Guthrie's song for a backup plan: "An' I give that rollin' Ford a shove, An' I's a-gonna coast as far as I could."

We headed down Gold Hill, ever down, with the temperature gauge's needle staying in friendly territory. Our worry now was overheating brakes. We hedged slowly around the hairpin turns. At most, a straight section would last a hundred yards, then it would lurch sideways and plunge downward in the dark.

"In the morning, this car gets a bath and a mechanic," Peter said, patting the dashboard.

"First we have to find a place to sleep," I reminded him. "And I don't think we should drive too far tonight."

"There's nothing in Oatman," he reminded me in turn.

"We should pick a side road, park, and sleep in the car. Use our sleeping bags. Morning will come soon enough. Do you snore?"

"It would surprise me if others found you fun to travel with."

"Well, what's *your* idea?" I asked.

Peter's belief in an intervening god seemed to be strengthened by our travels. As we drove, he was muttering, "Please God, deliver me from . . . "

Suddenly Oatman rose out of the dark. We coasted into that shadowy dimness that buildings take on at night. The buildings were closed and mostly dark, but one light shone. It lit a sign that read: JUDY'S SALOON AND POOL HALL.

"Like a beer?" asked Peter.

"I'm driving," I said.

"Not for much longer, if we're lucky."

We pulled over and decided to explore. Peter pushed open a gate that led through a small courtyard and into the saloon. A couple of movie posters, a wall map of Arizona, three watercolors by a local artist, and a few torn black-and-white photographs of early Oatman covered two sides of the room. A buffalo head was mounted at the far end, overlooking the pool table. Three striped balls sat alone in defeat on the green felt. The fourth wall was stocked with liquor, and two beer taps sat behind a polished bar.

"Evening," said a middle-aged woman who leaned against the liquor cabinet. She wore black denim slacks and a checkered blouse that offered no protection from the night's cold.

A young man slouched on a stool at the bar, with two nearly empty glasses in front of him. His eyelids were half-closed, and his right elbow slipped on the counter when he turned toward us. He was the only other occupant of the room. His blond hair, angular good looks, and clean shirt made him seem out of place here, but when he slurred a greeting it was clear he'd lost himself to the bottle.

"You Judy?" Peter asked the woman, ignoring the man.

"Paula," she said. "What would you like?"

"A beer. A Coke. Food."

"Got beer. Got Coke. Might have a leftover burrito out back in the freezer. Could microwave it."

"I'll take those peanuts," said Peter, pointing to the shelf behind her.

The drunk persisted. "You-ou nott ak-knowlg-ing mee."

We sipped our drinks and pondered our situation.

"Busy here during the tourist season," offered Paula. "It's a pretty town. Lots of history. This building's the post office. Real slow this time of year."

"Any place to stay?" I asked. It was worth a try.

"Nope. Used to be. Hotel had a couple of rooms. No more. Most people visit awhile, buy souvenirs, and leave. Good breakfast places, though. Two of 'em." She stopped at that, hesitated, and thought out loud. "Gary's got a place up the hillside. Sometimes he rents it." Without saying anything further, she picked up the phone and dialed Gary. When she had him on the line, she handed me the phone.

"Hi, Gary, I hear you might have a place for the night," I began.

Peter watched me, his apprehension turning to nervousness as he heard only my side of the phone conversation:

"Don't worry about clean sheets. We've got sleeping bags."

"No, that's okay. We like 'old.'"

"Really? . . . 1908."

"Ha. That's funny. Peter's tall, but I think he'll fit."

"Sure. Fifty bucks sounds fair."

"Right. We'll wait here. See you in five."

I clicked off the phone and gave it back to Paula.

"What was *that*?" asked Peter.

"Gary's coming by. We've got us a place for the night. He'll pick us up in five minutes and take us there to see it. It's a cabin."

"Sort of . . . a cabin," said Paula. "It used to be a migrant's shack."

Peter ordered another beer.

Gary hobbled into the pool hall, hand extended. Peter noticed Gary's limp, and right away Gary said, "I lost two toes." No explanation given; none sought. The three of us, all big men, climbed into the two-seated cab of Gary's truck. It was a roundabout drive through town. We bounced up a hillside path into silent surroundings and the pickup pulled in next to a stave-sided shack. "This is the cabin," Gary confirmed as we climbed out of his rig to be greeted by the growls of nearby dogs.

Gary's partner, Karen, was there to meet us, shushing the neighbors' pets when they poked aggressively against the loose boards in the fence. "Hi. You here for the night? Great." Her boisterous greeting confirmed that we'd chosen a safe and decent place. "Miner built it in '08," she said. "*Nineteen* '08," she laughed. "Other folks added on in the thirties—you can see it here." She pointed to a place where sideways-nailed planks greeted upright wooden slats. "Added more again in the fifties."

She asked about the drive we'd taken up the other side of the mountain to get here, having asked, "You know you're on the original Route 66?" Then she offered an anecdote of her own. "In the 1940s, my grandfather drove up Sitgreaves Pass *backwards* so that gravity would keep the car's fuel flowing to the engine."

We smiled, so she continued. "Reverse is actually a lower gear than first, and that helped on the steep parts."

We entered the shack under a low overhang of plywood, through a door that had a broken lock, and walked into a tiny kitchen with a sink, a wood stove, and a table covered with a green plastic table cloth. Peter walked through the little living room, past the television, and into the back bedroom. He threw his bag on the bed.

There was a side room off the living area. It had a low bed and two bunks. I had the room to myself and took the lower bunk.

"There's no key," Karen said from the kitchen as I returned, "but the latch will keep any critters out."

The main room had clapboard walls. There were strips of tongue-and-groove lumber on the ceiling, the same kind of boards as the floor.

Peter asked Gary how much.

"Fifty dollars," said Gary.

Peter feigned, "Fifty?"

"Fifty," said Karen.

Peter's face said he wanted to negotiate.

"Fifty," I said.

"Don't drink the water," said Karen, shifting away from a done deal on the night's rent. "The gold mine. Chemicals," she explained. "They'll kill you, eventually. Brush your teeth with bottled water."

"Um, we're fresh out of bottled water," I said, glancing at Peter.

Gary drove us back to the saloon. "Go have dinner and get bottled water. I'll come down in an hour and lead you back to the cabin. You should bring that Mustang up to the cabin for the night. You're not going to find a mechanic here." He laughed at the thought. "Get it looked at first thing tomorrow in California."

When Paula saw us return, she smiled.

"Got that burrito?" I asked. "We'll share it."

She frowned, but went in search of the mystery food—it was not her preferred offering, just her only one. She returned holding two wrapped offerings, and winced at the minuscule portions—or did she wince at the contents? We were too hungry to say no. I ordered a draft beer and asked her to start pulling a second one.

"Thanks for introducing us to Gary," I said.

"His place is haunted," Paula told us. "That shack has ghosts."

"Tell me the ghosts are in the back room."

"Yes," she said. "That's where. In the back bedroom."

Peter looked at me uneasily.

"Sleep well, my friend," I said, raising my beer. I looked at the draft's pull tab behind the counter; it was Free Style Pilsner from Santa Fe Brewing.

For the first time this evening, I heard noise and laughter coming from nearby. A small party, louder than its size would warrant, was underway in the room behind the bar. From that room emerged a man in his late-twenties. He brashly ordered a bottle of Mike's Hard Lemonade—a liquor-loaded drink—not his first of the night. He laughed as Paula took his drink from the fridge.

"Paula, I'd tip you, but I'm not my dad. Dad tips. I don't. He's got money. Can I have two of those?" He leaned away from the bar and plunged backward into a seat, two stools over from Peter and across from me.

"I'm Mike!" He laughed, as though discovering his identity for the first time. "Motormouth Mike." Looking straight at us, he giggled some more, thinking that we too must find it funny. "Name's 'cuz I talk all the time." His face bent into the fun of the moment. He quaffed his drink while Paula set the second bottle on the counter.

"You guys travelin'?"

"From Chicago," said Peter. "Ten days on. We're driving all the old parts of Route 66. We'll wrap up in L.A. in two days."

"Wow. I'd luv to do that. . . . Not many people do *all* 66, ya know. Driving'z life. Life iz a highway. We get lotsa tourists here in s'nummer. Too many!" Oatman seemed to be a drinking town with a tourist problem.

"You live here?" asked Peter.

"Not me. Visitin' my dad. I work outta town. I'm a mechanic. I can fix anything."

Peter and I looked at one another.

"Can I buy you a drink?" I offered.

Five minutes later, Mike and I were out on the street. I drove the Mustang a bit farther, at his insistence, moving it near a storefront light so that Mike could look under the hood.

"The v-viscosity of your oil is bad," he said, slipping the dipstick back in, missing twice, then finding home. "Change it. Wait—you said rental car? They'll change it. Put STP, blue label, in it. T'morrow."

Mike collapsed on Route 66, slowly and harmlessly, and bent the Mustang's licence plate fully upward, forcing it out of his way. He looked up, under the engine, at the base of the radiator. "Mud. Gotta get that offa there. That's yur problem. Plus, now you've got real water in the radiator from fillin' it yurselfs. Ya need anti-freeze in there. Anti-freeze keeps water from heating too much." He poked around beneath the grill, talking all the while. "That's yur problem. Fer sure. Hose it here." He was still lying on the road, peering up at the radiator. "Don't spray too close. Hold back the power wash, but skim it full."

Mike and I strolled back to the saloon together. Back inside, Peter offered our rescue mechanic another drink, noting that he'd been enjoying his Mike's Hard Lemonade. "Mike, another Mike's?"

"Ha, you noticed! Mike. *Mike's*. Sure. I love that stuff. America at its best."

"Actually, it's from Canada," Peter said, explaining the drink's origins while signaling to Paula the order with two fingers. He then pointed at me. "'Nother beer for my older brother."

Looking at my shirt he said, "First time you've fixed the car and not gotten all covered in dirt."

"Mike did that," I said, raising my beer in Mike's direction. "Leaned right under the car. Fell. Tinkered. Gave good advice."

Mike held up his Mike's and tilted the yellow bottle our way, mud coating his elbow. Just then, a short, lean man came in from the back room, an evening of drinking behind him and within him. Hair sprang from everywhere on his face to form a beard, and on top of his head he wore a round cloth hat that sprouted more hair at its edges. His eyebrows were shaven, his eyelashes were not there. It didn't take long to guess that he and Mike were family, even before Mike said, "That's-a ma dad."

I shook the man's hand and put in an unneeded good word for Mike. "Your son helped us with our car."

"He can fix anything," said Mike senior. "'Cept he could break a hammer in a rubber room."

Gary returned to the saloon in a three-wheel ATV, saying, "You're better to move that Mustang off the road. Who knows what the morning brings on America's Main Street. Follow me."

Peter ordered half a dozen beers to go, and we jostled in the Mustang, bumping over the inclined road, dodging holes the size of a ditch. Gary's three-wheeler rocked back and forth ahead of us, its headlight bobbing. The ATV stopped at the back of Gary's shack, and I drove into the driveway. The dogs again barked furiously at our arrival.

Seeming to be a caricature of outback America when we first met him, Mike (left) quickly proved his worth by fixing something we could not: the Mustang. Even his "dad" (right) was proud of the encounter.

Gary and Karen had left one light on, the door unlatched, and a couple of bottles of water on the counter. And Gary had made good on his promise: "We'll put clean sheets on the bed."

Still, I tossed my sleeping bag on the lower bunk and opened it. I found a little lamp on a chest and put it near the bed so that I could read a 1950s paperback that had been left on the table: *Outlaws of the Wild West*.

“Come out here,” I heard Peter call from the backyard. “Look at this.”

Behind and above us, shadowy in the dark, loomed the mountains, much like those we’d driven through to get here. Above them the sky arched deep and dark. There were no nearby lights. These desert mountains seemed to drift from the ground into the sky in shades of darkness.

“I could sleep outside,” I said, lying on top of a picnic table.

“Here, help me with this,” Peter said, and we pulled a home-built, iron A-frame swinging bench from the cabin porch out into the yard. I sat on the bench, and Peter slumped into a garden chair. A light breeze blew. Wind chimes tinkled. Next door a dog growled.

Evening took as long to whisper its way to silence as morning had taken to rise and find voice.

I heard the cap crack off a long-neck beer bottle. And soon, another.

11

The Backbone of America

"Route 66 is an expression of going somewhere . . . "
—Stirling Silliphant

We woke to find that our shack's backyard was in the shadow of the peak known as the Elephant's Tooth. I tried to walk quietly on the deck behind the shack, so as not to disturb the dogs. But its boards creaked, and I heard a snarl at my feet, then a growl. That really woke me up.

Retreating to the Mustang, I lifted the trunk lid and immediately smelled wet jeans. "We might want a Laundromat today."

"Mold setting in?" Peter asked.

"I think the radiator spew killed that."

I showed Peter the empty water jugs and suggested we top them up from the sink in the cabin.

"Karen told us not to drink the water," he said. "The gold mine's tainted the wells."

"I don't mean for us. I mean for the Mustang."

"If you won't drink it, why would I serve it to our car?" he said.

Down the hill and on America's Main Street, the town of Oatman was slowly coming alive. It has not seen the glory days since the Yucca Bypass of Route 66 took place in October of 1952. That day, the traffic through Sitgreaves Pass was so drastically

A shanty cabin, built with a miner's needs in mind and never planned for a century of additions and compromises, turned out to be our most satisfying stay of the journey.

reduced that only one of seven gas stations in Oatman remained open twenty-four hours later.

We went to Karen's recommended breakfast room at the Oatman Hotel—an establishment no longer offering its rooms for let, but rumored to have the best restaurant within fifty miles in either direction. "If you like movies and trivia, go to the hotel," she had said, continuing a rumor that's become myth. "That's where Clark Gable and Carole Lombard spent their wedding night. Room 15. Imagine!"

The first thing we encountered on the road was a somewhat tame herd of wild burros, descendants of the original pack animals brought here by miners. Peter captured the carnival on camera, gratuitously introducing me and the first donkey that came near: "Ass, meet jackass."

I'd stepped onto the boardwalk and noticed the burro droppings on it. I didn't say anything to Peter, who was behind me, thinking he might step in it. My scheme had a good chance of succeeding, as he was looking across the narrow strip of Route 66 and skyward at a sign.

Across from us hung a painting of a woman marked by a tattoo that looked like both a goatee and a cattle brand.

"Would you look at her!" Peter exclaimed.

"That's Olive Ann Oatman," I said, hoping to keep Peter's eyes on the painting.

Peter sidestepped the burro's scat.

In 1851, at age thirteen, Oatman was captured by Indians who had attacked her family's wagon. It had willingly become separated from a larger contingent of wagons when, days later, the massacre of her family occurred. She was kidnapped and enslaved.

The woman portrayed in the painting looked frightful, though in truth and spirit the facial adornment was not intended to be degrading. Her black hair seemed artificial, as though it had been wrapped tight and pulled onto her head like an overstuffed shower cap. Her face appeared scarred, the result of the ceremonial, striped lines of a Mojave tattoo. This "goatee" was a not uncommon feature of face painting among the tribes of New Mexico, Arizona, and California in the 1800s. It's reputed to once have been a Mojave truth that someone without "marks on the face" would not be accepted into "the land of the dead." Tattoos could be a rite of passage, an accent to body beauty, or an indication of stature.

The Oatman family had traveled west in a large wagon train, protected from hostility by its size. Splitting off from this group, as part of a ten-wagon contingent, the Mormon parents and seven children continued to enjoy relative safety. But their fellow travelers did not approve when Olive's father decided that the family would strike out on its own and head to Arizona's Fort Yuma.

Once alone, the family's hardships included dwindling food supplies, difficult terrain, vanishing paths, and cumbersome river crossings—all with constant fear of an Indian attack. Having forded a river and moved their supplies forward in several shifts, they found themselves being watched, then approached for food by nineteen Indians. The cautious greetings became confrontational. The family was bludgeoned and stabbed. Olive's mother and father were killed immediately, as were four of the children. A roughed-up brother, Lorenzo, thought to be dead, was tossed over an embankment and left behind. Olive and her younger sister, Mary Ann, were taken away.

One can speculate about how they were treated—and there is no lack of innuendo in the writings of the day, but there is nothing to prove that it was inhospitably. They were rumored to be with the Apaches—and were in fact with the Yavapai Indians, who within two years had traded them to the Mojave, near what is now Needles, California. During a celebration the Mojave, as Olive later described it, "put marks on our faces" by pricking her chin "in small regular rows." When the bleeding stopped, the wounds were stuck anew, this time using reeds to ink them with a turquoise powder. The blue chin tattoos (known as *ki-e-chook*) provided identification in case the girls were stolen by another tribe. And it may also have ensured that they would have to endure a certain shame if they escaped back to white society.

Nearly six years after the deaths of her family and two years after her sister died, Olive, now barely able to speak English, was "ransomed" to the U.S. Army. The exchange of the young woman for a horse and blankets is said to have taken place a mile north of what is now Oatman, at a place then referenced as Ollie Oatman Springs.

The horrific story of murder, kidnapping, and forced assimilation turns into that of a nineteenth-century celebrity upon Olive Oatman's reintegration with the society from which she was stolen. Later a popular lecturer, writer, and mother, she understandably never shed memory of the haunting events, despite an eventual happy marriage and a comfortable life in Texas.

Peter had moved on from considering the tattooed woman and was looking at

Thirteen-year-old Olive Oatman was the survivor of an 1851 Indian attack on her family's wagon. She was traded to the Mojaves, had her face tattooed, and six years later was ransomed back to American authorities. The Arizona Historical Society provided this rare image, donated by Warren J. Harris in the 1930s. The donor wrote on the back that this original photo had been purchased by his grandmother from Olive herself.

the cowboy-town facades. Quoting from a pamphlet he held in his hand, he said, "This is where they filmed *How the West Was Won*."

I remembered that 1962 film: tempestuous Debbie Reynolds in one role, serene James Stewart in another, with John Wayne, Carol Baker, and a host of other Hollywood stars who garnered the film many nominations for the Academy Awards. The movie intermingles family stories that arc over sixty years, beginning in 1839, as prospective settlers left the eastern seaboard states for the glamour of California. Its storyline parallels the grand narrative of westward movement in the United States during the nineteenth century: crossing rivers and plains, making war, building a railroad, and fighting outlaws—and, of course, unwelcoming Indians. It is fiction, and therein reinforces America's habit of telling and retelling the nation's adventurous history in a dramatization of "what might have been."

"Too bad that movie didn't tell the real-life story of Olive Oatman," I said, only then realizing that her westbound settler story was much more dramatic than anything fictional.

The mountain portion of Route 66 gently delivered us, in our top-down Mustang, over a rolling landscape, a comforting contrast to the nerve-wracking climbs and unsettling descents of the evening before. Leaving the mountains, we entered the expanse of the Mojave Desert. The early heat was already intense. The plateau, which had looked wonderful from the heights, became intimidating when we landed in it. The Mojave is the southern portion of the Great Basin Desert, the largest desert in North America—covering 190,000 square miles in four states. From ground level, we could see everything and nothing. Here the 1930s migrants must have gasped in disbelief: "*THIS? This* is California?"

Crossing the Colorado River, we left the state of Arizona at Topock. It was at this border that 1930s migrants from the

Midwest were routinely denied "immigrant" status in their own nation—Americans thwarted by Americans. They were dumped in camps and tenements like so much driftwood. They had believed California to be a land of endless plenty, endless jobs, and endless welcome.

A poignant movie scene is set in this very spot.

John Ford's film version of *The Grapes of Wrath*, released in 1940, was shot in seven weeks and was nominated for as many Academy Awards—including one for best director, which it won. It was shot at many locations along Route 66, including in Oklahoma—though never with the presence of lead actors such as Henry Fonda, who said that for this film, they never ventured far from Los Angeles for a shoot. "The river outside

Jane Darwell (Ma Joad), Henry Fonda (Tom Joad), and Russell Simpson (Pa Joad), in John Ford's Academy Award–winning film *The Grapes of Wrath* (1940). (*Photograph © Bettmann/CORBIS*)

Needles, California, where we'd take a bath, was the farthest away we went," Fonda recalled. Gramps is so happy in this scene that he proclaims, "Land of milk and honey!" The camera pans to feisty Grandma, who spits.

It is a movie of parched earth, endless telegraph lines, pipe-smoking women, and humbled sharecroppers—and of Steinbeck's best dialogue. ("Listen. The wind's fixin' to do something.") For today's travelers, those who see the movie before driving Route 66, it becomes a compass. For those who see it upon returning home, it creates unresolved emotions.

Steinbeck felt the movie to be photographically harsher than his writing could convey, and his wife, Carol, said it captured the "salty quality" of his writing. Steinbeck had come to believe that "the only heroes left are . . . the poor," and he praised Ford's portrayals. The land was large; the people were small. Steinbeck and Ford made the people large, too.

Film producer Pare Lorentz, quoted in *U.S. Camera* in 1941, said that "[Dorothea] Lange . . . and [John] Steinbeck . . . have done more for these tragic nomads than all the politicians of the country." It would not be amiss to add John Ford's name to that short list.

Woody Guthrie called the movie the "best cussed pitcher I ever seen."

Peter had become one with the Mustang, as the Joads had with their jalopy; the large flatbed truck with the canvas canopy almost became a character in *The Grapes of Wrath*, with spare tires strapped to its sides and suitcases piled on top. A canvas water sack, like the one I remember my dad taking on car trips when I was a kid, hung off the hood of their vehicle. More than once, it occurred to me that Peter should have brought one along.

Peter swung the car into a gas station in Needles, mindful about our vehicle's suitability for the long desert drive ahead.

I topped up all the fluids, including Motormouth Mike's recommended blue label STP, while Peter pumped gas—precision teamwork that was nine days late in coming. We doglegged around town to see the older Route 66 patches, the flashes of faded fame apparent in sad motels and closed restaurants.

Twenty minutes west of Needles we were on Goffs Road, the earlier 66 passage here, beginning a thirty-mile drive without seeing another car on the desert highway, neither ahead nor behind us. The sense of emptiness was an illusion, of course, as the desert is full of life.

Crossing what Steinbeck called "the bright and terrible desert" today, as before, many travelers choose to pass through in the evening or during the night. Even with air conditioning, the heat is oppressive. The sun's glare destroys concentration and drains energy. It is easy to believe that "California" may be a derivative of the Spanish *caliente forno*: "hot furnace."

We left the Mustang's top down despite the intense sun. Eleven days into our journey, we had only one day left and were not going to spend it sheltered, not even in the shade! We had reached California, the eighth and final state in our litany of experiences. We began to feel the sadness that accompanies the anticipation of the trail's end, but also the satisfaction of our trip's near-completion. The coming miles were to be the last medley of open road; the essential song of America is that of tires humming on pavement. We'd greet the San Gabriel Mountains, Steinbeck's "good mountains," go through busy Cajon Pass, and approach the Los Angeles Basin. We were far away from Broadway's image of America and very near one created by Hollywood.

George Maharis and Martin (Marty) Milner drove their basic-white Corvette into the living rooms of America every Friday night for four years. The television drama *route 66* combined portraits of carefree road adventures and a dash of romance

The construction of plank roads such as this one, photographed in 1961 near the Arizona/California border, enabled automobiles to cross the shifting sands, though the elements caused erosion, warps, and deterioration, limiting the roads' useable life span.

with edgy scriptwriting to convey the uncertainties of America in the early 1960s.

Buz Murdock (Maharis) and Tod Stiles (Milner) balanced one another sharply, playing out as characters with compatible contrasts rather than tension-driven differences.

Buz—black-haired, wearing an unbuttoned shirt over his T-shirt—was tough and troublesome. He was the show's bad boy. Hailing from New York's Hell's Kitchen, he had been left fatherless by the man who died in his arms of a drug overdose. He looked upbeat-poor, a streetwise drifter.

Tod, blond and carefree, had come through Yale and was usually dressed in a tailored blazer. He was invariably at the wheel of the sports car, which had been left to him in his father's will as a last vestige of the family's wealth. His narrow chin pointed to naïveté and optimism.

The back-story for these two characters is that they met up when Buz was working for Tod's father while the family's shipyard business was failing. Tod had come home from Yale for a summer stint of dockside work when his father died suddenly. The two adult "orphans" then left in search of America, themselves, and the 1960s.

Their car (soon to be considered the series' third character) was a Corvette sporting a white soft-top and white horizontal coves on its sides. Chevrolet offered the vehicle as part of General Motors' sponsorship of the television show. The lone Californian among the New Yorkers planning the series, Milner had pitched for something more upscale, advising "Let's get a Ferrari. A Corvette is too common." He was overruled.

George Maharis (left, as Buz) and Martin Milner (as Tod), stars of the original TV series *route 66. (Photograph © Bettmann/CORBIS)*

People still debate the original car's year and color. It is variously identified as a 1961 and a 1960 model. Milner, interviewed decades later, thought it was a 1959. The first one, he said, was "baby-blue-silver," two-tone powder blue, and pale white, which showed up well on CBS's black-and-white television screens, as the network lacked NBC's (then) new color broadcasting capabilities. In fact, when the show first aired on October 7, 1960, Milner and Maharis were in a 1960 "horizon blue" Corvette—a factory color. It crashed in the season's finale—a ploy to facilitate a new season in 1961 featuring that year's Corvette, factory-painted "fawn beige." Each season, General Motors replaced the vehicle, providing two new cars to the TV studio.

The image of the much-loved red (or "more manly" red-and-white) Corvette came not from television's *route 66*, but from related promotional paraphernalia such as kids' lunchboxes, a spin-off board game, and non-TV-show merchandise such as toy cars and model car kits. A reasonable source reports that due to the popular misperception of a red Corvette on the television show, along with the growth of color television's viability (increased color TV set purchases by the public as well as CBS's technical uses), a "red-on-red" Corvette was on order for a following season—though it was rerouted to other purposes when the show was cancelled.

Some references erroneously identify the popular Corvette cars used in the TV series as Stingrays. However, a GM prototype of that name (using a tight lettering of StingRay), developed in 1959, was active only on the race circuit. The Corvette Sting Ray (spelled as two words) was not in commercial production when the TV series began. That car began production in 1963, which was the start of *route 66*'s last television season. The Sting Ray never appeared on *route 66*. ("Stingray," one word, was first used as the Corvette's name in 1969.)

The acclaimed 116 episodes of *route 66* ran from October 1960 to March 1964. The first three episodes were aired immediately following the Richard Nixon–John F. Kennedy presidential-election debates in 1960, ensuring carryover viewers for the premiere season of the series. The hour-long drama aired at 8:00 PM Eastern Time, positioned against ABC's already successful *77 Sunset Strip*. And with that, the real Route 66, *the* road, took center stage in the modern media world.

The idea for the television show originated with two partners who were already making TV history in New York. Scriptwriter Stirling Silliphant had an idea that suited the times. "Why don't we put together a show about two guys riding around the country in a car?" He crafted a script around their odd jobs, dangerous encounters, and mysterious women, ending each story with a Lone Ranger-type, feel-good departure scene.

The producer, Herbert Leonard, shot the pilot as a part of his award-winning *The Naked City* series in the spring of 1960. The last episode of that season's *Naked City*, "Four Sweet Corners," was about a discharged army serviceman taking off to see America. The pilot's plot was set in Alabama and filmed in Kentucky. Originally proposed by Silliphant and Leonard as a new series to be called *The Searchers*, that title was considered a confusing one to introduce on television that season, given John Wayne's recent major motion picture of the same name. That shortcoming, coupled with Columbia's feeling that the pilot lacked clear family values, doomed this first attempt.

Silliphant and Leonard recast their approach, heightening the highway angle, and re-pitched the idea. Repackaged and renamed, the show hooked the CBS executives.

CBS pre-launch discussions led to a road-warrior mystique for the two characters. Always, the show began with Tod and Buz cruising down the paved two-lane highway, earning the show's reputation for "two-lane American morality." Over the years, when viewers tuned in once a week to enjoy an adventure on the renowned Route 66, that was seldom true. Many fans from long ago are surprised to learn that only two of the 116 episodes actually take place *on* Route 66: one in Needles, California, and the other on a pre-1937 Route 66 stretch near Santa Fe, New Mexico. The cast and crew moved on location to eighty-one U.S. communities in twenty-three states. They also made two side trips to Canada, to film episodes in Toronto and Niagara Falls, Ontario.

Early on, Bobby Troup heard that the new show would use "Get Your Kicks . . . " as its theme song. It seemed a natural tie-in. However, to his dismay, "They had Nelson Riddle write the music so they wouldn't have to pay me royalties." He called it "one of the big disappointments of my writing career." On the other hand, Riddle's jazzy composition became an instant hit, and in its own way fuelled generations of "open road" dreamers.

Guest stars lobbied to be on the program: Robert Redford (who was almost cast as Tod instead of Milner), Lee Marvin, Gene Hackman, and Martin Sheen were among those who appeared on the show early in their careers, anxious for exposure on an international television series.

In the latter part of season three, without a word of public explanation, George Maharis disappeared (in real life, suddenly coping with debilitating hepatitis). Nine episodes were quickly written to feature only the Tod Stiles character. Then, again without any explanation to viewers, Glenn Corbett replaced Maharis for the last quarter of the series, taking up as Lincoln (Linc) Case, contrarian sidekick to Milner's Tod.

Route 66's international reputation as a highway was secured with this series, which was dubbed in half a dozen languages and exported around the world. It spoke of America, of freedom, of a land where good won over bad.

NBC (rather than CBS) gave the show a short-lived reprise in 1993, the year after Route 66 celebrated its sixty-sixth anniversary as a highway. The network wrote in Nick, an illegitimate son of Buz Murdock who inherits *his* father's 1961 Corvette in a will. (The show actually used a 1960 Corvette, the last model with a radiator grill that conveyed "teeth." This made it similar to the original season's vehicle.) This time, the 'Vette was suited up in the manufacturer's "roman red" and white to satisfy, even validate, the continuing myth about its color in the 1960s series. And the new show finally capitalized the "R" in its title: *Route 66.* But this time, only four episodes were aired before the new series was cancelled.

Throughout *route 66* 's television run from 1960 to 1964, the formula was a straightforward law of transition: sports car plus two guys equals open road equals freedom. America. Wrapped in the Route 66 aura of restless romance and uncertain outcomes, it became a hit. Scriptwriter Silliphant saw the symbolism implicit in the show's name: "Route 66 is an expression of going somewhere . . . it's the backbone of America."

We drove that backbone at its barest. The National Old Trails Road traverses vacant lands and holds tenuous dots to the map—spots such as Essex, which are so barren and inhospitable that this is where General George Patton's troops trained before they were shipped off to Africa in search of Germany's elusive General Erwin Rommel, the Desert Fox.

Danby came next, then Amboy. Nothing brightened the travelers' day but the unforgiving sun. Here Route 66 is renowned for its failed settlements—the shells of buildings, the desert overcome by graffiti, small towns in commercial purgatory.

As lunchtime neared, we continued to endure the endless drama of flatness. This is where that backbone weakens, where the body America kneels to Mother Nature. There was, however, a diversion to look forward to.

The Bagdad Café is written about more than it is talked about. It is "spotted" by travelers because that is what guidebook writers and mapmakers encourage them to do. The odd stops are often highlighted regardless of their worthiness. On this trip, we'd learned that the smattering of operating businesses generally offered less of interest to us than did deserted, falling-down buildings. One such artificial experience was the Bagdad Café. You wouldn't stop there if you weren't parched. But it existed, so we went in.

Peter ordered the buffalo burger and ate it with relish (the sauce, not the emotion). I poached his french fries and had a wilted salad of my own, graced with recovered chicken. As is our wont in such places, we redesigned the interior of the place in our conversation.

"First I'd clean the windows. Then I'd fix the blinds." Peter took another bite of his burger, and continued with his mouth full. "The lady wasn't busy when we came in, so might she be persuaded to clean up the leftovers on those tables?" He motioned his head toward several messy tabletops and their unappetizing display of past meals.

"It'd take nothing to straighten the pictures on the walls, wash the T-shirts on display, and maybe add a few posters for ambiance. Maybe they don't have the money to fix the torn vinyl on the seats, but a hundred bucks would buy a lot of Route 66 mementos to patch over the gouges in the walls. Then there's the concept of paint."

Noteworthy as the site of the movie of the same name (mostly, though, that was filmed in nearby Newberry Springs), Bagdad Café (an opportunistic renaming of the Sidewinder Café) rests ridiculously on those laurels. Were it not for the name and the movie connection, it'd be bypassed quicker than you can say "interstate." I wondered what their service would be like if the Harvey House were still operating at the Bagdad Depot. Were a Dunkin' Donuts shop to open next door, this place would close within twenty-four hours for lack of customers. If it had to rely on its references rather than its remoteness, it would starve.

Our pace seemed to quicken as we neared the population centers. The route's wild aloneness faded in the rearview mirror; roads mattered more here—at least, the one we were on mattered to more people.

We decided on a last, slow piece of travel, Swarthout Canyon Road, dodging the interstate for a final experience of the "old road." It began near the Cleghorn Road exit and swung out of sight of the freeway. This short glimpse lets anyone with an uncommitted quarter hour in their life (and who doesn't have that?) feel the purity of Route 66. We drove along Cajon Creek, over the venerable span, past tarnished blue rocks and views below of pieces of Route 66 that remained from its first and second decades. When this road ended, something else ended, too. We got out of the car and took to our feet. We strolled fifty paces on the old road and up to the woods, where we spontaneously urinated on a tree stump near the final abutment, and out of sight of the freeway, marking the shoulder of Route 66 as our own—a respectful graffiti of sorts. Boys will be boys.

I read verbatim from Peter's cherished *EZ66 Guide* (yelled, actually) as we left Route 66's last vestige of tranquillity and shot onto the interstate. "Join I-15 southbound. QUICKLY move to the middle/left lanes (signs: 'Riverside/San Bernardino I-215'). I-15 splits right: BEAR LEFT with I-215, but QUICKLY take the NEXT off ramp (signs: 'Devore Road/Glen Helen Park Right Lane' and 'Historic 66 Next Right'). Once the offramp merges with the other road QUICKLY get in the RIGHT LANE and EXIT again to DEVORE. TURN LEFT on Cajon Boulevard . . . " Whew. This eventually got us into San Bernardino.

After passing through San Bernardino, Route 66 takes a bow to history and heads west to prosperity. It might be here that the road is most heavily laden with a mixture of sorrow, stillborn dreams, laughter, and hope. For the migrants of the 1930s who made it this far, the journey's terrible memories were replaced with anticipation.

California's insatiable appetite for growth has always benefited from a transient underclass willing to do its menial jobs—pick its fruit and vegetables, wash up after its consumption, mind its children, mend its socks. The trouble is, the members of this class want to stay. California is the transients' end-terminal. Few want to return home, wherever home may have been. The greatest influx of immigrants to the state today is from Latin America—it has been so for decades, as it is in other U.S. states that border Mexico. They're welcome when wanted, and illegal when they arrive in surplus numbers. Migrant Latinos have become the new Okies, and today they see Route 66 as simply a line to be crossed when heading north.

California has long had a leading role in building four-lane expressways and paving over precious land (hands up, those surprised). It competed with Illinois for that role and, to be fair, has many cities in which residents wanted enhanced mobility, faster movement of goods, and greater safety. Ironically, those very reasons for the creation of Route 66 eventually pushed it into the margins of U.S. transportation.

Route 66 stopped being about the future and started being about its past when President Dwight Eisenhower signed the National Interstate and Defense Highways Act on June 29, 1956. As it had evolved, trail by trail, road by road, Route 66 had been held together by politics. That political engineering was near an end. Eisenhower himself had endured awkward and dangerous crossings of the United States in military vehicles that got stuck in the mud on poorly constructed roads. Later, with the allies in Europe, he had admired the German autobahn for its efficiency and reliability, a concept he brought home to America after the Second World War. But it was not his only reason for wanting to reconfigure the road system. He was also aware that the Nazis had used the autobahn to land armed forces planes and supply planes.

I recalled a roadside coffee shop we'd visited a few days back and the cranky couple sitting next to us, eavesdropping on our banter. They sat shifting food around their plates as though they'd been married too long to want to converse with each other. When Peter left the table to use the washroom, the man looked over at me. He pulled his suspender with his thumb, let it go with a hardy slap and began to brag about the interstate, which surprised me. I'd guessed that, by age and disposition, he'd be a fan of Route 66.

"Interstate brought me here. Brought us here," he added, after noticing his wife's stare. "We weren't local way-back-when, so Route 66 doesn't have the same cachet for us. I like the wide, wide road. I paved it . . . well, helped pave it. That was my job."

"Only in the east of the state," his wife said.

He ignored this clarification and boasted, "You know, these interstates came from the Defense Highway Act. After World War Two, the government mandated that one mile in every five of the interstate be straight as an airplane landing strip in time of war."* He then suggested cautiously, "Or . . . civil unrest. I was a Nixon man." I could not figure this out, and wondered if he harbored fears of student unrest or felt that an uprising was in the works.

He released his re-extended suspender again and it slapped against his wrinkled shirt. He had said his piece. Both he and his wife turned away from me and again stirred their food with their forks.

---

* One authority I later found on *HistoryNet.com* clarified this myth, saying that "no law, regulation, policy, or sliver of red tape requires that one out of every five miles of the interstate highway system be straight." The impracticality of the requirement would be evident to road builders who engineer around mountains and in treacherous areas.

By 1984, Route 66 had been bypassed by rival roads I-55, I-44, I-40, I-15, and I-210, which together formed a continuous super-path. In 1985, federal transportation administrators cast a formal vote, altering the national road network and eliminating this favored road, the only highway ever deleted from the original 1926 grid. It is not that they began to erase existing maps; they simply forgot about the road when updating grids or reprinting maps or creating new maps. Route 66 went from being chock-a-block busy, carrying tens of thousands of vehicles per day, to becoming a spur line to suddenly-remote locations. The only thing that remained unchanged was that Route 66 passed through three time zones.

It was still daylight when we arrived on Foothill Boulevard and spotted the Wigwam Village Motel at Rialto. Peter, clearly excited, said, "Let's stop!"

I drove on in silence, ignoring him, thinking I'd be able to invoke the Ten-Second Rule if only I kept my mouth shut.

He said it again. "Go back! We should stay there." I counted in my mind *seven, eight, nine . . .*

"Seriously. I know you don't believe this," he wheedled, "but I'd like to see that place." He was within the ten seconds—barely—and I turned around.

The Disney/Pixar movie *Cars* has a teasing reflection of this motel. It is, in keeping with the Route 66 car-road motif of that movie, called the Cozy Cone Motel, and its design evokes these teepees. Here, we had twenty-foot-high teepees, never meant to shelter Native Americans. The Wigwam chain began operations in 1933, and eventually operated seven such motor courts. This Wigwam was the last one built, in 1950.

This motel's managers, from the *real* India, told us they had rooms available and handed us a couple of rooms' keys to have a look. The rooms are clever, in a 1950s way—great fun for kids (or adults) not schooled in the nuances of this country's indigenous people. They seemed to express the trinket mentality popularized by early railroad marketers, and highway boosters who wished to portray native people as caricatures. Peter came to this conclusion, all on his own, and we left.

As the day progressed, we cruised Route 66 on Foothill Boulevard in a sequence: Rialto to Fontana, Rancho Cucamonga to Glendora. Eventually Foothill yields to Huntington Drive, and later the road reclaims the designation of Foothill, then yields again, this time to become Colorado Boulevard, on which we entered Pasadena. Here there is no sorrow for the bygone days of Route 66. There are many glimpses of the route's iconography—its rise, fall, and resurrection. Beautiful old signs here are being revived as part of a program to emphasize the road's heritage.

Remarking on this, George Maharis said to interviewer Ron Warnick about Route 66, "It's a great old road. It's too bad what [the interstates] did to it. Now they realize the impact that it's had, and they're trying to preserve it. That's good. It's part of our history."

In Pasadena, we headed to the Saga Motor Lodge, hoping for a last night on the road in old Route 66 style. We drove under the 1950s portico, thinking there'd be rooms available, if the lack of vehicles parked in front was any indication.

"We're closed tonight," the front desk manager said as we walked in. "Power's off."

"That's fine with us. Give us the keys and a good rate," said Peter. "We'll stay wherever you tell us."

"We're closed tonight. Power's off."

That should have been our hint. The man told us he didn't know which rooms were rented and which were not. "Computer's off."

Peter tried to get us keys, advising the manager on how simple it was to solve the problem ("Send a housekeeper to knock on the doors. If two are empty, we'll take them."). I can't imagine what the price might have been.

Soon we were heading back to a spot on the road swarming with motels and motor courts. The first two were Best Westerns, and we parked between them. Peter opened the trunk to fiddle with papers in his briefcase.

I was the first one into the lobby, for the only time on the trip.

"You got two rooms?"

"Yes," said the girl behind the counter.

"Great. We'll take them." And I put my credit card down.

Peter came in carrying his luggage, saw my credit card on the counter, and felt I'd usurped his negotiation role. "Did you get us a good price?"

"Best rate in Pasadena."

12

America's Main Street

"Route 66 was and is the best of us, and perhaps even the worst of us . . . "

—National Historic Route 66 Federation

One of the best parts of any journey is packing for home—so long as you can tuck satisfaction into your old kit bag alongside the sadness of completion. Soon, the commotion of travel will be over. Regrets—the missed Laundromat being one—were there in the smells and skipped opportunities. The last morning of our drive, as I walked toward the motel office to square our bill, I stopped and saluted the road. I bowed to Route 66. It had taught me. America is more than the sum of its flaws; America, as seen via Route 66, is at once compound and intriguing, frustrating and invigorating, truthful and false. There was much more of America's Main Street available to travel today than we had known about before our drive. We had been forced onto the interstate for only a few hundred miles of our journey. Amid it all, the route has kept its dignity as a destination, if not as a highway—over 2,000 of the original highway's 2,448 connected miles were still approachable, if not always drivable. It has avoided becoming merely an asterisk of tourism; it remains an exclamation mark of travel.

I leaned against the lamppost in front of the motor court. It was time to say goodbye to memories of the making and unmaking of the road. Our trip had resulted not so much in a journey as in a discovery.

Early routes across the United States inevitably became focus points for commerce, and commerce meant housing nearby. Villages became towns; some towns became cities. And so it was that the main useful street for the cluster of businesses was, as often as not, capitalized into Main Street.

A steady stream of traffic linked the Main Street of one town to the Main Street of the next in a continuous string of service centers. Route 66 introduced both a practical and a philosophical thread in America. It was not the longest of highways, so perhaps it was the diversity of the states and communities it linked that garnered the world's attention and, later, its respect. Miles of myths have earned Route 66 its designation as "America's Main Street."

Peter showed up in the motel's lobby unshaven and wearing the same shirt for the third day. His shoes were scuffed, and one shoe's lace was undone.

America's Main Street became for me a series of stories, symbolized by a baseball player, a roadbuilder, a novelist, a photojournalist, a humorist, a political poet, a songwriter, a jazz musician, two actors, and a Corvette. There is more, to be sure, yet it is through these images and characters that we can learn much about such a public road. Each of them recognized that Route 66 was America's podium. Mickey Mantle, Cyrus Avery, John Steinbeck, Dorothea Lange, Will Rogers, Woody Guthrie, Bobby Troup, Nat King Cole, Martin Milner, and George Maharis fold into one another as neatly as the pleats of a fan.

It is easy to misjudge a nation by resorting to stereotypes. John Steinbeck, after much soul-searching and many encounters with his country's people, wrote in *Travels With Charley*:

> Traveling about, I early learned the difference between an American and the Americans. They are so far apart that they might be opposites. Often when a European has described the Americans with hostility and scorn he has turned to me and said, "Of course, I don't mean you. I am speaking of those others." It boils down to this: the Americans, the British are the faceless clot you don't know, but a Frenchman or an Italian is your acquaintance and your friend. He has none of the qualities your ignorance causes you to hate.

Nothing breaks down bigotry and prejudice quite like meeting face to face with those you don't understand, leaning on their fence post, and listening to their stories.

The opposite of the people's love for Route 66 is government indifference. Government and time have conspired to hide much of the route from public view. Technically, it no longer exists, in the eyes of federal gazetteers. It may have been airbrushed from government maps—but not from travelers' maps. Route 66 has held on to a stubborn belief that it has not died.

All told, Route 66 is embraced in over a dozen organizations' mission statements. That's before one adds publications, local businesses, tourism aficionados, and political commentators. The overarching entity for many years, though not having any such governance structure or mandate, was the National Historic Route 66 Federation. Related, but not directly connected to it, are the eight state Route 66 associations.

The federation was sparked to life in 1994 by David and Mary Lou Knudson, who lamented: "We drove from Chicago to L.A. and we could *not* find Route 66. Maps ignored it. The signs treasured from [our] youthful travels were gone. The road seemed to have disappeared. When we did find fragments, the once-thriving businesses and small towns seemed deserted. Their abandoned structures stood as silent reminders of America's Glory Road."

The Knudsons rededicated their lives to "save as much as possible of Route 66 before it was completely gone." It was as though the ghostly hand of Cyrus Avery had reached across seven decades and passed the torch.

The federation's role became one of public advocacy, the badgering of elected officials for funds, and the creation of a checklist of requirements: heritage property refurbishments, zoning assistance for historic districts, and the replenishment of Route 66 symbols on the road, as well as the erection of new metal shield signs, replicas of the original stamped steel or porcelain-enameled ones. The federation's simple message appears to have been "Don't mess with Route 66." It partnered with, even followed, the leadership activities of state associations and governments. "Sometimes you lead, sometimes you follow—always you cross-support one another," says David Knudson.

The federation's Adopt-A-Hundred Program now covers all the surviving sections of Route 66 with bite-size jurisdictions where volunteers focus on biannual reviews and ongoing preservation projects.

However, it is with the federal government's National Route 66 Preservation Act that the rubber meets this road. The act's $10 million investment can reach every nook and most crannies of Route 66. The federation's role in all this is that of provocateur: "We spearheaded that bill for four years."

Lobbying by the federation and by others resulted in the National Route 66 Corridor Preservation Act of 1999, which in March 2009 was extended for a second ten-year mandate, though with an allotment of only $10 million—a measly amount, federal budget dust.

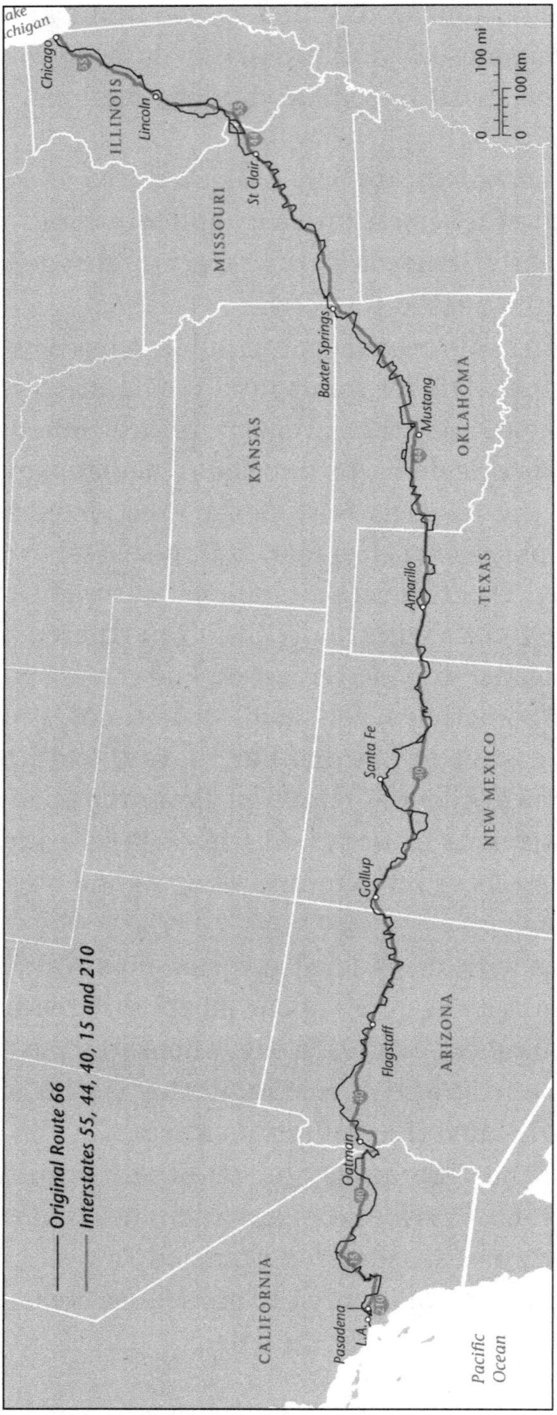

"America's Main Street" then and now, with most of the old route still reachable, though not always driveable. Note how Route 66's original, meandering course has been forsaken, paved over, or disassembled by the five superhighways. Place names designate Rick and Peter's overnight stays.

As the federation notes, "Route 66 was and is the best of us, and perhaps even the worst of us, but it will always be a part of our American Dream."

The morning of day twelve, the last morning of our trip, I was driving, following the tacit agreement we had made when Peter began our journey behind the wheel. My goal was simply to get us safely to Will Rogers Park, the modest memorial to a great man, where it overlooks the blue waters of the Pacific Ocean, bringing green grass to the faded boardwalk of Santa Monica Pier.

First, though, we glided along and onto Santa Monica Boulevard, setting a peaceful pace. We were pleased to see more designation signs noting California's claim to Route 66. They continued to be the most consistent and continuously formalized symbols of the route's delineation. In clear agreement, stores and plazas too claimed the Route 66 brand as their own—both in their signage and in their context.

Route 66 has no brand manager, no brand steward. The untamed highway appears to have an untamed brand. Almost everywhere en route, this is left to the vagaries of opportunists and misappropriation. It seems too important to allow that inconsistency to continue as Route 66 comes to terms with its past. A brand is a promise, not simply a marketing slogan. Route 66's brand promise is unequivocally: "Get your kicks on Route 66 . . . "

Route 66 is a beer, a root beer, and fridge magnets. In the past I have seen Route 66 cigarettes on sale at a train station in Warsaw, Poland, and have bought Route 66 Rum at a liquor store in Nassau, The Bahamas. I saw neither for sale on the actual Route 66.

If you were to list the insignias in the "Brand U.S.A." portfolio, that list would include the American flag, Coca-Cola, the Statue of Liberty, McDonald's golden arches, Bourbon Street, the Empire State Building, Golden Gate Bridge, Mickey Mouse, and a few mistakes. The Route 66 shield deserves to be among the top ten positive symbols.

But the "shield" is a logo, not a brand, and 66 is not alone in its use of the sheriff's badge design for its road signs. Unique about its designation are the matching digits and a high-profile combination of brown and white that claims immediate recognition.

Early in the 1900s, road signs were hand-lettered, and even official ones used fence posts or tree stumps as props. The continuity required for a nation-wide grid of roads demanded consistent signage. At a Kansas City meeting in May 1925, E. W. James, the Bureau of Public Roads' chief of design, presented a concept that he and Frank Rogers had developed from a Maine shield labeled "U.S. 56." It received encouragement at the meeting, and that positive response would have an unforeseen, immeasurable further impact.

Oklahoma's Cyrus Avery and Missouri's highway commissioner, B. H. Piepmeier, were seated at that table. Avery, foreshadowing his later proposal of "66" as a highway number, tabled a sample for the look of the new national signs. Having seen James's concept earlier that year, Avery had worked up an Oklahoma rendition in black on yellow. It showed "U.S. 66." Avery conceded that the black-and-white elements were superior; however, he had put down a soft hold on the "66" moniker.

"Stay on Colorado, eyes left, and then we'll take the Arroyo Seco Parkway. It's from 1940. It was one of the first U.S. freeways." This from Peter.

"Still there?" I asked.

"Just drive." As the trip wore on, there was more of a twinkle in his eyes when he was blunt or passed judgment about me, something that implied, "Sorry, I had to say that," without, of course, mouthing the word "sorry."

This road has forged many friendships over nearly a century, and it furthered ours. Not that either of us said that out loud; it was there in the unspoken interpretations. Over beer the night before, we'd reminisced about a stretch of abandoned Route 66 back in Oklahoma ("or was it Missouri?" Peter asked, uncertain as the days merged in his mind). It was perhaps half a mile long, and was blocked by an embankment, but we noticed it as we drove on a more recent, but still old, alignment. We stopped and walked over the dirt obstacle to get to it.

Trees encroached on the road; some were over six feet high and had grown through cracks in the pavement. Peter pointed to a laneway through a ditch and up a slope where we could drive, so we got back in the car and made it onto this brush-covered piece of history, warts, warps, and all. I drove carefully, winding my way around the small trees, bumping over a fallen tree.

Peter walked the pavement behind, taking pictures. He climbed into the Mustang when I was stopped by the overgrowth, and I started to back up along old Route 66, pushing the scrub brush out of our way with our bumper. That's when he said it, the telling comment: "I'd never do this on my own. Just wouldn't happen in my life."

This day's drive, particularly in comparison, was efficient. Route 66 peters out the closer it gets to its climax. Hollywood and environs still post the route, and the streets, though very busy, feel like Route 66 in their sense of place for 1960s-vintage snapshots. It is as though these parts went oh-so-modern at that time and have since then been trapped in a time warp. You could park this street full of cars from the 1960s, and the stage would be set. Housing, businesses, transportation—it would all fit.

As we drove through Hollywood and Beverly Hills, it surprised us that we were still, technically, on Route 66. Along the movie-making strip, with its studios and post-production shops and agencies, any driver would slow to enjoy the art deco designs. It is no less special because of its "everydayness."

The CD *More Songs of Route 66* set our mood, and for the umpteenth time the Steve James recording of "66 Highway Blues" cycled through: "Been on this road for a mighty long time . . . " is sung over and around simple guitar-picking that is extraordinary for its quickness, though the tune is not complicated. The songwriter tells us: "I'm going down this road with troubles on my mind . . . "

It was a ballad with an enviable provenance and timely truths. On a summer evening in 1940, Woody Guthrie and Pete Seeger picked at strings and plucked at emotions after Woody had brought Seeger to his hometown of Okemah, Oklahoma. One result was this song about the working man, the hungry man, but they let the song drift afterwards, recorded, but not released. Then James and others picked up the message and the music, and regifted it to contemporary folks.

Toward the end of his biography of Woody Guthrie, Joe Klein writes about "Woody's gift to his descendants: the freedom to walk away, go off to some other town or a different place inside your head; the freedom to come back home again and do what you were doing in the first place. The freedom to try any old thing; the freedom to start over. There is nothing more American than that."

Route 66 has its long-standing California terminus at Lincoln and Olympic. We knew this from the guidebooks. Were it not for the write-ups, a passerby would be oblivious to the importance of this intersection. There are no signs, building names, or street names that acknowledge its importance. There is no mention of what is happening when one drives down Lincoln and crosses Olympic. The lack of awareness of the westward "end" and of the corresponding eastward "start" of Route 66 was odd to us.

The original western terminus of Route 66 was in Los Angeles at 7th Street and Broadway, right downtown. That eventually shifted south and west to Lincoln and Olympic, and four years later, the theoretical end of Route 66 was moved again, on a promotional whim, to Santa Monica Pier, thus providing an emotional, if unofficial, anchor tenant for the commercial property. Then, in the fall of 2009, during celebrations of the eighty-third anniversary of America's Main Street, the new Route 66 Alliance formally endorsed the Santa Monica Pier as the "End of the Trail."

Having crossed over dozens of bridges on the open road, we now ended on a pier, an inconclusive jetty of wood pointed at Asia. Of course, it is much easier to park your car, reflect, and applaud the accomplishment on a pier than it is at the original terminus's busy intersection. It is easier to take photographs on the pier, where onlookers and self-absorbed motorists pose no hazard to speeding vehicles.

After I parked on a slip of Ocean Avenue, it was over.

I stared at the last piece of pavement that could claim lineage with Route 66 and found myself humming Woody Guthrie's "So long, it's been good to know yuh . . . "

Peter looked over at me and I thought he was going to say something cutting, so I prepared a sarcastic remark in retaliation. But we just stared at one another until he finally nodded, and I nodded—at both the unstated end and the overwhelming satisfaction. Dorothea Lange articulated feelings I shared when she once wrote after a road journey, "I wish I could work the whole trip over again, go to the same places—knowing what I know now . . . "

Friendships can bind or slip when much time is spent together. Ours weathered the weeks of close quarters, perhaps because we always had separate rooms. Peter had given up an overscheduled life to come on this freewheeling trip. What had he gained? Much respect for the looseness of time, I thought. A stronger friendship, I hoped. Yet, looking at his face, I thought it betrayed some anxiety, perhaps at leaving the road, more likely at returning to the constant demands of his business life.

I opened my mouth to say something but he raised his hand, "Don't you go getting sensitive on me."

We lunched amidst Santa Monica Pier's hyped-up vigor with a friend who had lived in Santa Monica for two years. His awareness of Route 66's relevance in this part of town was skimpy, yet his response to our accomplishment was hearty. We swallowed big mugs of Alaskan Summer Ale with codfish and chips. As Peter picked up a piece of fish and bit into the greasy crust, he reminisced, "I think I'll miss the shiny food places we found along Route 66."

It was more than the route's geographic directness that made this road stand out from the others; it was more than the name. But what was it? There are other twin-digit designations; the assignment of consecutive identical digits eventually included U.S. Routes 11, 33, 44, 77, and 99, U.S. Highways 22 and 88, and Interstate 55. Only the latter and Route 66 were graced with songs of their own. Many of the other federal highways were subsequently devolved to state status.

When I first read of Will Rogers's association with Route 66 and the work undertaken by his admirers to attach his name to it, I'd thought it presumptuous to replace the established name. From further reading, though, I became aware that there were gaps along the route—statewide gaps, where there was no mention of the Will Rogers Highway. There is, however, Palisades Park, where a brass plaque sits atop a chipped cement slab to commemorate the man. It reads: "Will Rogers Highway, dedicated in 1952 to Will Rogers, Humorist, World Traveler, Good Neighbor. This Main Street of America, Highway 66 was the first road he traveled in a career that led straight to the hearts of his countrymen."

I'd like to paraphrase columnist Damon Runyon's comment that Will Rogers was the "most complete American" and suggest that Route 66 is the "most complete American road."

Route 66 highway signs had long been scavenged by collectors and vandals, but a methodical removal had been underway with each increment of interstate. Overlooking the road's culture, history, heart, and pulse, the states it ran through consciously eliminated the recognition of its having been there. It had fallen victim to an evolutionary trend in transportation, "survival of the fastest."

On January 17, 1976, a *Chicago Sun-Times* photographer clicked the seminal shot of Route 66's demise: two Chicago city employees taking down the last of the highway signs that for fifty years had welcomed cross-country travelers to the eastern terminus. The photograph, taken at Grant Park, was newsworthy because Route 66 was also coming off the map—in atlases, on service station walls, and from federal government charts. The road was on its way to history's dustbin, and the road signs were on their way to the city archives.

The photograph shows Chicago civic worker John Chesniak's gloved hand passing the unhinged sign down the ladder to hard-hatted Gus Schultz, who is standing in the snow. It is poignant, not for the magic "66" shield, but for the definitive message that had so long graced that particular lamp standard at the intersection of Jackson Boulevard and Lake Shore Drive: END OF ROUTE 66. Now the sign took on a whole new meaning.

Route 66 was once—and it is again today—one long, rambling sentence that describes America, with Chicago its capitalized start and Los Angeles its ending period. The dashes in the sentence are cities such as St. Louis, Oklahoma City, and Albuquerque; its necessary commas are spots such as Joliet, Commerce, Depew, and Santa Fe. And then there's the rest—let's say McLean, St. Clair, Arcadia, Gallup—places where we pause to catch our breath in the story.

Peter swerved the Mustang into the rental agency at Los Angeles International Airport. Once again, it was a squeaky-

More telling than intended, the removal of this sign in downtown Chicago in 1977 reflected the demise of a through-road that once linked a nation. *(Photograph © 2012 Associated Press)*

clean vehicle, it had a full tank of gas and its engine fluids were topped up, and the hand-wiped dash shone. The convertible roof was clamped down. Preparing to abandon our travel companion in the corral of sameness that becomes a car lot, Peter and I grabbed our bags from the trunk.

Then Peter slammed the trunk lid shut—a final, firm pat for our reliable friend. There was a sound, and I turned to look. A clump of red Oklahoma mud had fallen to the pavement under the Mustang.

Epilogue

A 2,400-Mile Declaration of Independence

"Anyone who has ever bet against this country has lost."

—John Ibbitson

Route 66 still kicks. As does America.

Peter and I bent to clichés. By traveling on America's Main Street, we "traveled the road [once] most traveled." And we let a 2,400-mile journey become "the destination."

I'd embarked on this trip convinced that America is more hung up on myths than on reality, more tied to perceptions than to facts. The trip validated that, though it left me with a sense that this situation was okay. It is fine to be confused if you're complex, and America is certainly complex. Will Rogers said of his America: "There is no other country with as much air, and not knowing where it's going, as this country."

It is a familiar conversation topic to say that the United States is flagging, diminished. Well, that's a debate. America may be in a rough patch, but as columnist John Ibbitson writes, "Anyone who has ever bet against this country has lost."

Route 66 is in a class of its own, compared with the homogenized freeways of easy American travel. It has been called everything from "The Migrant's Highway" to the "Heart Line of the Nation" and "America's Byway," even "America's Longest Traffic Jam." It has never been called the "Carefree Highway."

Route 66 symbolizes one of the great ironies of America. It once carried unwilling refugees over roads once used by unwanted settlers. This state-to-state emigration contributed to America's sense of itself as a rootless society. And it made Route 66 the most human of highways.

Route 66 became America's pathway from its generational past to its future; it is not only the Mother Road, it is the grandmother road. It is a mainstay of American legend, on a par with the Alamo. It is a teacher road, a giver of perspective and lessons.

Perhaps Woody Guthrie portrayed the highway euphemistically in a seldom-heard stanza of "This Land Is Your Land," one that had been part of his "theme song" during his short-lived (twelve-week) New York radio show over the winter of 1944–45: "Nobody living can ever stop me/As I go walking my freedom highway/Nobody living can make me turn back/This land was made for you and me."

If, as the truck driver told me years ago, "You'll never understand America until you've driven Route 66—that's *old* Route 66—all the way," is it a corollary that once you've driven this sliver of road, you *do* understand America? I think not—not fully—but you are given tantalizing hints, clues, and suggestions. Traveling Route 66 is not about *understanding* America; it is about *contemplating* America. The difference is vast. America is not to be understood.

This, though, I do understand: Route 66 is a 2,400-mile declaration of independence. Perhaps that's what the truck driver meant.

Afterword

A trip often brings perspective and understanding only much later, and many months afterward I realized it had been one helluva drive. That's when I began writing snippets to find out what this book wanted to be. I replayed all the songs Peter and I had found along the route, listening between the chords and choruses; learning, always learning from the ballads and folksongs about an America often forgotten but not gone. I leaned on Woody Guthrie's words as I wrote: "There's a feeling in music, and it carries you back down the road you have traveled and makes you travel it again."

In 2012, the titular Route 66 experience arrived in a condensed form, available to anyone with a few hours to spare after their visit to Disneyland. Next door, Cars Land opened, featuring a four-and-a-half-minute Route 66 trip that zips and dawdles over a "journey." The film *Cars* bursts into "auto-animatronics" life as part of the billion-dollar amusement park known as Disney's California Adventure.

The Radiator Springs Racers are the attraction, and those who have seen *Cars* can imagine the Disney "Imagineers" cackling over a ride that has Mater, the reverse-only towtruck, backing away from guests while bantering with them. Visitors can sample the landscape of Radiator Springs' Texas Panhandle-New Mexico-Arizona-like setting without having to leave the twelve-acre California lot. Get ready for Route 66-lite. And settle back for Mater's Junkyard Jamboree.

Lightning McQueen and Sally invite you to their small world.

Ten months after our road trip, Peter was still fighting the Chicago parking ticket.

Chronology

1838—Cherokee Trail of Tears

1853—Wipple Expedition (exploration along much of a similar routing to eventual Route 66)

1866—Atlantic and Pacific Railway begins, envisioned as a transcontinental railroad

1892—National League of Good Roads is formed

1902—Founding of the American Automobile Association

—Founding of the National Old Trails Association

1914—Ozark Trail (St. Louis to Tulsa) and National Old Trail (Santa Fe to Los Angeles), predecessors to Route 66

1916—Federal Aid Road Act

1917—United States enters First World War (conflict begun in 1914)

1924—American Association of State Highway Officials chooses Cyrus Avery to lead the new federal highway system's layout and number designations

1925—Initiation of Burma-Shave promotional highway signs

—Disputed transcontinental "U.S. 60" designation for Chicago route to Los Angeles. American Association of State Highway Officials adopts "shield" sign designed by E. W. James and Frank T. Rogers, which would eventually be infamous with use as "Route 66"

1926—Formal designation of U.S. Route 66, November 11, nationwide highway numbering system adopted

1927—Founding of National U.S. 66 Highway Association

—Santa Fe bypassed with new Route 66 alignment

1929—U.S. stock market crash
1932—U.S. Highway 66 map published in combination with National Old Trails Road map
1930—Introduction of Phillips 66 logo, which mimics that of Route 66
1935—*"The worst of dust storms that ever filled the sky,"* April 14
1938—Paving of Route 66 from Chicago to L.A. (Santa Monica) completed, including the new portion west from Santa Rosa direct to Albuquerque
—Route 66 declared "The Will Rogers Highway"
1939—John Steinbeck publishes *The Grapes of Wrath*
1940—Woody Guthrie writes "This Land Is Your Land"
—John Ford releases *The Grapes of Wrath* film, starring Henry Fonda
1941—United States enters the Second World War (conflict begun in 1939)
1944—National System of Interstate Highways act passed by U.S. Congress
1946—Bobby Troup, at the inspiration of his wife Cynthia, writes "(Get Your Kicks) On Route 66"
—Nat King Cole records "(Get Your Kicks) On Route 66"
—Publication of *A Guide Book to Highway 66* by Jack D. Rittenhouse
—Post Second World War–travel boom hits Route 66, lasts until mid-1950s
1956—National Interstate and Defense Highways Act passed
1960—Premiere of *route 66* television series, starring Martin Milner and George Maharis
—Nelson Riddle's orchestra releases "Route 66 Theme"
1965—Highway Beautification Act passes U.S. Congress
1977—*Chicago Sun-Times* publishes "End of Route 66" photograph

1984—Final bypass of last section of Route 66 constructed at Williams, Arizona

1985—American Association of State Highways and Transportation votes to decertify Route 66

—Official decommissioning of Route 66 as a highway designation, June 26

1990—Route 66 restoration needs acknowledged by the U.S. Congress with passing of the Route 66 Study Act

—Premier issue of *The Mother Road Journal*

—Publication of *Route 66: The Mother Road* by Michael Wallis

1993—Premiere issue of *Route 66 Magazine*

1994—National Historic Route 66 Federation is created

1995—Jason Eklund releases song "What's Left of Route 66"

1999—National Route 66 Preservation Bill (National Route 66 Corridor Preservation Act) passed by U.S. Congress

2001—National Park Service Route 66 Corridor Preservation Program established

2003—Bob Moore and Rich Cunningham publish *The Complete Guidebook to Route 66* and *The Complete Atlas to Route 66*

—Route 66 Preservation Foundation active (lasts until 2011)

2006—Release of Disney/Pixar feature film *Cars*, featuring Route 66

—First issue of *Route 66 Pulse* newspaper

2007—America's Most Endangered Historic Places lists a range of Route 66 motor courts

2008—Route 66 named to World Monuments Fund's watch list of endangered sites

—Jerry McClanahan publishes *EZ66* Guide, 2nd edition

2009—Congress extends National Route 66 Corridor Preservation Act for ten years

2011—"About 5.5 million people live within one mile of Route 66 (the Route 66 Corridor)," according to Rutgers study

2012—Cars Land, featuring Route 66, opens next to Disneyland, in California

2014—Musical Road section created, "singing road at 45 miles per hour," in Tijeras, New Mexico, near Albuquerque
2015—Road Ahead Partnership formed to "rescue and protect" portions of the old road
2017—*America's Longest Small Town* published, Jim Hinkley, Voyager Press
2018—U.S. Bicycle Route 66 system, underway; parallels historic Route 66
2020—Route 66 Centennial Commission Act passed by senate: route66-centennial.com
—*Route Magazine* launched, building upon *Route 66 Magazine*'s legacy
2021—*Route 66 Magazine*, launched 1992, no longer published with passing of Paul Taylor, co-publisher with his wife Sandi.
2023—Lou Mitchell's diner at start of Route 66, Chicago, 100th anniversary
2024—Proposed Congress legislation: The Route 66 National Historic Trail Designation Act aims to formally designate Route 66 as a National Historic Trail
2025—Route 66 RoadFest AAA, launched
2026—Route 66 Centennial 1926–2026

Acknowledgements

This book's introduction says that "Road trips, like marriages, are about compromises," and my first acknowledgement needs to be for my travel companion, Peter Armstrong. If there are times when the writer seems to take liberty with his characterization of Peter, that may be true—and if there are retellings herein that embarrass him, my apologies (sort of). There were two of us on the journey; one got to write the book about it. The fact that Peter was astounded to find out eight months after the trip that I was writing about it makes the experience of recounting even better.

Peter

There was a third partner on the trip, our Mustang. What is not apparent in the book is that Peter nicknamed the car "Shadow" early on in the journey, and then said, "I've never named an inanimate object before."

I said, "Relax, NASA does it all the time," after which he frequently spoke to Shadow during the rest of the trip, often forgetting I was in the car, too.

John Eerkes-Medrano brought a sage editor's guidance to the manuscript, often seeing where a fuller story needed to be told and urging the author to undertake the research and the telling. And when the manuscript grew, and he began to recommend pruning, he advised, "Rick, we still have room for fewer words." This book has no better ally.

Robert Mackwood of Seventh Avenue Literary Agency liked the idea for the book before the manuscript existed, and worked with Kirk Howard, publisher of Dundurn, to make *Route 66 Still Kicks* part of the multi-book commitment between them and the author. Robert brought about the arrangement with Tony Lyons of Skyhorse Publishing of New York for the U.S.A. rights, creating a strong relationship behind the title for its primary audience. Those three individuals anchor the book's launch into the world.

Michael Carroll, associate publisher and editorial director for Dundurn, was the book's editor and architect of its publishing, wisely ensuring a balance of images and text and seeing the book into your hands. The return of Shannon Whibbs as the book's copy editor, a role she undertook on *To Timbuktu for a Haircut*, was welcomed for the professionalism, patience, and wisdom she brought.

Brian Peterson of Skyhorse Publishing designed the book's cover to capture the trip's mood, and Yvette Grant and Cory Allyn oversaw the book's interior development and the thoughtful layout. My respect and appreciation to all three.

Dania Sheldon, permissions editor, undertook the complex task of securing "permissions" for quoted matter, acquiring the historical images, and preparing the permissions acknowledgements, and proved a timely accomplice.

And for a friend's help with consistency and quality of the photographs for reproduction, I thank Don Waite, a professional photographer and researcher whose advice has made this a better book.

All photographs are identified and credited at the book's end, yet I wish here to thank their creators. A special recognition: The "trip photographs" were all taken by my travel buddy Peter Armstrong (except for those sharp interruptions where he tossed me his camera and said, "Quick, catch that").

Cartographer Eric Leinberger's maps were tailored to the story and will assist future travelers, as well as readers. Illustrator Simon Anderson-Carr's portraits were commissioned for this book to further the reader's understanding of those characters. Both continued their professional roles to complement my storytelling, roles begun with *To Timbuktu for a Haircut*.

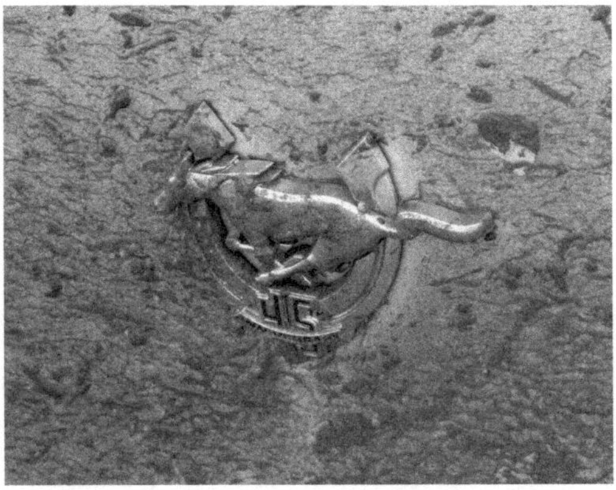

Our faithful Mustang, Shadow.

When writing, it is wonderful (crucial even) for an author to have trusted "readers" who critique the manuscript as it is unfolding. For their candor I wish to thank Jon Hutchison, Jess Ketchum, Russ Johnson, Paula Salloum, Darren Johner, Karen von Muehldorfer, Gary Grimmer, Tina Powell, and Jonathan Walker.

The willingness of Peter Greenberg and Keith Bellows to lend their stature and words to endorse this book's well-being contributed notably to its early acceptance. I tip the brim of my hat their way.

A quartet of leaders in Route 66's preservation and renewal befriended this book. Each read the manuscript and provided advice. They saved the author from errors and the overlooking of recent changes, ensuring a clearer and more factual rendition for the reader. Thank you to Paul Taylor, publisher, *Route 66 Magazine*; Bob Moore, co-author, *The Complete Atlas to Route 66* and *The Complete Guidebook to Route 66*; David Knudson, executive director, the National Historic Route 66 Federation; and Jim Conkle, director, *Route 66 Pulse* newspaper and TV. I salute their love of the route, their belief that it can be preserved for future travelers, and the role each plays in making it so.

I extend heartfelt respect and appreciation to the people along Route 66—those whom I met and those who call it home; they are between the lines of this book on every page.

There is a small focus group I frequently use to bounce around ideas and insecurities when writing, and that brings together the advice of my two sons, Brent and Sean, and my older brother Brian—they proved fundamental to the book's coming about and emboldened my writing. And for many-a-supportive-reason, I thank my wife, Janice, though of particular note for ending months of indecision about this book's title when we sat one day over lunch in an American diner, listening to fifties' music fill the background, and I began yet again to offer up title ideas that did not work. And she said, "From everything you've talked about since your return—Route 66 still kicks. So why not use that for the title of the book?"

About the Author

Acclaimed travel writer Rick Antonson is the author of ten books including *Full Moon Over Noah's Ark: An Odyssey to Mount Ararat and Beyond and Train Beyond the Mountains: Journeys on the Rocky Mountaineer*, and co-author of *Slumach's Gold: In Search of a Legend—and a Curse*. He is the former chair of the board for the Destination International, based in Washington, DC, and was deputy chair for the Pacific Asia Travel Association, based in Bangkok, Thailand. He served as president of Pacific Coast Public Television, affiliated with PBS, Seattle. Rick and his wife Janice make their home at Predator Ridge in the Okanagan Valley surrounded by 250 wineries. HYPERLINK "http://www.rickantonson.com" www.rickantonson.com.

Rick

A Note on Sources

The primary sources I relied on in writing this book are interviews or personal observations, and I obviously also relied on the books I mention. Increasingly, information, fact-checking, and corroboration of stories comes from online sources. In this Google and Bing world, the plethora of leads and articles tossed up by Wikipedia, Dogpile, Lycos, and other online searches is overwhelming—including the checking of satellite image maps. Each source mushrooms with traces to links and more sites, some obscure—and one can get lost in the chase. I frequently did. My research and writing benefited from all of this.

As examples, artists such as Woody Guthrie and Nat King Cole are covered by extensive biographies on a wide range of websites—some official, many not. In particular, National Public Radio's site offers recordings and scholarly observations; YouTube video clips of recordings abound. When I was writing about the murder in Depew, some of the sources were American Opinion Publishing, Oklahoma's News Channel 8, KTUL, *Tulsa World* newspaper, KPRC Houston, and reporters Matt Elliott, Ralph Maler, and Rhett Morgan. For Times Beach background, sources included the *New York Times*, media releases from the Environment and Natural Resources Division of the federal Justice Department, and the Environmental Protection Agency's website, plus references attributed to the *St. Louis Star-Times* newspaper (no longer in existence). The Navajo Code Talkers' Dictionary comes from the Department of the Navy—Naval Historical Center in Washington, D.C., though that is but one of the ways to track it down, and publications including *The Republic* and the online *Newsfinder,* as well as the River of Time Museum newsletter, extend the list of places to find reference points on this important topic.

For a novelty source, I single out a report on Flagstaff's Hotel Monte Vista by the Ghost Hunters of Northern Arizona. And tracking down confirmation of Bobby Troup's original words for "(Get Your Kicks On) Route 66" sent me many places, including listening to the old recording of *Perry Como Live at The Supper Club* on a disc released more recently by Submarine Records of England under the Sounds of Yesteryear label.

Importantly, there are the national and state Route 66 associations that have websites and provide literature. Anyone interested in more information is encouraged to check the respective Route 66/state name online, and enjoy the ride. There are also Route 66 organizations in France, The Netherlands, Japan, and beyond, each providing details for their nation's travelers heading to the United States. Lorrie Fleming, founder of the Canadian Route 66 Association, was particularly forthcoming with information.

Notable among publications is *Route 66 Magazine*, a quarterly with some twenty years of articles and interviews.s And the Route 66 News site tracks helpful articles such as that by Ron Warnick and his interview of George Maharis.

The documentaries and videos I referred to are *Route 66: An American Odyssey*, *A Journey Down Route 66*, *Route 66 Revisited*, and *Route 66 Turns 75*, as well as samplings from the *route 66* television series collection.

David K. Dunaway's three-CD set, *Across the Tracks, A Route 66 Story*, is impressive.

While several books are referred to in the text, most helpful, both on the journey and in my research, was the *Here It Is! Route 66 Map Series*, by Jerry McClanahan and Jim Ross. They also created the DVD, *Bones of the Old Road*. Two books I wish we'd had prior to our trip are the pair by Bob Moore and Rich Cunningham, *The Complete Atlas of Route 66* and *The Complete Guidebook to Route 66*; they would have provided guidance and direction, as they did to the eventual writing of my travel narrative.

Sources and Recommended Reading

Clark, David G. *Images of America: Route 66 in Chicago.* Chicago: Arcadia Publishing, 2007.

Clark, Marian. *The Route 66 Cookbook.* Tulsa: Council Oak Books, 2000.

Connolly, Billy. *Billy Connolly's Route 66.* London: Sphere; Little, Brown Book Group, 2011.

Crump, Spencer. *Route 66: America's First Main Street.* Corona del Mar, CA: Zeta Publishers, 1996.

Curtis, C.H. Skip. *Birthplace of Route 66, Springfield, Mo.* Springfield: Curtis Enterprises, 2001.

Dedek, Peter B. *Hip to the Trip: A Cultural History of Route 66.* Albuquerque: University of New Mexico Press, 2007.

Donovan, Sandy. *Will Rogers: Cowboy, Comedian, and Commentator.* Minneapolis: Compass Point Books, 2007.

Dregni, Michael, ed. *Greetings from Route 66: The Ultimate Road Trip.* Minneapolis: Voyageur Press, 2010.

Ehle, John. *Trail of Tears: The Rise and Fall of the Cherokee Nation.* New York: Anchor Books/Random House, 1988.

Epstein, Daniel Mark. *Nat King Cole*. Boston: Northeastern University Press, 2000.

Fletcher, Robin. *The route 66 TV Series*. Port Richey, FL: Route 66 Magazine, 2006.

Gordon, Linda. *Dorothea Lange: A Life Beyond Limits*. New York: W.W. Norton & Company, 2009.

Guthrie, Woody. *Bound for Glory*. New York: Penguin Group, 1943.

Haskins, James, with Kathleen Benson. *Nat King Cole: A Personal and Professional Biography*. Chelsea, MI: Scarborough House, 1984.

Hinckley, Jim. *Route 66 Backroads*. Minneapolis: Voyageur Press, 2008.

Hinckley, Jim, with James Kerrick, photographer. *Ghost Towns of Route 66*. Minneapolis: Voyageur Press, 2011.

Jensen, Jamie. *Road Trip USA: Route 66*. Berkeley: Perseus Books Group, 2009.

Klein, Joe. *Woody Guthrie: A Life*. New York: Dell Publishing, 1980.

Knowles, Drew. *Route 66 Adventure Handbook*. 3rd ed. Santa Monica: Santa Monica Press, 2006.

Knowles, Drew. *Route 66 Quick Reference Encyclopedia*. Santa Monica: Santa Monica Press, 2008.

Krim, Arthur. *Route 66: Iconography of the American Highway*. Santa Fe: Center for American Places, 2005.

Lange, Dorothea, and Paul Schuster Taylor. *An American Exodus: A Record of Human Erosion*. Reprint. 1939; New York: Arno Press, 1975.

Langguth, A.J. *Driven West: Andrew Jackson and the Trail of Tears to the Civil War*. New York: Simon & Schuster, 2010.

Levy, Buddy. *American Legend: The Real-Life Adventures of David Crockett*. New York: Berkley Books, 2006.

Love, Paula McSpadden, ed. *The Will Rogers Book*. Waco: Texian Press, 1972.

Mantle, Mickey, with Herb Gluck. *The Mick: An American Hero: The Legend and the Glory*. New York: Doubleday, 1985.

Mantle, Mickey, with Mickey Herskowitz. *All My Octobers*. New York: HarperCollins, 1994.

McClanahan, Jerry. *EZ66 Guide For Travelers*. 2nd ed. Lake Arrowhead, CA: National Historic Route 66 Federation, 2008.

Meltzer, Milton. *Dorothea Lange: A Photographer's Life*. New York: Farrar, Straus and Giroux, 1978.

Mifflin, Margot. *The Blue Tattoo: The Life of Olive Oatman*. Lincoln: University of Nebraska, 2009.

Moore, Bob, and Rich Cunningham. *The Complete Atlas of Route 66*. Port Richey, FL: Route 66 Magazine, 2003.

Moore, Bob, and Rich Cunningham. *The Complete Guidebook to Route 66*. Port Richey, FL: Route 66 Magazine, 2003.

Olsen, Russell A. *Route 66 Lost & Found: Mother Road Ruins and Relics—The Ultimate Collection*. Minneapolis: Voyageur Press, 2011.

Parini, Jay. *John Steinbeck: A Biography*. New York: Henry Holt and Company, 1995.

Poling-Kempes, Lesley. *The Harvey Girls: Women Who Opened the West*. New York: Marlowe & Company, 1991.

Rittenhouse, Jack D. *A Guide Book to Highway 66*. Reprint, Albuquerque: University of New Mexico Press, 1989.

Robson, Ellen, and Dianne Halicki. *Haunted Highway: The Spirits of Route 66*. Phoenix: Golden West Publishers, Inc.

Rosin, James. *"Route 66"—The Television Series, 1960–1964*. Philadelphia: Autumn Road Company, 2007.

Rowland, Jackie. *Oatman: History, Recipes, Ghost Stories*. Laughlin, NV: Route 66 Magazine, 2006.

Rowsome, Frank, Jr. *The Verse by the Side of the Road: The Story of Burma-Shave*. New York: Plume/Penguin Group, 1990.

Scott, Quinta, and Susan Croce Kelly. *Route 66: The Highway and Its People*. Norman: University of Oklahoma Press, 1990.

Snyder, Tom. *Route 66 Traveler's Guide and Roadside Companion*. New York: St. Martin's Griffin, 2000.

Steil, Tim. *Route 66*. Minneapolis: Voyageur Press, 2000.

Steinbeck, John. *The Grapes of Wrath*. New York: Viking Press, 1939.

Steinbeck, John. *Travels With Charley*. New York: Viking Press, 1962.

Taylor, Paul. *Route 66 Place Names*. Port Richey, FL: Route 66 Magazine, 2006.

Wallis, Michael. *Route 66: The Mother Road*. New York: St. Martin's Griffin, 1990, 2001.

Witzel, Michael Karl, and Gyvel Young-Witzel. *Legendary Route 66: A Journey Through Time Along America's Mother Road*. Minneapolis: Voyageur Press, 2007.

Credits and Permissions

The author and the permissions editor would like to thank the following individuals for their kind assistance: Dean Black, Oatman, Arizona; Mrs. Lucille Slack, Tulsa, Oklahoma; Anna Canoni, Woody Guthrie Publications, Inc.; Tiffany Colannino, archivist, Woody Guthrie Archives; Beth Freeman, library director, Oklahoma State University Tulsa Campus; William Furry, executive director, Illinois State Historical Society; Wendi Goen, archivist for Photograph Collections, Arizona State Library, Archives and Public Records; Nora Guthrie, director of the Woody Guthrie Foundation and Archives; Nathan Kerr, intellectual property coordinator, Oakland Museum of California; Susan Kirkpatrick, author; Richard Michelson, R. Michelson Galleries; Kate Reeve, head, Library and Archives, Arizona Historical Society; staff at the Library of Congress in the U.S. Copyright Office and the Music Division, especially Patricia A. Rigsbee, senior copyright research specialist, and Chamisa Redmond Nash, senior information and reference specialist; Nancy Sherbert, acquisitions, Archives Kansas State Historical Society; Chris Smith, Michigan Department of Transportation Photography Unit; Catherine Stevanovich, president, Route 66 Association of Illinois; Marshall Trimble, author and official state historian of Arizona; John Weiss, chairman, Route 66 Preservation Committee; and Terry Zinn, Photo Archives, Oklahoma Historical Society.

Page xiii: ENJOY YOURSELF (IT'S LATER THAN YOU THINK)

Music by HERB MAGIDSON

Words by CARL SIGMAN

"Enjoy Yourself (It's Later Than You Think)"

By Herbert Magidson and Carl Sigman

Edwin H. Morris and Co., Inc. (ASCAP).

ENJOY YOURSELF (IT'S LATER THAN YOU THINK)

Lyrics by Carl Sigman

Music by Herbert Magidson

Pages 43, 44, 242, 244–245, 249, and 346: ROUTE 66

By Bobby Troup

Page 49: Interior view of the Harvey House in the Bisonte Hotel, Hutchinson, Kansas, showing customers and Harvey Girls. Photograph taken between 1920 and 1929. Courtesy of the Kansas State Historical Society.

Page 66: Missouri farm wife, quoted in *Proceedings of the Twenty-second Continental Congress of the Daughters of the American Revolution* (Washington, D.C.; April 14–19, 1913). Available at: *www.archive.org/stream/proceedingsofcon1913daug/proceedingsofcon1913daug_djvu.txt.*

Page 69: Quotation from President Andrew Jackson's Message to Congress, December 7, 1829. Available at: The American Presidency Project (University of California, Santa Barbara), *www.presidency.ucsb.edu/ws/index.php?pid=29471#axzz1fyp2KQuN.*

Page 71: Max D. Standley, *Trail of Tears*, courtesy of R. Michelson Galleries, Northampton, MA, *www.RMichelson.com*

Page 84: Telegram from Cyrus Avery to W.C. Markham, February 8, 1926. Used with permission of Oklahoma State University Tulsa Campus Library, Department of Special Collections and Archives, Cyrus Stevens Avery Papers.

Page 86: Telegram from Cyrus Avery and B.H. Piepmeier to Bureau of Public Roads Chief Thomas H. MacDonald, April 30, 1926. United States National Archives.

Page 108: Mickey Mantle photo. Source caption: "Mickey Mantle is flanked here by his twin brothers Roy, left and Ray, in front of their Commerce, Oklahoma, home. (October 21, 1952)." © Bettmann/CORBIS.

Pages 141 and 152: John Steinbeck, "If only I could do this book properly it would be one of the really fine books and a truly American book." From *Working Days: The Journals of the Grapes of Wrath*, by John Steinbeck, edited by Robert Demott. Published by Penguin Books, 1990.

Page 148: "Chapter 12," from THE GRAPES OF WRATH by John Steinbeck, copyright 1939, renewed © 1967 by John Steinbeck. Used by permission of Viking Penguin, a division of Penguin Group (USA) Inc., and by permission of Penguin Books Ltd.

Page 148–149: From *The Harvest Gypsies*, by John Steinbeck (1988; first pub. 1936). Reprinted by permission of Heyday, Berkeley, California.

Page 151: Dust Storm, Hooker, Oklahoma, June 4, 1937. Photo by G.L. Risen. Reproduced by permission of the Research Division of the Oklahoma Historical Society.

Page 163: Photograph of car stuck in the mud. Photographer and date unknown. Photo courtesy of the Michigan Department of Transportation. Copyright © State of Michigan.

Page 166: Family on the Road. Photo by Dorothea Lange, 1938. © The Dorothea Lange Collection, Oakland Museum of California, City of Oakland. Gift of Paul S. Taylor.

Page 187: Boise City, Oklahoma, April 15, 1936. Reproduced by permission of the Research Division of the Oklahoma Historical Society.

Pages 191 and 314: From *Woody Guthrie: A Life* by Joe Klein, published by Dell (Random House), 1999.

Pages 225 and 228: "This Land Is Your Land" by Woody Guthrie. Courtesy of the Woody Guthrie Archives. © Copyright 1956 (renewed), 1970 and 1972 by Woody Guthrie Publications, Inc. & TRO-Ludlow Music, Inc. (BMI).

THIS LAND IS YOUR LAND. Words and Music by Woody Guthrie. WGP/TRO Copyright 1956, 1958, 1970 and 1972 (copyrights renewed) Woody Guthrie Publications, Inc. & Ludlow Music, Inc., New York, NY; administered by Ludlow Music, Inc. International Copyright Secured. Made in U.S.A. All Rights Reserved Including Public Performance For Profit. Used by Permission.

Various pages: Words by Woody Guthrie
© Copyright Woody Guthrie Publications, Inc.

All rights reserved. Used by permission.

Page 228: Holograph of lyrics for "This Land Was Made for You and Me," dated February 23, 1940. "This Land Is Your Land" by Woody Guthrie. Courtesy of the Woody Guthrie Archives. © Copyright 1956 (renewed), 1970 and 1972 by Woody Guthrie Publications, Inc. & TRO-Ludlow Music, Inc. (BMI).

Page 246–247: Quotations from "The Route 66 Lyrics Debate." This article appeared on pages 22 and 23 of the Winter 2010/11 issue of *Route 66 Magazine*, and is reproduced courtesy of *Route 66 Magazine*.

Pages 249 and 346: Image of the original copyright deposit provided by the Library of Congress via their U.S. Copyright Office and Music Division.

Page 288: Olive Oatman, *circa* 1858. Courtesy of the Arizona Historical Society/Tucson. AHS# 1927. The photograph was retouched for clarity at the author's request.

Page 290: *The Grapes of Wrath* motion picture, 1940. © Bettmann/CORBIS.

Page 293: Photograph of plank road on California–Arizona border, by James (Jim) Slack. Courtesy of Mrs. Lucille Slack.

Page 294: Source caption: "Hollywood, California: Scene from the TV show Route 66, starring Martin Milner and George Maharis. Basically Route 66 is an adventure series built around a pair of young fellows wandering around the country in a sports car. This scene shows Martin Milner (L) [*sic*; should be R] and George Maharis laughing together seated in the car." © Bettmann/CORBIS.

Page 308: Quotation from TRAVELS WITH CHARLEY by John Steinbeck, copyright 1962, renewed © 1989 by Elaine Steinbeck, Thom Steinbeck, and John Steinbeck IV. Used by permission of Viking Penguin, a division of Penguin Group (USA) Inc., and by permission of Penguin Books Ltd.

Page 318: "Workers remove signs that mark the end of U.S. Route 66 in Chicago, Ill., Jan. 17, 1977. The highway connecting Chicago with Los Angeles, Ca., is replaced by interstate highways across the nation." © 2012 Associated Press.

Great care has been taken to locate the owners of all material held under copyright and used in this book and to gain permission for republication. The author apologizes for any errors that may have occurred in the permissions process and will rectify any incorrect references or credits in subsequent editions. Please contact Skyhorse Publishing, 307 West 36th Street, 11th Floor, New York, NY, 10018, if you have any inquiries regarding the material included in this book.

A mud-covered Rick preparing to be towed from the mud hole by truck owner Vince on an old, never-paved alignment of Route 66 in Oklahoma, having just climbed under the vehicle to carve out space to secure the tow chain.

A portion of the author's royalties from *Route 66 Still Kicks* will be donated to the National Historic Route 66 Federation campaigns to protect, preserve, and revitalize the route, which can be found at *www.national66.org*.

FEB 27 1946

"Route 66!---"

Words and music by
Bob Troup

Chorus: If you
Ever plan to
Motor west
Travel my way, take the highway
That's the best
Get your kicks
On Route Sixty-Six!

It winds
From Chicago
To L. A.
More than two thousand miles all the way
Get your kicks
On Route Sixty-Six!

Now it
Goes through Saint Louis
And Joplin, Missouri
And Oklahoma City is mighty pretty
You'll see
Amarillo
Gallup, New Mexico
Flagstaff, Arizona
Don't forget Winona
Kingman, Barstow, San Bernardino

Won't you
Get hip to
This timely tip
When you make that California trip
Get your kicks
On Route Sixty-Six!

- o -

Carl Fischer, Inc., New York.
No. 4-12 lines.
Printed in U. S. A.

Original words (typed) for "(Get Your Kicks On) Route 66," filed as part of the copyright deposit submitted by Bobby Troup on February 27, 1946.

Index

To Timbuktu for a Haircut; A Journey Through West Africa

"Great Characters, great stories, and truly great adventures. Not to mention...a great read."

—Peter Greenberg,
Travel Editor, *CBS News*

"*To Timbuktu for a Haircut* is a great read – a little bit of Bill Bryson, a little bit of Michael Palin, and quite a lot of Bob Hope on the road to Timbuktu."

—Professor Geoffrey Lipman, former assistant secretary-general of the United Nations World Tourism Organization

Full Moon Over Noah's Ark; An Odyssey to Mount Ararat and Beyond

"Packed with historical facts and anecdotes, enhanced by excellent maps and photos, this is a fascinating travel adventure to one of the most ancient areas of the world . . . A reader's feast that is not to be missed."

—John A. Cherrington,
author of *Walking to Camelot*

"An educational, amusing and inspiring tale told by an experienced and worldly traveler . . . a fabulous weaving of adventure and research."

—Shannon Stowell,
president of Adventure Travel Trade Association

Walking With Ghosts in Papua New Guinea; Crossing the Kokoda Trail in the Last Wild Place on Earth

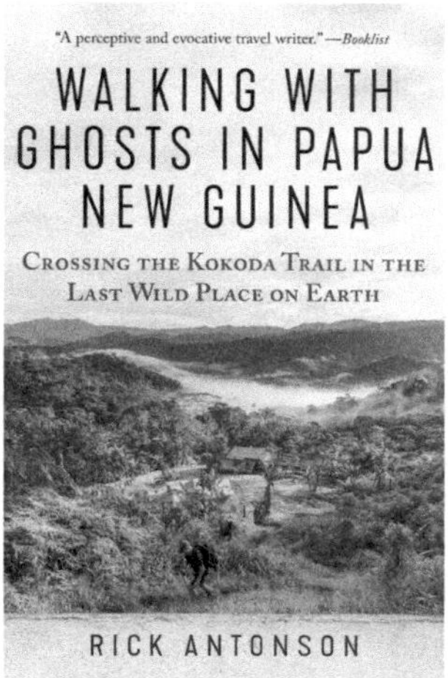

"*Walking With Ghosts In Papua New Guinea* is among the best travel narratives I have read. Rick Antonson beautifully creates a sense of the environment in New Guinea as well as the local people he encountered. He effortlessly weaves in the dramatic wartime history of the Kokoda Trail as his party treks across rushing streams and up and down the mountainous terrain. I highly recommend this book to armchair travelers anxious to experience life in a truly wild, and in many ways, primitive world."

—James P. Duffy, author of
War at the End of the World

"A wild and forbidding terrain reveals its dramatic history. Vancouver-based travel writer Antonson vividly recounts a two-week, 60-mile journey on the formidable Kokoda Trail in Papua New Guinea, a rugged terrain marked by jungle, bogs, gullies, cliffs, malarial mosquitoes, rigorous ascents, and steep, slippery descents . . . An absorbing account of a physically and spiritually challenging journey."

—*Kirkus Reviews*